WHAT YOUR MINISTER IS AFRAID TO TELL YOU ABOUT THE BIBLE

by
Terry Cain

A Theory of Biblical Interpretation

R&E Publishers
Saratoga, California

R & E Publishers
P.O. Box 2008, Saratoga, CA 95070
Tel: (408) 866-6303   Fax: (408) 866-0825

Book Design by Diane Parker

Cover by Kaye Quinn

Library of Congress Card Catalog Number: 92-056389

ISBN 0-88247-958-10

Grateful acknowledgment is made for permission to reprint the following:

The Bible in the Making by Geddes MacGregor, Harper Collins Publishers, New York, NY.

The Outline of History by H.G. Wells, on behalf of The Executors of the Estate of G.P. Wells, A.P. Watt Ltd., London, England.

The Zend Avesta of Zarathustra, translated by James Darmesteter, Holmes Publishing Group, Edmonds, WA.

Buddhist Mahayanna Texts edited by Cowell, Dover Publications, New York, NY

The Upanisads translated by Muller, Dover Publications, New York, NY

The Velveteen Rabbit by Margery Williams, Bantam Doubleday Dell Publishing Group, Inc., New York, NY.

A Rabbinic Anthology by C.G. Montefiore and H. Lowe, Random House, Inc., New York, NY.

Scripture quotations are from the Revised Standard Version of the Bible, copyright 1946, 1952, 1971 by the Division of Christian Education of the National Council of the Churches of Christ in the USA.

Permission to quote from *The Lost Books of the Bible* and the *Forgotten Books of Eden* is granted by the publisher, World Bible Publishers, Inc., Iowa Falls, IA.

The Book of Hymns. Copyright ©1964, 1966 by the Board of Publication of The Methodist Church, Inc. Words used by permission.

The Koran, translated by N J Dawood (Penguin Classics, Fifth revised edition, 1990), copyright © N J Dawood, 1956, 1959, 1966, 1968, 1974, 1990.

Bhagavad-Gita, Vedanta Press, Hollywood, CA

Acknowledgements

I want to express my deepest thanks...

...to Mom and Dad. They raised me with a profound respect for all persons, the highest regard for truth and honesty, and an understanding for the meaning of love. However, they cannot be blamed for the sentiments of this book.

...to Robert Cain of Omaha. Without cousin Bobby's expert guidance in matters of grammar, style and word choice this work would be unreadable. Any errors or weaknesses in this area that might occur in the book will be found only in sentences here and there that were added after Bobby read the manuscript. Neither can he be held responsible for the ideas.

...to L. Edward Mattingly who was my religion professor at Wesleyan and very good friend. Matt provided much inspiration and encouragement which helped me become a serious theological student and an independent thinker as well as a struggling Christian. Matt cannot be blamed for my wild ideas. I'm sure he is in heaven at this moment shaking his head woefully and asking, "Why did they let Terry near a typewriter?"

...to the members of the churches I have served. In spite of my preaching unorthodox ideas, they continued to love and support me in my ministry. They cannot be blamed. Many a Sunday morning they would challenge my sermons in an effort to lead me back into the path.

...to my loving wife. Sue acted as a sounding board for my thoughts. She offered so many helpful suggestions and is probably responsible for any original or good ideas found in this book. (There must be one or two: I think she is also responsible for the bad ideas—someone has to take the blame.)

This book is dedicated to my family:

My father, Harold Cain,

My mother, Dorothy Cain,

My wife, Sue Cain,

My son, Terry Cain,

My daughter, Sherry Cain.

Contents

Introduction: See no evil, Speak no evil, Hear no evil

When a book is full of goofy ideas—as the Bible is—and when a great many people believe this book to be the accurate and unadulterated "word of God", then we have trouble! Our Bible has spawned some crazy notions in the heads of too many folks. Some of these insane ideas include:

- God is busy killing little children in automobile accidents in order to "teach us lessons."

- We don't need to be concerned about population problems because God tells us in Genesis that we must reproduce and "subdue" the earth.

- Only Christians and no one else will be saved.

- Occasionally some of us become possessed by demons.

- Spouting gibberish—sometimes known as "speaking in tongues" is evidence that the spirit of God is in you.

- All of us perfect folks should shun the sinners.

The list goes on. Witch burnings, inquisitions, white supremacy, and other such enormities supported by "Bible proof" still have their equivalences today.

For God's sake—but really more for our own—it is about time we made a serious effort to become honest with our Bibles. It is certainly time that we "grow up" and begin to use common sense in our study of scripture. We must abandon our "ostrich" approach to Bible study and face the problems and embarrassments of scripture openly. After all, "Honesty is the best policy." Give the many accusations concerning the Bible in these pages a chance; who knows, the author may have stumbled by happenstance upon some truths. You won't like this book—but read it anyway!

The many responsibilities a clergy person has include opportunities to preach and teach from the Bible. We call the Bible the "word of God," and as Christians we should be spending a certain amount of quality time appropriating from the Bible knowledge about the kind of person God wants us to be. Our ministers should be helping us with this task. It is even rumored that some ministers have spent significant time and money on an education to prepare themselves for just such a responsibility, not to mention their personal on-going study of the Bible throughout their ministry. We need this kind of help from our clergy in interpreting the Bible for the following reasons:

1. It is a difficult book to read with its ambiguities, strange imageries, and contradictions,

2. It originates in a time and culture much different from our own, and for clarification requires much background from sources outside our Bible,

3. We are not always motivated to do our own homework in Bible study.

There have been times in the history of the church when lay people did not have access to the scriptures due to lack of printing, absence of translations in their own language, or inability to read. Priests and ministers became the chief sources of disseminating Biblical knowledge to the people, and they welcomed such control over the scriptures because it allowed them to avert any confusion or misunderstanding that might come from the casual reading by the unlettered or unenlightened laity.

Today the clergy still have a certain amount of control over what the rest of us know about our Bibles, and they don't always tell us the truth. It is much like parents telling their children that storks bring babies. Two reasons might be suggested why our ministers do not give us the full scoop: 1. Some of them themselves believe that storks bring babies, and 2. the others who know differently think that most of us are not yet "ready" to know the truth that babies are found under cabbage leaves.

First, some pastors still believe that everything we read in the Bible is literally true: for instance, that God wanted a large number of people in the Old Testament times to die in a flood, or on other occasions to be killed by "the chosen people." These ministers also believe that there are no contradictions in our scriptures. They have ways of rationalizing as to why major differences exist between the ethical teachings of the Old and New Testaments, or sometimes they even boldly suggest in the face of contrary evidence that there are no differences. They either totally ignore them or try to explain away the discrepancies found in the facts and stories. Such pastors cannot accept the fact that the Bible is both human and divine. It contains inspiration from God as well as human errors and prejudices.

Religious leaders who need the Bible to be a perfect book to be taken literally find themselves trapped into doing some very unpalatable things in the name of "the Bible tells me so." This practice leads to superstitions as well as stupid and erroneous beliefs concerning scripture. Examples of such foolish or wrong beliefs about scripture include not allowing children to have proper medical care, playing with poisonous snakes, excluding women from leadership roles in the churches, revealing from the pulpit on Sunday morning to the entire congregation the name of one of the members along with the embarrassing "sin" that person confessed to the minister in private counseling, and advocating capital punishment as a Christian practice. We are not out of the woods.

Then there are the pastors who, knowing that the Bible contains errors, myths, contradictions, and cruel doctrines and deeds attributed to God, still tip-toe around the unsavory or difficult passages for a number of reasons. Among such reasons is the fear that because the Bible is held in such reverence, any minister who would dare say anything resembling a derogatory remark concerning scripture would find her or his Christianity seriously questioned. She or he even might find herself or himself out on the streets, pink slip in hand, looking for a new church to lead astray.

Another reason such a pastor may consider for not leveling with us is that the pastor believes that if the church member hears the Bible is not perfect her or his belief in the scripture will weaken, perhaps be shattered. Many church members reason that if we cannot count on everything we read in the Bible being true, then in what can we believe?

Other pastors try to educate us with the truth about the Bible, but feel that they must proceed slowly so as not to alienate any of us. Coming all at once upon the truth, we might find the shock to be too great. Consequently, these pastors will sneak up on us so slowly, they don't even frighten the bunny rabbits away.

What has been said of ministers who either close their eyes to the truth about the Bible due to their own ignorance, fears, or prejudice, or those who gloss over the human mistakes in the book to protect our faith can also be said of most of the Bible study books written for us. Seldom do we encounter the frank and honest approach to our scriptures that is necessary if we are to have a more realistic and dependable faith to meet the challenges of our complex and dangerous world. Stepping in to fill that void is this brilliant little volume you now hold in your hands.

It is the contention of this book that "knowing the truth will make us free." So let us look honestly at our Bible in the glaring light of reality, and let us allow it to be true to what it really is and what it can do for us. Make an honest man or woman out of your pastor; ask him or her to level with you! Better yet, read this book and shock your minister with your new and dangerous knowledge!

Being honest with the Bible should clear up confusion about religion and theology and lead us to a more mature faith. Such honesty and subsequent clarification of God's truth for us should go a long ways toward resolving the unnecessary differences, not only between individual Christians but between denominations. The vast differences that plague Christiandom today, between "liberal" and "conservative", ("mainline" and "evangelical"), destroy the unity that the Christian Church must have if it is to be effective in the struggle against evil in our world. Liberal and conservative ministers in most communities won't even fellowship together for fear a demon might jump from one to the other (the direction in which the demon jumps might be either way).

We will look at some mistaken notions, contradictions, and myths of our Bible in order that we might glean from the chaff the real grain of truth or "word of God." Our ultimate reason for reading the Bible should be to find out as much as possible about what God is like; what God wants us to be and do; what the "good news" is; what are our hopes, inspiration, comfort and challenges are; as well as what is the nature of creation or the universe.

Approaching The Bible dishonestly and unrealistically as we so often do, we have accepted some ridiculous, erroneous, and even tragic ideas. We have allowed those ideas to become devicive in the Christian family.

Buckle your seat belts and read on!

1. Good God or Perfect Book?

You can't have both! Take your pick. Which do you want? Between the covers of the Bible can be found the most significant and profound ideas ever recorded in literature; we call these ideas the "word of God" because we believe them to be the truth about what God is like as well as how God wants us to be and live. However, we also find there ideas about God that are not only not true but also are disgustingly blasphemous, as well as some terribly mistaken notions about how we should conduct ourselves as Christians.

When we make comparisons with the sacred writings of various other religions of our world, the high ethical teachings of Jesus, for example, stand head and shoulders above all of them. Naturally, as a Christian I will be biased in my assessment of non-Christian scriptures, but I hope that I have approached the reading of them as open-minded as possible. I have sincerely and with high expectations searched for truth and great ideas in the sacred writings of other religions. After all, millions of people revere their own religious writings as something special, and I read with eager anticipation those writings hoping for new insights. Unavoidably, no matter how open we try to be, our evaluations will be strongly subjective at best. With that as the inevitable given, we have to strive for whatever objectivity is possible in our appraisal of other religious works.

In my search through other sacred writings such as the *Ta o Teh Ching*, the *Bhagavad-Gita*, *The Koran*, *The Upanisads*, *Buddhist Mahayana Texts*, the writings of Confucius, and many others, I found nothing that could compare with the great moral teachings of Jesus. These others writings contained an occasional great idea, but they were generally filled with much trivia, repetition, nonsense and outright mistaken ideas concerning proper ethical conduct and the nature of reality.

It is often suggested that some of the world's great religious literature cannot be translated from its original language without suffering loss. This is certainly true of its poetic value and perhaps certain imagery, but when it comes to teachings about ethical conduct, the value of persons, and the significance of all creation, great ideas and truth will be preserved when translated into the world's major languages. Suggesting otherwise is just an excuse for the glaring inadequacies in the religious value of the literature. Such an excuse has never been made for the Bible which has been translated into a great many languages and dialects while faithfully retaining the power and meaning of its great ideas.

Elements of ideas similar to those that comprise the teachings of Jesus are occasionally found elsewhere in the Old Testament and other religious writings, but nowhere are they articulated with the same poignancy and perfection. Nowhere has a greater spirit of living on such a high ethical plane as found in the teachings of Jesus been so comprehensively developed. The concept of God as loving and forgiving and the high call to sacrificial living growing out of our love for one another are theological concepts presented in such a way in our New Testament as to be unmatched elsewhere.

Now for the bad news! Our Bible contains ideas that rank alongside of the worst we can imagine! In it are beliefs about God which make God out to be the worst kind of vicious monster. It also contains totally erroneous beliefs about what is right and wrong in terms of personal conduct and ethics.

First of all, many passages in our Bible attribute to God such terrible conduct that if a human being were to do such a thing as God is depicted as doing that person would be judged either crazy or terribly cruel and either locked up or executed.

For example, the book of Joshua describes how God commanded the Israelites after they had been led out of Egypt by Moses to invade the land of the Canaanites and to take it from the peoples living there by destroying them (Joshua 1:1-6). The destruction of Jericho (Joshua 6) is a well-known story in which God not only gave instructions to destroy all of the people of the city (6:17,21) but even joined the Israelites in their slaughter. God instructs the people to repeat this kind of destruction over and over again throughout Canaan. Many times in the Old Testament, reasons are given as to why God did this. God had promised the people of Israel a nation with land (Joshua 23:5, 24:13). Unfortunately, the land happened to belong to the Canaanites. Then God decided the Canaanites had to be destroyed because they worshiped pagan idols which would threaten to corrupt the Israelites (Joshua 24:14-20, Judges 2:1-2,11-12). Finally, such destruction would show the world how powerful God was (Joshua 4:24). We are told God even made the sun to stand still (Joshua 10:12-13) for them during their campaign to crush the Canaanites. We could find it in ourselves to fear a god like that, but hardly to love and respect one.

No manner of interpretation can dignify the concept that God sent a "chosen" people into Cannan to take over the land through the wholesale destruction of the inhabitants. Attributing such a campaign to God is blasphemy. The God I worship is not capable of such vengeance, else I'd be too frightened to even write these words.

Similarly, Israel's "greatest" historical event, the exodus, is fraught with despicable acts being attributed to God. The story is related as to how God used many miracles to convince Pharaoh, king of Egypt, to finally let the Israelites leave the country. One engaging problem that emerges from the story is that God would use a miracle to persuade Pharaoh to let the people go. Then, just when God (through Moses and Aaron) gained Pharaoh's approval, *God would change* Pharaoh's mind so that he refused to let the people leave. The reason seemed to be that this gave God just one more opportunity for an additional miracle in order to show off:

> And the Lord said to Moses, "See, I make you as God to Pharaoh; and Aaron your brother shall be your prophet. You shall speak all that I command you; and Aaron your brother shall tell Pharaoh to let the people of Israel go out of his land. But I will harden Pharaoh's heart, and though I multiply my signs and wonders in the land of Egypt, Pharaoh will not listen to you; then

I will lay my hand upon Egypt and bring forth my hosts, my
people the sons of Israel, out of the land of Egypt by great acts of
judgment. And the Egyptians shall know that I am the Lord. . . ."
(Exodus 7:1-5).

Throughout chapters eight, nine, and ten the cycle is repeated:
each time that a plague convinced Pharaoh to let the people go,
God changed Pharaoh's mind so that God could perform yet
another magic trick and introduce another plague. One last time
God "hardened Pharaoh's heart" (Exodus 11:10) in order to bring
on the final plague—God kills all of the Egyptians's first-born sons
(12:29). I do not imagine that even some of Egypt's gods—Nu,
Nut, Isis, Osiris, or Ra—would play such sick games!

If all this is not abhorrent enough, after the people were
allowed to leave Egypt, Pharaoh changed his mind once more
(remember God was at the controls and pulled the strings) and had
his army pursue the Israelites in order that God could destroy the
army in the Red Sea (Exodus 14:26-28).

This kind of theology permeates the Old Testament. Everyone
knows the story of the flood so well. I believe there is no way that
the God of loving forgiveness that Jesus revealed to us—the God
that I John tells us about:

Beloved, let us love one another; for love is of God, and he who
loves is born of God and knows God. He who does not love does
not know God; for God is love (I John 4:7-8)

—would simply and intentionally destroy almost all life on the
earth because God was upset with the people's sin (Genesis 7).

That proverbial "bolt of lightening from God" can even strike
do-gooders! The story is related twice in the Old Testament of an
instance wherein God killed someone who was only trying to do
something kind (II Samuel 6:1-9 & I Chronicles 13:1-12). The
story starts with God's first church, the house God moves into after
deciding to come in out of the rain. It was an ark, a chest made out
of wood, God's first indoor dwelling place. Until God moved into
the temple in Jerusalem, the ark moved around a great deal, even
for a time being captured by the Philistines. At the time of our

story, David is having the ark and God moved towards its ultimate home in the Temple. As the ark is moving along on a cart pulled by oxen, the oxen stumble and one of the men, named Uzzah, who was commissioned to guide the cart on the trip, was walking alongside the ark. When the the oxen stumbled, the cart and ark apparently began to wobble. In what would have been a knee-jerk reaction for all of us, Uzzah puts out his hand in a gesture of concern to steady the ark from tipping over. For the audacity of touching God's house, God in a fit of anger strikes Uzzah dead. David is angry at God at first, but after a moment's reflection repents of his hasty outburst and appropriately fears God. David decides it is too dangerous to carry around a god whose temper flares at such a little provocation. David leaves the ark there for a while giving God time to cool off. You can think about this story with fear and trembling the next time you sneeze in church!

The most shocking story in the New Testament in which cruelty is attributed to God may be the account in Acts wherein two new Christians, Ananias and Sapphira, husband and wife, do not turn all the proceeds from a sale of their property over to the church as they were supposed to do. Then they lied to cover up their deed. When the disciples confront Anaias with his deceit, he drops dead, presumably by the hand of God. His wife enters center stage, she also lies to the disciples, and apparently God in the same manner strikes her dead (Acts 5:1-10). This story is followed by a very significant verse (11): "And great fear came upon the whole church, and upon all who heard of these things." We can imagine! Some readers will say to themselves, "I've done worse than that. When am I going to get mine?"

This last verse captures the appropriate response any person would have to a god that does these kinds of things. Indeed, the "hell and brimstone" preachers have always played upon fear as the motive for obeying God: we are "sinners in the hands of an angry God" and we will burn in hell if we don't get right with God. In the face of the overwhelming love that God has for us as revealed in the teachings of Jesus, the contrasting idea of an angry and cruel God sends us mixed messages about the nature of God.

Is God a terrible cosmic police officer (this is not in any way to denigrate police officers, though some Christians will not hesitate to denigrate God in such a manner) to be obeyed out of fear of retaliation, or is God loving and forgiving and to be obeyed in return simply out of a response of love and devotion?

The key for Christians must always be the teachings of Jesus. Jesus uses the image of a parent in his parables and other teachings about God to denote the nature of God. Jesus makes it very emphatic to us that God is love and treats us as a loving parent treats a child—even more so:

> If you then, who are evil, know how to give good gifts to your
> children, how much more will your Father who is in heaven give
> good things to those who ask him? (Matthew 7:11)

Sentiments such as these emanate from all of Jesus' teachings. It may help us get closer to the truth to ask the question: "Is it better to respond to God out of fear or out of love?" Would we want our own children to obey us and relate to us from a posture of fear or of love? Should their conduct result from threats of punishment making them to cower and be afraid, or should it be because they love us and want to express that love in behavior they know pleases us? Jesus taught us to understand the nature of God by illustrating with the best of human love between parent and child, and then he tells us that God loves us even more.

Yet there remains this very serious contradiction in our Bible: God is seen as hard and cruel at times and at other times gentle and loving. Can God be both? Some say, "Yes," the explanation being that God is so great that we cannot begin to understand God's ways and reasons. Such an idea is tantamount to saying that we simply do not have an adequate explanation. In other words, we are unable to answer the challenge that God seems to do very cruel things. Either the Bible is wrong about God when it presents God as cruel because God is not cruel according to our understanding, or God is actually cruel according to our human values and understanding, but if we could know all about God and the reasons for God's behavior, we would find that God is not cruel at all.

I suspect the former is true. But let us first examine this notion that God may seem unreasonable and unloving at times when in reality it only seems so to us because God's motives and purposes are so far beyond our ability to comprehend them. This argument is central to much of our theological discussion and paramount in the defense of the conservative and fundamental positions; therefore we should look at the argument's chief fallacy, an examination which should subsequently lay the argument to rest.

Jesus is operating on the premise that we can know God and be able to understand God's expectations for us and the manner in which God wants us to live. If we do not accept this premise, it seems foolish to study the teachings of Jesus in order to understand what it means to be a Christian. God has created our universe as a marvelous design that operates physically and spiritually according to reason and logic. What sometimes seems like a mystery to us for a while becomes very reasonable as we learn more about God's world. Little by little, as our knowledge of the universe unfolds before us, we see it revealed as a glorious and wonderful creation that runs according to physical and spiritual laws. Those physical and spiritual laws make sense as we come to know them more fully. What may seem unreasonable at first—such as "turn the other cheek" one of God's spiritual laws about the power of love and pacifism that Jesus taught—when examined more carefully and understood more clearly becomes very reasonable and logical.

In other words, so much about how we need to be and how we should live is understandable. It is reasonable and logical. It has to be.

To say that God will do things that seem cruel according to our human perspective but would seem very reasonable and consistent in terms of the beautiful love that Jesus revealed to us if we could only have the mind of God is to contradict all that Jesus did and taught and is to destroy the basis for our response to God and the foundation of our ethical conduct. It is much like God saying to us, "Do as I say, not as I do. Be good, and ignore the image I have given you as one who destroys and seeks revenge." Shouldn't we at least expect God to practice what God preaches?

The other alternative would be that the Bible is wrong in instances where it depicts God in dire contradiction to the love and forgiveness that Jesus revealed to us. Of course, this is unpalatable to the conservative and fundamentalist who strain to maintain a belief in a perfect book; but perhaps it is not as unpalatable as seeking to preserve a perfect book at the expense of attributing atrocious conduct to God—which is blasphemy.

It is amazing that people will believe that God could do such reprehensible things (as we read in the Bible), that if you or I did the same things, we would be hated, condemned and executed. And the carry-over is that, because God did it in the Bible, God is credited with atrocious acts still today—a tornado hits a community, a young child drowns, a plane crashes, and God did it!

Our dilemma then is do we have a good God or a perfect book? Some will say that we can have both; we simply do not understand God. I say that we have a perfect God, and that the book at times is wrong. I believe that all we know about God should harmonize with love and goodness as they are understood in human terms because love and goodness as we understand admirable qualities necessarily originate in God.

Not only does our Bible sometimes tells us untruths concerning the nature of God, but the fall-out from this blasphemy is that subsequently certain unethical codes of conduct are promulgated for our behavior.

While we have outgrown such ignorance as believing that God wants us to burn witches or mediums (Leviticus 20:27) (actually stoning them to death would be more scriptural), or thinking that there is anything immoral or impure about someone who is lame, blind or disfigured in any way (Leviticus 21:16-20), or believing that we should kill and burn animals as an act of worship to God, or believing that we can own slaves (Deuteronomy 15:12), or believing that we should have our disobedient children stoned to death (Deuteronomy 21:18-21), yet there remains the fact that we do justify certain unethical and unjust conduct because we believe the Bible tells us that it is permissible.

Moses (or whoever it was) was wrong when he gave us laws demanding capital punishment (Leviticus 24:17) as God's will. Jesus clearly negates in his entire teaching the practice of capital punishment (Matthew 5:38-48, John 8:1-11). Paul is mistaken when he gives women a second-class position in society by making the husband the master of the household (Ephesians 5:22-24, I Corinthians 11:3,7-9) or by saying that women should not have leadership in the churches (I Corinthians 14:34-35). The Bible in these instances is wrong—not only wrong for today, but also wrong for the day in which those passages were written. God never intended animal sacrifice, polygamy, second class citizenship for women, or capital punishment at any point in history. The Bible was also in error when it gave justification for war. These are all mistaken notions perpetuated by those persons who wrote our Bible literature.

Do we have a good God or a perfect book? The perfect book concept is untenable, while the good God position is a must. We have a choice to make. The conservative position is an attempt to preserve a perfect book while, however, saying terrible things about God. In an interesting turn of events, one could easily imagine that if the conservative's theology were true, they could be struck down for believing it! However, their motive is commendable. After all, our faith comes from our Bible initially. If there are defects in our Bible, what can be said about our faith? Well, we know that we do have defects in our faith and beliefs. Just look at the serious contradictions and disagreements between individual Christians as well as between various denominations today. Everyone cannot be right! In a later chapter we will deal with the problem of how we can have a significant faith, based on an imperfect book.

One outgrowth of our believing that the Bible is a perfect book is the superstition that now surrounds the book. It is viewed as magical. Depending upon what the individual's interpretation of the word "holy" is, the title "Holy Bible" probably contributes considerably to the revered status of the book. I recall a war veteran showing me a pocket New Testament with a bullet imbedded in it and telling me that the book was in his breast pocket when the bullet struck him and the book saved his life. He, of course, believed it to be a miracle and not a coincidence: the New Testament had magically saved his life; any other book would not have been up to the task. (I've heard the story many times as has most everyone. Do I just happen to be the lucky person to have met the person who had the actual experience and to have seen the actual bullet embedded in the New Testament or has it really happened many times over and, thus, I am, in fact, in error in believing the Bible is not magical?)

We have made the Bible into God when it is only a vehicle that points to God, and sometimes it points errantly. We worship the Bible at times. For some persons, reading this material will cause their blood pressure to soar to new heights because they view anything critical being said about this book as sacrilegious. But the fact remains that the only way we will ever get away from the divisiveness in the church and the contradictory beliefs that Christians hold is to be honest in regards to the Bible—with what it really is and what in it can be, as well as cannot be, trusted to be the word of God.

However, if we love and respect the book, we will do justice to it and be honest with it. Parents who love their children do not overlook their faults! Every religion should have its sacred literature scrutinized carefully and challenged! If it cannot stand the heat, and light, get it out of the kitchen and get a new cook book.

Most Christians will have a more healthy attitude about the Bible when they know that it is not a perfect book dictated word for word by God to expert stenographers who made no mistakes in receiving and recording the dictation. When we know how this book came to be, whom it was written for, the kind of material it contains, and how we can come to know God from its pages, our faith will be much stronger because we will be closer to the truth about God and what God expects of us. It also means clearing out the baggage of some of our erroneous beliefs that clutter and confuse our appreciation of the book. Such is the MODEST attempt of this book.

2. Two Religions: Two Books

Not only is the Bible mistakenly seen as infallible, it is also assumed by most Christians that it is one book from Genesis to Revelation, uniform and with all of its parts being of equal value. Despite knowing that it contains sixty-six different books (or thereabouts), many believe that it is just one complete, unified book from cover to cover; everything necessary is included, and nothing is left out. It is viewed as one book by most Christians in the same sense that they understand *David Copperfield* by Charles Dickens to be a single book. Such a notion is sustained by the fact that the Old Testament and New Testament are usually published as a single volume under a single title, The Bible.

For very good reasons, it is important for Christians to be clearly aware that what we usually acknowledge as our Bible, the Old and New Testaments, is in fact, at the least, two different books or canons representing two very different religions. (Canon, among other things, means an authoritative list of scriptures or sacred writings established by an official religious council.) It is important to keep clear in our minds that the Old Testament is the sacred writings of the Jewish faith, and it is not in any sense a Christian book or Christian literature, while the New Testament is an entirely different religion's sacred literature. The two books represent very different histories, theologies, and ethical systems. There is an obvious relationship and connection between the two books historically, but we may have been doing a serious disservice to the Christian church by publishing both testaments in a single volume with the implication that they are an organic whole, which has led to much confusion.

For those who have become familiar with the Old and New Testaments, the differences in theology between the two should be readily apparent. In the New Testament, Jesus presents a concept of God as loving and forgiving that even goes too far for some Christians. The many teachings and parables showing God to be a God that forgives, too easily according to some Christians, will make it seem that justice isn't being done. People who do "bad things" should suffer more than they do, according to our sense of what is fair. It doe not seem right that the "good people" and the "bad people" share the same fate. We wonder if perhaps Jesus' God is too lenient. Has God "gone soft" or gotten too mellow in old age?

Jesus' parable of the man whose son took his share of the family inheritance and foolishly squandered it and returned home receiving his father's forgiveness and blessing makes us want to cry out, with the son who stayed home, that there is no justice (Luke 15:11-32). Surely the foolish son should have performed more penance. The elder son thought that there was some inequity in that the father had never held a celebration for him.

Another of the beautiful stories of God's love and of how we are to love one another in turn is told by the Gospel of John concerning a time in Jerusalem when the religious authorities brought to Jesus a woman who had been caught committing adultery (8:1-11). The Old Testament law made it very clear that the woman should be stoned to death. However, Jesus makes it equally clear that that is not what God would have done. After reviewing the qualifications of the crowd for would-be executioners, Jesus suggests that only a person who had never sinned could throw the first stone. You and I not having been born yet, no one seemed to qualify, so Jesus indicates that the woman should be released, thereby not only escaping capital punishment, but escaping any punishment at all. Is there no justice?

If your sense of justice has not been offended yet, then recall to mind the parable that Jesus told concerning the man who hired people to work in his field, hiring persons at different times of the day so that some worked all day and others worked a shorter portion of the day (Matthew 20:1-16). At the end of the day, the employer paid all of the workers the same amount of wages—the ones who worked only one hour were paid as much as those who worked all day. Is God's love too impartial? If God is going to be so foolish with the dispensing of blessings, some of us will surely try to take advantage of God.

If God wants foolishly to love too much, should we really be expected to make ourselves vulnerable with the same kind of behavior? Jesus suggests that we should turn the other cheek when someone slaps us, give whoever sues us more that they ask for, carry burdens for those who force us into service twice as far as they demand, and even love our enemies (Matthew 5:39-41,44).

Jesus' version of God is one of loving forgiveness—God loves us with the love of a parent for a child elevated to a perfect state, and God wants all of us to emulate that love as much as possible. That is the God of the New Testament.

The Old Testament version of God is generally quite different. God is seen as cruel and God does not hesitate to order the slaughter of large masses of people and even joins in the fray. The Old Testament law is filled with harsh and unjust punishments. Punishment for cursing one's parents is death as is the punishment for adultery (Leviticus 20:9-10). Foreigners who curse God should be put to death (Leviticus 24:10-16). Punishment must be in kind: "an eye for an eye" is the rule. If someone breaks another person's bone or puts out the eye of another person, the punishment is to be the very same for the guilty party.

Whereas Christianity preaches love for all persons and anyone can become one of God's chosen simply by responding to God,

There is neither Jew nor Greek, there is neither slave nor free, there is neither male nor female; for you are all one in Christ Jesus (Galatians 3:28),

the Old Testament has a concept of God's "chosen people," the Israelites, whom God loves more than other people and to whom God has given special privileges. For example, the Israelites must never enslave a brother or sister Israelite, but it is permissible to own non-Israelites as property (Leviticus 25:39-46).

Such harsh laws and such harsh notions about God would encourage us to unkind behavior that is totally contradictory to the teachings of Jesus. Belief in a cruel and harsh god fosters similar conduct in the followers of such a god. The Old Testament clearly encourages the use of capital punishment, war, and acts of revenge. Like God, like people.

One Old Testament example of vicious retribution blasphemously attributed to the will of God is found in I Samuel 15. Samuel, when he tells Saul that he is to be anointed king over the people, also tells Saul that he must attack and destroy the Amalekites because the Amalekites attacked the Israelites some 100 years or more earlier. God holds a grudge a long time! God wants everything belonging to the Amalekites completely destroyed: all women, men, children, babies, and all animals. It sort of gives new meaning to that favorite hymn:

O brother man, fold to thy heart thy brother!
Where pity dwells, the peace of God is there;
To worship rightly is to love each other,
Each smile a hymn, each kindly deed a prayer.

For he whom Jesus loved hath truly spoken:
The holier worship which he deigns to bless
Restores the lost, and binds the spirit broken,
And feeds the widow and the fatherless.

Follow with reverent steps the great example
Of him whose holy work was doing good;
So shall the wide earth seem our Father's temple,
Each loving life a psalm of gratitude.

Saul, obedient to a loving and merciful God, kills all of the people, but spares the king, Agag, and a few of the animals. God is upset that Saul did not obey the order to the letter and sends Samuel to reprimand Saul. Samuel then requests that King Agag be sent to him. The text tells us,

And Agag came to him cheerfully. Agag said, "Surely the bitterness of death is past" (I Samuel 15:32).

In this case it almost seems that Agag is a "bigger person" then both Samuel and (excuse the anthropomorphism) God. Agag hopes that killing and revenge are now over. Then we read, "And Samuel hewed Agag in pieces before the Lord in Gilgal." It all sort of makes us feel that we would have been proud to have known the prophet Samuel, doesn't it? What is God really like—vengeful or loving?

The truth is that there are many beautiful and inspirational passages in the Old Testament. Many of the writing prophets— Isaiah, Amos, Jeremiah, Hosea, and others—soar to great heights in understanding God's loving nature. But such passages are found in the midst of such bloody and vicious activity attributed to God that permeates the Old Testament.

The Psalms preserve for us some of the stark contrast that exists in Old Testament beliefs about God. Many Psalms are very beautiful songs of faith and inspirational prayers. Yet they reveal the same human weakness that throughout the Old Testament so often ascribes to God monster-like behavior. One of the most beautiful Psalms is the 139th. After describing an exceptionally wonderful relationship that exists between God and us, the psalm takes a nasty turn in the versus near the end. Apparently the same author who prays this beautiful song still believes that God wants vengeance:

O that thou wouldst slay the wicked, O God. . . Do I not hate them that hate thee, O Lord? And do I not loathe them that rise up against thee? I hate them with perfect hatred. . . (Psalm 139:19, 21-22).

One of the great English preachers, Leslie Weatherhead, quotes John Wesley on Wesley's thoughts about the Psalms. Wesley felt that parts of some of the Psalms were "highly improper for the mouths of a Christian Congregation."[1] Wesley can say that again.

Is all this to say that the Old Testament is bad and the New Testament is perfect?—No! The Old Testament has its high moments as well as its low moments. One of the great passages in the New Testament found in Romans 12 is a quotation from the Old Testament and is certainly consistent with the high ethical teachings of Jesus:

If your enemy is hungry, give him bread to eat; and if he is
thirsty, give him water to drink; for you will heap coals of fire on
his head, and the Lord will reward you (Proverbs 25:21-22).

This assumes, of coarse, that the emphasis is on the love of
another and not the reward only.

There are many other beautiful moments in the Old Testament:
the suffering servant of Isaiah (42:1-7, 50:4-10, 53:1-12) and the
hope of Micah (4:1-4), as well as many others. Unfortunately these
moments of light are almost lost in the midst of the "eye-for-an-
eye" Old Testament theology.

The New Testament, along with its great passages, also has its
embarrassing moments, such as the pathetic theology expressed in
the story of Sapphira and Ananias (Acts 5:1-10) that was
mentioned in our first chapter. The Old and New Testaments
contain truth about God but also contain some very human and
very mistaken ideas. Both books are a mixture of very different
kinds of literature with different values. There is no chronological
order or orderly progression from bad to good as we move through
scripture. Harry Emerson Fosdick said it well:

> . . . the retrogressions in Biblical thought, the irregularities of
> change, with its ups and downs, its persistent lags, and its moral
> surrenders. There is no smooth and even ascent in the Book.
> There are, instead, long detours, recrudescences of primitivism,
> lost ethical gains, and lapses in spiritual insight. There are even
> vehement denials of nascent truth. . . [2]

The important point for Christians to remember is that we have
in the Bible, actually two entirely different books: the Christian
New Testament, the Christian's Bible; and the Old Testament, a
pre-Christian book of another faith that has historic relationships
with the Christian book. Christians must become more aware of
this difference because of the contrast in the nature of God that
each book portrays, as well as the ethical conduct each book
promulgates. The Old Testament is a bloody, vengeful book,
despite its many great truths. The New Testament, in contrast,
depicts a great loving God who expects sacrificial and loving

conduct. While glimpses of this latter theology is caught at times in the Old Testament, it is in minor proportions; but the New Testament overwhelms us with love, peace and equality. For those persons who cannot recognize the stark contrasting difference between the Old and New Testaments, they are either not familiar enough with the Bible or their elevator doesn't stop at every floor.

Some may challenge the above conclusions. I have no doubt many will on the basis that there is some very harsh theology in the New Testament.

A strange account is given of Jesus getting upset and cursing a fig tree because he could not find on it any figs to eat even though it was not the time of year for the tree to bear (Mark 11:12-14,20-21). The tree whithers and dies because of the curse. Even though Bible scholars try to justify this entirely uncharacteristic behavior of Jesus by saying it was all meant as an opportunity for Jesus to teach a lesson (22-25), it remains a questionable passage. Stories such as this stand out in dramatic contrast to the rest of the New Testament simply because they are the rare exception.

Someone could argue that the New Testament also suggests some hard-line theology concerning God's love and mercy as they point out such examples as the story of Lazarus and the rich man (Luke 16:19-31), or the story of the sheep and goats in the last judgment (Matthew 25:31-46), where, in both cases, it seems that God has provided eternal torment for some of us in cases where the punishment does not seem to fit the crime. This does not conform well with the concept of God as the perfect, loving parent.

Any enormities of punishment depicted in Jesus' stories, such as the latter two mentioned, must be understood in the traditional Oriental style of teaching. Jesus often used dramatic and improbable imagery: camels passing through eyes of needles, or casting mountains into seas with prayer power. Jesus' parables are not concerned about eternal pain and suffering—the rich man's experiencing a hell of fire because he had not cared for Lazarus in his lifetime, or the "goats" in the final judgment being sent to eternal suffering—but rather, in both cases the message is that people are supposed to love and care for others when they have the opportunity. The focus must be on our conduct. The negative punishment is not germane to the parables; it is only dramatic imagery employed for emphasis. Moreover, it is the positive lesson of compassionate concern and service that is central.

While exceptions exist to the generalization made here concerning the dramatic differences between the two books, such dramatic differences do exist. The Christian must always remember it is the New Testament that is her or his Bible. Christians cannot allow themselves to be influenced by the Old Testament theology of hatred and violence, nor let it be a justification for our wars, or for capital punishment, or for revenge.

Some may suggest that God's nature changed from Old Testament times to New Testament times, or that if God did not change, God changed the expectations for us in terms of ethical conduct. If the latter is true, it is actually also a case of God changing. Human needs, emotions, problems, sins, and hopes have not changed in basic nature through the centuries. God's laws pertaining to the way God intends that we should live remain constant in history. God does not change, nor do God's ethical principles and values for human beings. Capital punishment, for example, is clearly against God's will according to the life and teachings of Jesus, and it always has been against God's will. Process theology can say what it will, God's will for us remains the same for all generations.

Roy L. Smith tells us that the word "testament" means "covenant" or "agreement," and that implies that the people of the Old Testament entered into an arrangement or contract with God that they would be a certain kind of people and live a certain kind of life.[3] The idea is that the New Testament is now a new relationship or covenant with God and it supersedes the Old Testament arrangements. Rather than being a new deal we have made with God, I would claim that the new covenant or testament is really what God wanted all along. The Old Testament lawyers simply did not read the contract carefully, or else they had some "fine print" clauses that God overlooked. The old erroneous beliefs about God found in the Old Testament were never accurate in the first place. Jesus came along and revealed God's real nature as God had always been.

Jesus clearly changes theology as the Old Testament knew it. God is no longer seen as angry and vengeful; God is forgiving and loving. Jesus even actually challenged and changed the Old Testament law itself. Some examples of this are found in Matthew 5. It seems quite clear that Jesus tightened the law concerning divorce (31-32). The Old Testament is very lenient concerning the ease of getting a divorce, at least from the man's perspective though later rabbis tried to make it harder to procure a divorce.[4] A man could divorce his wife for just about any reason by just "giving her a certificate." Jesus clearly makes divorce allowable only for rare and unusual circumstances:

> But I say to you that every one who divorces his wife, except on
> the ground of unchastity, makes her an adulteress. . . (Matthew
> 5:32).

Next, Jesus summarized the Old Testament on the point of our not swearing falsely, and followed this by saying that we should not swear or take oaths at all (33-37).

Jesus even more poignantly revealed the major difference between the two books by quoting the Old Testament position of revenge, "an eye for an eye," and then turned our ethics completely around by telling us to love and forgive as we "turn the other cheek" (38-42).

Jesus continued on this line of thought by pointing out the general tenor of the Old Testament concerning treatment of enemies. Hostility and retaliation had been the norm. Jesus changed our understanding of God's will using his familiar formula, "But I say to you. . .", and proceeded to tell us to love our enemies (43-48).

There can be no doubt that Jesus intentionally brought a new, and very different, understanding about what God is like and how God wants us to live. To deny this would be irrational and would be dealing dishonestly with the Bible. There is no doubt that there are major differences between the two books.

Everyone would agree that there are Old Testament laws and practices that definitely are not applicable for our day. I would say that they never were appropriate. However, the question I would like to ask is, "Just what are all of the specific changes that the New Testament is supposed to make in Old Testament theology or law?" Some of them are obvious, I suppose. For example, the Christian faith (speaking here only generally because there are too many denominations and sects within Christianity to allow for anything other than generalizations) believes that it is no longer wrong to eat pork, believes that it is now wrong to practice polygamy, and believes that animal sacrifice is definitely ridiculous. These, at least, are givens. Or are they?

If we were to read, following some ritual law, the words that this law or statute was "a perpetual statute" (or in the King James: "a statute for ever") would that mean it definitely was not one of the laws that Jesus should have changed or a law that Christians could give up on? These words refer to a law of purification from uncleanness in the Old Testament where we are told to kill and burn a "red cow" along with some "cedarwood and hyssop and scarlet stuff" (Numbers 19:1-10). Is this really a ritual that law requires us to practice "forever?" We so seldom burn red cows any more in the church where I serve. Should I feel guilty? What is the punishment for ignoring this law?

Seriously, I would like to see a list of all the changes that persons believe were appropriate for Old Testament times but not for us today, and the scriptural explanations that go with them, particularly concerning moral conduct and proper behavior. What is supposed to have changed and what has not, and why? Surely, someone somewhere has compiled such a list.

Even later Judaism thought it necessary to modify the extremities of Old Testament theology. For centuries, following the Old Testament period, Rabbis found it necessary to make extensive commentary on the Torah (which usually refers to, but sometimes may be more inclusive than, the law or instructions given in the first five books of the Old Testament called the Pentateuch) either to clarify or to actually change the nature of the law. These later scriptural traditions were circulated orally for a long time before finding written form under the headings of Talmud and Mishnah. Some authorities consider the Talmud as embracing both the Mishnah and Gemara.[5]

As an example of the changes that needed to be made, the Talmud had to seriously curtail the Old Testament license of the death penalty for punishment for so many crimes, such as adultery and the disobedience of children. One modern Jewish writer, C. G. Montefiore, in commenting on the work of this early Rabbinic literature which tries to make the Old Testament more palatable, says that:

> Considering the unfortunate fetters in which the Rabbis were bound—that all that is said of, and by, God in the Old Testament is perfect and inspired—they came out of this terrible dilemma very well.[6]

He believes that both the Old and New Testaments may have some harsh theology and that neither Jews nor Christians satisfactorily meliorate the problem by their interpretation:

> The modern man is not taken in or satisfied by these attempts to show that a God who annihilates, or sends to eternal hell, a single soul which He has made, is, nevertheless, a God of love.[7]

Montefiore acknowledges, concerning the Old Testament, the truth that many Christians will not admit, that there are "imperfections and crudities in the Hebrew Scriptures"[8] as well as "contradictions and inconsistencies within the Scriptures."[9]

Montefiore comments on the relationship between these two books and two religions:

> For one thing Judaism was growing when Christianity was born, and it continued to grow after Christianity had diverged from it. And, for another thing, the two religions are distinct, and Christianity did not just quietly and regularly develop out of Judaism. This would be agreed to by passionate advocates of either religion. . .[10]

We need to have clear in our minds just what the connection is between these two books and two religions that some theologians have merged into a "Judeo-Christian" tradition. Some have suggested the distinction as one of seeing the Old Testament as a history of a people, in contrast to the New Testament which is a religious movement. Such an attempt at differentiation must be very careful not to overlook the Old Testament as being the development of a religion, also. It certainly is the history of the origins of the Jewish Faith beginning with God's call to Abram to leave his home in Babylonia and to be led into a new land in order to bring about a new nation of people, as well as a new religion (Genesis 12). The rudiments of Old Testament history begin with Abram and continue through many great religious leaders who were at times in touch with the Spirit of God (and at times not). Judaism as a religion took shape in its early formative years between the time of Abram, (sometime after 2000 B.C.), and about a century and a half before Jesus at the close of the Old Testament period.

Two things must be remembered. Judaism did not end its development at that time. Unlike Christianity, which had its foundation very well laid during the New Testament period, Judaism continued to evolve well beyond the Bible period. For Judaism, the Old Testament was not a finished product. It was only a beginning with its share of errors, mistaken notions, and weaknesses. It became a "jumping off" point for an ever-growing body of sacred literature that matured through the centuries into a more sound and sensible theology.

The second thing to remember is that there remains even now confusion over the issue of rather Judaism is a national movement, a religion, or, to be more exact, a combination in some complex way of these two entities.

Whatever the case, Judaism did become one of the world's major religions, and its theology continued to grow, as mentioned, beyond its Old Testament origins. Indeed, one Jewish scholar, Jacob Neusner, opens his book with the statement that the Talmud, which includes the material that follows the Old Testament in time, "is the single most influential document in the history of Judaism."[11] However, we are not concerned so much with Judaism in terms of what it became, but Judaism as we know it in the Old Testament! It was into this religious tradition that Jesus stepped!

Jesus grew up in the Jewish Faith, attended the synagogues, probably even worshiped in the Temple (at least he was there doing interesting things), and seemed to have had significant parts of the Old Testament memorized. His family and his whole culture were of the Jewish Faith. After his death, his disciples and followers began to meet on the first day of the week as well as the traditional sabbath of Judaism at the end of the week. Very soon, serious conflicts arose concerning the nature of this group of people who finally came to be called Christians. Were they a group within Judaism? Were they being faithful to Judaism, or were they doing things differently? To make a long story short, the Christians eventually became totally divorced from the Judaic religion.

However, the point to be emphasized is that Jesus was of the Jewish Faith. He began with the Judaic theology of the Old Testament as the foundation for his teachings about God and about God's will for our ethical conduct; but he definitely made many changes and modifications in the ideas of that tradition. He was like Michelangelo of Florence, who in the early 1500's took a block of marble that another sculptor had started and almost ruined by cutting too far into the middle of the block and created the magnificent statue of David. Jesus took a religion and gave new shape, meaning, and life to it to the point where it became a new "covenant," a distinct new religion.

Judaism had, as a part of its theology, a concept of a messiah, an instrument of God who would come and right all of the wrongs of our world. Because they had suffered cruelly under the hands of several nations during their history, this savior would come to bring peace and justice. The Jews did not, and do not, believe that Jesus was this messiah. But Christians do believe Jesus fulfilled everything that we could hope for in a savior. Well, not really! In our weak moments, we would rather that Jesus would have destroyed all the "bad people" or else made them all into "good people" (like you and me) and just generally turned the world into a place of perfect peace and justice. Only reluctantly do we

acquiesce to the idea that Jesus probably did the far more significant thing of dying on the cross—it may not be our way, but it
seems to be God's way.

As Christians we have roots, through the background of Jesus,
in the Jewish faith, but we must remember that it is a religion apart
from Christianity, that the Old Testament belongs to the Jewish
faith, and the New Testament alone is our Bible. We have in the
Bible two religions and two books.

One of the great Methodist preachers of England, Leslie
Weatherhead, was very hard on the Old Testament when he said of
it:

> . . .it must be admitted by all honest readers that much of the Old
> Testament is dull, meaningless, irrelevant and hopelessly sub-
> Christian in its sentiments. . .[12]

Even though he was Methodist, he was right. We as Christians
must never elevate the Old Testament to the level of the teachings
of Jesus. It leads only to theological confusion to attempt to equate
the ethical systems and the descriptions of God found in the two
books.

Even though the literature is composed of many "books," it can
be thought of as two distinct books—the Old Testament and the
New Testament. Consequently, I would be so bold as to propose
that the name of "Bible" be used exclusively to designate the Old
Testament while Christians find another name for the twenty seven
books that we now call New Testament.

However, in the rest of this book for convenience in discussion
and reference I will generally refer to the two as one book, the
Bible, as it is so often published. However, I categorically believe
that the Old and New Testaments should never be published in one
volume under one title as the Bible. Furthermore, I believe that
Christians should never use Old Testament stories such as David
and Goliath, and The Flood, for church school children! Although I
will give the Old Testament (and the New Testament as well) this:
on the whole it never glosses over nor attempts to cover up the sins
and embarrassments of its heroines and heroes. The shortcomings

and weaknesses are hung out for everyone to see. This honesty is a refreshing change from almost all other kinds of literature, including sacred writings of other religions.

If this chapter has sounded somewhat critical of the Old Testament literature, I am sure that no thoughtful person would jump to the irrational claim that it is anti-Semitic. To critique a literature is not to denigrate a people, and to ignore faults and errors in a literature is not being honest with it. Wait until you see what I do with the New Testament!

NOTES:

[1] Leslie D. Weatherhead, The Christian Agnostic (New York: Abingdon Press, 1965), p. 193.

[2] Harry Emerson Fosdick, A Guide to Understanding the Bible (New York: Harper & Row, Publishers, 1956), p. xiii.

[3] Roy L. Smith, Know Your Bible Series # 1: How Your Bible Grew Up (New York: Abingdon Press, 1955), p. 7.

[4] The Interpreter's Bible Volume 7 (New York: Abingdon Press, 1951), p. 299.

[5] Morris Adler, The World of the Talmud (New York: Schocken Books, 1963), p. 50.

[6] C. G. Montefiore and H. Loewe, A Rabbinic Anthology (New York: Schocken Books, 1974), p. xxviii.

[7] Ibid.

[8] Ibid., p. xxiii.

[9] Ibid., p. xxix.

[10] Ibid., p. xiii.

[11] Jacob Neusner, Invitation to the Talmud (San Francisco: Harper & Row, Publishers, 1984), p. 1.

[12] Weatherhead, p. 191.

3. It Ain't Necessarily So

In 1935, George Gershwin wrote the American folk opera, *Porgy and Bess*. "It Ain't Necessarily So" is one of the popular songs from this musical hit. The words are cute and catchy and bare a striking resemblance to the truth:

> "It ain't necessarily so,
> It ain't necessarily so, De t'ings dat yo' lible
> To read in de Bible, it ain't necessarily so. . .

The kind folks who hold the copyright to this song were not gracious enough to allow me to quote the verses for you. Consequently, I am limited to paraphrasing the ideas. Verse one refers to David killing Goliath; verse two tells about Jonah being swallowed by a whale; verse three mentions the fact that Moses was found in a stream by Pharaoh's daughter; the last verse says Methuselah lived 900 years. Included in the song is a cute refrain about taking the gospel whenever it's possible—but with a grain of salt.

Some of the following chapters will deal with different reasons why we might agree with the words of this 1935 song. It is important in the light of the fact that so many of us are guilty of taking a position on an ethical question and of then turning to the Bible for confirmation. That confirmation is usually some verse or short passage that we can quote to show how the Bible justifies our opinions.

If the Bible cannot be taken literally (and it can't), if it contains errors or mistaken ideas (and it does), if we find in it myths that we have mistaken for history (and we do), and if some of the material must be recognized as allegory or figurative (because it is), then we have to approach the book much more carefully and thoughtfully. Rather than looking for proof texts to substantiate our already formed prejudices, we must, instead, come to scripture seeking to understand the nature of God as revealed in the life and teachings of Jesus so that we will grow in our Christian faith to the place where the spirit of God's love will lead us into appropriate Christian living and decision making. This means studying our scripture with the "blue-pencil."

One way of discrediting the literal interpretation of scripture, which assumes equal weight and value to all passages and thus leads to confusion, is to point out the errors, contradictions and inconsistencies that exist. There are many minor errors in our Bible that are of little consequence since they do not enter into any ethical concern, and they are of no theological or historical significance. An example of such an error is seen in the attempt to answer the question of who is the prophet Zechariah's father. In Zechariah's own book, named coincidentally, Zechariah, his father is listed as Berechiah and his grandfather as Iddo (Zechariah 1:1). Zechariah lived close to the time of Ezra and Nehemiah. All three were concerned with rebuilding the temple at Jerusalem after the Persians released the Jews and encouraged them to return to their homeland in the latter half of the sixth century and the fifth century B. C. Both Ezra and Nehemiah claim that Iddo was Zechariah's father and not his grandfather while Berechiah is not mentioned at all (Ezra 5:1 and 6:14, Nehemiah 12:16). Who is right? Well, it is not really important—except perhaps to Zechariah.

This mistake along with many other errors in our Bible simply shows that it is a human book, written by human beings, and consequently it contains human errors. Discrepancies are sometimes found between what two or more writers say about the same event or person because of the different perspectives in which things or persons are viewed or the different vantage points from which observations are made. Anyone reading the four gospels will quickly pick up on the contrast between John and the three synoptic gospels. Matthew, Mark, and Luke are called synoptic because they are so similar in nature, with Matthew and Luke probably having relied heavily on Mark, the earliest gospel. John gives us a far different perspective on the life of Jesus than do the other three.

In the Old Testament an example of this different perspective is the way in which the two books, Joshua and Judges, record the campaign by which the Hebrews returned to Palestine after Moses brought the people out of Egypt and through the desert. Joshua tells the story as one in which the people fairly successfully conquered the land in two major campaigns. Judges gives the picture of a long and more drawn-out process. This is a case of different writers recording history with different motives and allowing their biases to influence the facts.

How did Saul die? How did Judas die? You may have difficulty in answering these questions. While both deaths are recorded for us, each death, Saul's and Judas's, has two versions.

I Samuel ends with the story of Saul being badly wounded in a battle with the Philistines, and Saul asks his armor-bearer to kill him with the sword to end his misery and prevent the Philistines from finishing the job. The armor-bearer was afraid to take the life of Saul, it being an awesome thing to kill a king even upon request, so Saul has to commit suicide (I Samuel 31:1-4). II Samuel begins immediately with the story of an Amalekite who claims that he killed Saul at Saul's request as an act of mercy (II Samuel 1:1-10). To avoid the apparent contradiction in this incident, one could simply say that the Amalekite was lying about his part in the death of Saul. *But* the scripture does not say that he was lying. We are left assuming that he was telling the truth. In order to rationalize away the differences between the two stories we must, in fact, read into the the second account that the man was lying. Can we in good conscience *read into* the story any facts that are not actually stated? Perhaps we can, but then we must admit that we are not taking the story entirely literally and that we are adding something that isn't there.

We cannot so easily dispose of the inconsistencies in the two accounts of Judas's death. Fundamentalists and conservatives have to do some fancy dancing around the discrepancies between how Matthew and Acts both tell us Judas died. Matthew tells us that Judas tried to return the thirty pieces of silver he received for betraying Jesus because he repented of the terrible deed he had done. Judas throws the money down in the temple and goes out and hangs himself (Matthew 27:3-5). The book of Acts tells us that Judas used the money to buy a field and that he fell "headlong" (into the field?), "burst open," and "all his bowels gushed out" (Acts 1:18). The Bible isn't always delicate.

In order to reconcile the differences in these two descriptions of the death of Judas, one would have to do some fancy footwork, some contortion, or a little creative manipulation. One wonders, then, who it is that really takes the Bible literally in such instances as these. Is it the "fundamentalist" who must *read into* the texts ideas and facts that aren't there which will definitely change the obvious surface-value meaning in order to reconcile the contradictions? Or is it the "liberal" who accepts the literal facts of the two stories with their apparent contradictions? Interesting turn of events, wouldn't you say?

Matthew, more than the writers of the other Gospels, is anxious about proving that Jesus fulfilled all of the Old Testament prophecies concerning the messiah. Whenever he can find anything in the Old Testament that seems to parallel the life of Jesus, he will quote the Old Testament passage and comment on how this has come to pass through Jesus in order to fulfill prophecy. In the 23rd verse of chapter one Matthew quotes Isaiah 7:14 saying, "Behold, a virgin shall conceive and bear a son. . ." Only Isaiah does not say a "virgin" will conceive. Isaiah, in fact, says, "Behold, a young woman shall conceive and bear a son. . ." The Hebrew word from Isaiah, *almah*, means "young woman." The Greek word παρσενοδ that Matthew uses can mean either "a virgin" or a woman who is not a virgin[1], which adequately covers the alternatives. Of greater importance is the fact that Isaiah is giving a *sign* that does not concern either the messiah's coming or the life of Jesus. The sign of a young woman conceiving concerns a message that God is giving Ahaz, king of Judah. God wants to prove to Ahaz that he can trust what God is telling him concerning the threat of war with Syria and the immediate future. Ahaz tells God he does not want a sign because (having read Matthew 4:7 or Deuteronomy 6:16 in Sunday School) he does not want to "put the Lord to the test." God says Ahaz is going to get a sign anyway. A young woman will become pregnant at that time, and before that child reaches a certain age, God will accomplish certain things (Isaiah 7:1-17). The sign represents a few years, at most, in the life of a person, and it will all happen about 700 years before the time of Jesus.

Only Matthew and Luke record birth and infant stories about Jesus. Again, if one takes literally the language of these two gospels concerning where the family of Jesus lived before Jesus was born, one would have to honestly admit that Matthew and Luke imply entirely different scenarios.

Luke tells us that, Joseph "went up from Galilee, from the city of Nazareth, to Judea, to the city of David, which is called Bethlehem" where Jesus was born (Luke 2:1-6). The impression seems clear that the family was residing in Nazareth before going to Bethlehem. If that is not the case, then the text is very misleading—an accusation that ultimately must be mentioned repeatedly regarding many Biblical passages if one is going to try to resolve all contradictions found in the Bible.

In contrast, Matthew has Jesus being born in Bethlehem with no indication that the family had ever lived anywhere else. After the birth of Jesus, we have the story of Herod's attempt to kill the one that he felt was a threat to his future reelection to office. The family of Jesus has to flee to Egypt for safety. When some semblance of safety is restored, an angel calls the family out of Egypt and back into the land of Israel. It seems that there is still some danger in the area of Bethlehem so,

> . . .being warned in a dream he (Joseph) withdrew to the district
> of Galilee. And he went and dwelt in a city called Nazareth, that
> what was spoken by the prophets might be fulfilled, "He shall be
> called a Nazarene" (Matthew 2:22-23).

There is that formula again: Matthew is trying to make Jesus conform to what he believes the Old Testament says about a messiah. However, the clear impression is (besides the fact that Luke and Matthew never compared notes) that the family had not lived in Nazareth previously, but were going there for the first time to live. Again, that is the apparent or obvious interpretation. Are you going to *read into* these two passages something else?

Also concerning the birth of Jesus, we have some serious discrepancies in the two genealogies. For starters, Matthew lists Jesus' grandfather, Joseph's father, as Jacob, while Luke tells us that Jesus' grandfather was Heli. That could be easily explained by simply saying that Jacob and Heli are two different names for the same person since Bible people had a thing about changing their names in mid-history. But there would be no point in trying to resolve that problem when there are so many other problems in the two lists of genealogies, not just with names only, but also with numbers of generations (Matthew 1:1-17 and Luke 3:23-38). Of course one could just ignore the genealogies altogether if Joseph is not the biological father of Jesus anyway—unless, of course, Mary is a blood relative of Joseph, in which case the genealogies would be relevant—or not!

Conservatives and fundamentalists have worked on many of these problems trying to straighten out the contradictions that appear throughout the Bible. The task is Herculean and requires so much patch work and creative additions to our scriptures that one wonders why they don't just give up and accept what is there and take the Bible literally!

When it comes to the calling of Jesus' disciples, it requires some interesting slight of hand to reconcile the call of Peter, Andrew, James, and John found in Matthew's account with that which appears in the Gospel of John. For openers, Matthew, which follows Mark's account closely (Mark 1:16-20) and is not very much different from Luke's account (Luke 5:1-11), tells us that Jesus was walking by the Sea of Galilee when he saw Peter and Andrew who were fishing. Jesus simply calls the two of them to follow him and become fishers of people and they immediately follow him. Going down the beach a little way, they see James and John, two more fishermen, in their boat. Jesus calls them also, and they, too, leave their work and follow him (Matthew 4:18-22).

The Gospel of John places the incident farther south near Jerusalem (1:28). Two disciples of John the Baptist are with him one day when Jesus walks by. John immediately recognizes Jesus as the "Lamb of God." The two disciples start following Jesus and soon become his disciples. One of these two is Andrew who now goes to tell his brother, Peter (Simon), about Jesus, and Peter becomes a disciple, also (John 1:35-42).

The implication is clear when one reads these two stories that this is the first call in each instance and that it is simply told with different facts. The story when remembered years later, having been told and retold through the years until it was finally written down, became modified and changed as it diverged in different directions. This accounts for the fact that Matthew (who copied Mark) differs from the same story as told in Luke and John and other gospels, such as the Gospel of the Ebionites. Some try to reconcile these contradictions by suggesting that both stories happened actually as recorded in Matthew and John. John's story happened first near Jerusalem, and Matthew's story happened some time later north in Galilee. However, this is not an honest reading of these two stories. If both stories actually happened at two different points in time, the impression given in each story, that this was a first call to the disciples by Jesus, makes the Bible very misleading, much the same as does the two different accounts of Jesus' relationship to Nazareth related earlier.

If this problem occurred only once or twice in the Bible, we could perhaps accept such rationale. However, since such clearly different facts and impressions surround too many incidents throughout the scriptures, it becomes somewhat tiresome to keep repeatedly resorting to devices in order to explain away the problems.

An interesting difference is found in the four gospel's accounts of Jesus riding into Jerusalem on Palm Sunday. Mark (11:1-7), Luke (19:29-36), and John (12:12-15) make it abundantly clear that Jesus came into the city riding on one animal, a donkey or a colt. It is very strange, then, to read Matthew's account that Jesus told his disciples to go and "find an ass tied, and a colt with her; untie them and bring them to me" (21:2). The disciples "brought the ass and the colt, and put their garments on *them*, and he sat *thereon*" (21:7, italics mine). Why does Matthew have two animals and the other gospels have only one? I will explain "The Mystery of the Palm Sunday Ride" later in chapter 5. This will keep the reader reading on—if she or he has not already given up by now. At this point I want only to note that there is a definite contradiction between the accounts.

Those worried about preserving the inerrancy of the Bible will probably say that there were two animals but that the other three gospels just don't mention it. But then the quotations of Jesus do not coincide. Luke actually is quoting Jesus as saying, "You will find a *colt* tied"; "untie *it* and bring *it*", while Matthew says "Untie *them* and bring *them*" (italics mine). Resolving the problem by a different strategy and saying that here we have a case of two entirely separate incidents in the life of Jesus also becomes burdensome after a while. Jesus seems to have led a life of events that always happen by twos and in parallels (the feeding of the 4000 and the 5000, and so forth).

Another example of these so-called parallel events would be the anointing of Jesus. Matthew tells the story as happening in Bethany at the home of a man named Simon where a woman pours expensive perfume over Jesus' head (26:6-13). A few details differ between Matthew and Mark (14:3-9), but essentially the accounts agree since Matthew probably copied Mark. However, John places the event in the home of Lazarus and has Mary washing Jesus' feet with the perfume and her hair (12:1-8).

Did the event happen on two different occasions at two different locations? Not likely. The parallels are a little too close for that contrivance. It was one event perhaps either remembered differently or retold so many times that changes occurred in the process. Perhaps it would be well to quote both stories here to show the similarities as well as the differences.

Now when Jesus was at Bethany, in the house of Simon the leper, a woman came up to him with an alabaster jar of very expensive ointment, and she poured it on his head, as he sat at table. But when the disciples saw it, they were indignant, saying, "Why this waste? For this ointment might have been sold for a large sum, and given to the poor." But Jesus, aware of this, said to them, "Why do you trouble the woman? For she has done a beautiful thing to me. For you always have the poor with you, but you will not always have me. In pouring this ointment on my body she has done it to prepare me for burial." (Matthew 26:6-12).

Mark adds to this account this significant information:
"For this ointment might have been sold for more than three hundred denarii, and given to the poor." (Mark 14:5).

Finally John says,
Six days before the Passover, Jesus came to Bethany, where Lazarus was, whom Jesus had raised from the dead. There they made him a supper; Martha served, but Lazarus was one of those at table with him. Mary took a pound of costly ointment of pure nard and anointed the feet of Jesus and wiped his feet with her hair; and the house was filled with the fragrance of the ointment. But Judas Iscariot, one of his disciples (he who was to betray him), said, "Why was this ointment not sold for three hundred denarii and given to the poor?". . .Jesus said, "Let her alone, let her keep it for the day of my burial. The poor you always have with you, but you do not always have me." (John 12:1-5,7-8).

Can you really say this is another one of those coincidences in the life of Jesus where a second separate event happens which very closely parallels an earlier event? If we approach scripture naturally and normally, we would honestly suspect that this is simply one event that time distorted by remembering the details through two different channels or traditions. But if one's faith is so fragile that it must hang on trivial details rather than on the greater truths and more important messages in scripture, we will have to explain away the problems with suggestions of strange coincidences and by ignoring the simple and obvious explanation.

While on the topic of Lazarus, we would all agree that the Bible clearly says Lazarus was unquestionably dead and that Jesus brought him back to life (John 11:1-44). This presents another problem: the New Testament contradicts this fact at least twice. I Corinthians (15:20) tells us,

> But in fact Christ has been raised from the dead, *the first fruits of those who have fallen asleep.* (italics mine)

and the book of Acts (26:23) confirms this idea:

> . . .that the Christ must suffer, and that, by *being the first to rise from the dead*, he would proclaim light both to the people and to the Gentiles. (italics mine)

The Bible tells us that Jesus was the first to rise from the dead when it is clear that he wasn't the first. Along with Lazarus we remember that Jesus also raised others—the only son of a widow in the town of Nain (Luke 7:11-15) and perhaps the daughter of Jairus (Mark 5:21-43). In the latter case, of course, we could always say that the girl was not dead for Jesus himself tells us that she was only asleep. We must not forget several others who even got out of their graves two or three days before Jesus and walked around (Matthew 27:52-53). Some Halloween! Was Jesus the first to rise from the dead, or second, or third, or was he even in the top ten? The Bible is irrefutably incongruous on the point.

I have not begun to exhaust the many discrepancies and errors in our scriptures. The reason for making a point of the existence of errors in the Bible is to caution us all concerning the danger of quoting facts or statements in order to substantiate some bias we may have or to prove an ethical point on an important social issue or for any other reason. All kinds of strange notions and misconceptions have come about because persons have misunderstood the Bible. It is not infallible and some of its ideas are blatantly wrong. The Bible is in error, for example, when it indicates that God ever wanted anyone to go to war and slaughter other children of God, our sisters and brothers. And what about the Bible's narrow concept of God's love when it suggests that non-Christians won't find salvation except by some special formula or profession? And should we believe Paul when he gives to women a second class citizenship? The list goes on.

The book is not perfect. Only God is perfect. The book is an unfolding revelation of what God is like and how God wants us to live, sometimes on target and sometimes missing the mark entirely. The book often sends mixed signals because it is a book produced by human beings who were at times inspired by God and were at other times totally out of touch with God and mistaken in their ideas. To find the "word of God" in our Bible study may require more work than we think—or at least a different kind of approach from that to which we have been accustomed.

NOTES:

[1] The Interpreter's Bible Volume 7 (New York: Abingdon Press, 1951), p. 255.

4. Nobody Actually Takes It Literally

We operate under the illusion that Christians are divided into two groups, more or less. One group of Christians believes that the Bible is to be taken literally: every word is true as it stands in the primary meaning of the word. All of the other Christians are supposed to believe that there are some things we cannot take literally in the Bible—that there are portions that must be understood as figurative in meaning. To understand something figuratively means that, while the primary meaning of the words or text directly expresses one idea, there is another meaning to the words—a secondary meaning.

As an example, imagine a group of young people in school the day after their school athletic team scored a decisive victory over a team from another school. One would not be surprised to hear one of the students say something like, "We really killed them last night." If we took their conversation literally, we would believe that the students used weapons in the contest and that their opponents were at this very moment lying in a mortuary somewhere.

The truth is no one really takes literally what they hear or read every day. We are all sophisticated enough to appreciate the fact that in our "everyday real world" we use figurative communication much of the time. Yet there are persons who think that the Bible is not a part of the "real world" and that it does not contain any figurative language.

We call those who believe that the Bible must be taken literally "fundamentalists," a group which includes many persons who have been labeled "conservatives." Those who think we should not take certain portions of our scriptures literally and who understand that some of the language is figurative have been labeled "liberals."

This chapter contends that, no matter how we label people, the fact is that there is no one who ever takes the Bible literally. Actually, everyone takes it to some extent figuratively. It becomes a matter of to what degree we take it figuratively—the point at which each of us draws the line.

I illustrated in the last chapter with instances of persons who claim always to take the Bible literally (fundamentalists), when in fact they must of necessity find themselves actually taking a situation figuratively while, with the same passages, the liberal will be reading the material literally. Such an example would include the two accounts of Saul's death mentioned earlier. The liberal will simply read the words in their primary meaning contending that these are two different stories preserved for us, one or both of which may be wrong. The fundamentalist, in order to eliminate contradictions in the two stories, must *read into* the accounts some information that is not actually there! She or he must create a situation, for example, where one of the persons in the story is lying even though our Bible doesn't indicate that.

Another example of this interesting reversal of roles is the way in which Old Testament "prophecy" is handled by the respective groups. Liberals tend to see the prophets speaking more directly to the day in which they lived—describing events, not of the distant future, but of the time in which they live. Does the reader recall Isaiah's reference to the birth of a child by a young woman that we discussed in chapter three? A literal reading of the situation (Isaiah 7) reveals it as an event that will happen in King Ahaz's lifetime, or very soon—about 720 B.C. However, fundamentalists do not read this passage literally, but rather figuratively! Isaiah's remarks are interpreted as having a secondary meaning suggesting that the reference is to a time some seven hundred years later, as if it were written in secret code. The question, I repeat, is, "Who takes the Bible literally and who takes it figuratively?"

The answer, of course, is that we all take some portions of the Bible figuratively. So why get our noses out of joint when another person chooses to see a figurative meaning in some passage, as for example, the word "day" in the creation stories of Genesis. Some interpret the word to mean "a long time" rather than a twenty-four hour period? All of us take such liberties with the scriptures at different times. Most of the fundamental or conservative books I have read concerning Biblical prophecy always interpret the words "day," "week," and "year" in books like Daniel and Revelation as indicating periods of time other than their primary meaning—twenty-four hours, seven days, and twelve months respectively. The justification sometimes given for a convenient broader definition of "day" as it is used in certain passages is found in passages like Psalms 90:4 or II Peter 3:8 where a "day" is likened unto a thousand years. Why is it that that kind of symbolism is never used by the fundamentalists in relation to the use of the word "day" in the creation stories of Genesis? I suspect the real reason is that the notion of evolution—even the word itself—raises the collective conservative blood pressure.

Then we have creatures in the apocalyptic works, books like Daniel, Ezekiel and Revelation, which have very strange and cryptic descriptions such as lions, oxen, eagles, bears, leopards and dragons which the literalists treat figuratively as symbolizing countries and persons. They often believe that these animals refer to entities in the twentieth century—the "last days" in which we are supposedly living at present, (though perhaps they will have to shift these predictions into the twenty-first century soon). Explaining the figurative interpretation of material such as that which is found in the book of Revelation is justified because this material is acknowledged as consisting of visions. The book itself even tells us so. Yet they remain just visions of animals, lamp-stands, and whirling wheels and are never in any way identified with entities and events of the present unless one stretches the imagination—which is not a very literal way of handling scripture.

For further evidence that Christians do not take the Bible literally, one only has to remember that there are passages even in our New Testament with which few of us would be willing to comply. We avoid the handling of poisonous snakes even though Paul was not injured in an encounter with a deadly snake (Acts 28:1-6), and we were told that we will not be harmed if we, as believers, handle poisonous snakes (Mark 16:18). In like manner none of us is willing to drink poison even though we are told it also will not harm us (Mark 16:18). Certainly we wouldn't expect to be safe drinking poison if our only reason for doing so was to "show off" our faith or prove to others that the Bible always tells the truth. On the other hand, there are many instances in our Bible wherein miracles are performed with no other purpose in mind than to impress others of the greatness of God. I am going to believe that the large majority of Christians—a very large majority—do not take the ideas about poisonous snakes or poison drinks literally—and no doubt with good reason!

Nor do we believe that we can move a mountain or do the impossible with faith alone (Matthew 17:20-21). Why have there been no mountains moved by faith at any time in history? Is it because there has yet to be any appropriate occasions for doing so? When will such an occasion occur? Why would Jesus make such a statement if it is only applicable once in every hundred thousand years or so? A probable explanation is that, in fact, we have here a very fine example of something that needs to be taken figuratively. "Moving mountains" does not mean moving mountains; rather it means simply that there is power in prayer to do wonderful things—but not everything.

Christians seldom cut off their hands or gouge out their eyes even though scripture clearly tells us that on occasion it just might be the expedient way to avoid hell (Matthew 5:29). Do these passages not apply to anyone today? Or do we simply take these passages figuratively in terms of their meaning for our actions?

If we were serious about this literal business, then Jesus taught us to pray without giving thanks (the Lord's Prayer, Matthew 6:9-13 and Luke 11:1-4).

While I have contended that no one actually takes all portions of scripture literally, one of the great Bible teachers of the mid-twentieth century, Geddes MacGregor, in a very interesting and insightful passage, comes down very hard on fundamentalism and the idea of literal interpretation:

A word should be said here on the subject of what is still called, in America—very misleadingly—"fundamentalism." By this is usually meant literalism in the reading of the Bible; that is, the practice of attempting or claiming to attempt to read the Bible as though it contained no figurative language. Since the language of religion is in nature of the case even more figurative than are most other kinds of language, though all language is figurative to some extent at least, such a claim is absurd. It also betokens a peculiarly non-religious frame of mind. It is true that some people are more literalistic in their thinking than are others: imagination and intelligence are not universal endowments. But to say that a person's thinking is literalistic is really to imply that he has a block against religious thought, a barrier, indeed, against even the beginnings of a religious attitude. The so-called "fundamentalist" is therefore the most irreligious of men. Not only is the "fundamentalist's" arrogance stupid; it is fundamentally opposed to the indispensable condition required for beginning to understand what religion is about. All religious men in every age have been in some sense poets, though they have been also much else besides. To undertake to read the Bible literalistically is to make certain of wasting one's time.[1]

Yet, such a literalistic posture in Biblical interpretation remains even today a malady that impedes any progress towards healthy faith and sane positions on social and ethical issues, as well as wholesome cooperation between the different churches.

An illustration of the foolish theological positions to which a literal rendering of scripture has led is that which concerns who is saved and who is not, as well as the mechanics of salvation.

Conservative Christians long have been guilty of a narrow and literal interpretation of statements regarding who will be saved while ignoring all other passages that offer a different perspective. This has led to a very unfortunate self-righteous attitude on the part of so many Christians who believe their brand of Christianity is right and all others are wrong. Only they will be saved because they have understood the proper formula for salvation found in the

Bible and responded accordingly. The rest of us have other, much warmer prospects.

Examples of such passages that have been narrowly and literally interpreted include these comments by Jesus:

I told you that you would die in your sins, for you will die in your sins unless you believe that I am he. (John 8:24).

I am the way, and the truth, and the life; no one comes to the Father, but by me. (John 14:6).

For God so loved the world that he gave his only Son, that whoever believes in him should not perish but have eternal life (John 3:16).

This central thought appears elsewhere, for example:

And they said, "Believe in the Lord Jesus, and you will be saved, you and your household." (Acts 16:31).

And there is salvation in no one else, for there is no other name under heaven given among men by which we must be saved (Acts 4:12).

Often these passages are understood to mean that only by a formal proclaiming of a faith in Jesus can we be saved. Without ever officially making such a pronouncement using this formula, one will be lost, most probably to an eternity of torture in burning fire. Talk about a loving God! Conservative Christians tell us we can live good clean lives, but, without exercising that formula, God will consign us to hell for an eternity of torture. I really cannot think of any persons I know who would be that vicious, excepting the conservative's god.

While these joyful literalist Christians are dwelling on the prospects of most of the rest of us being roasted as marshmallows for eternity, they proceed merrily on their way blatantly ignoring the many, many other passages in the teachings of Jesus that suggest obedience to a formula is clearly not necessary for one's salvation.

Jesus tells a significant parable (Matthew 25:31-40) about persons who are saved and do not even know it. And would you believe it almost sounds as if they are saved by work of all things? This parable tells us that the person who finds salvation is one who has fed and clothed poor persons, helped the sick, and visited those in jail. No doubt this is an excellent example of that marvelous passage found in James:

> What does it profit, my brethren, if a man says he has faith but has not works? Can his faith save him? If a brother or sister is ill-clad and in lack of daily food, and one of you says to them, "Go in peace, be warmed and filled," without giving them the things needed for the body, what does it profit? So faith by itself, if it has no works, is dead. But some one will say, "You have faith and I have works." Show me your faith apart from your works, and I by my works will show you my faith. . . You see that a man is justified by works and not by faith alone. (James 2:14-18,24).

Salvation (and we won't stop at this point to explore the meaning of salvation) depends upon "what you are" as a person. Faith is a process of "being" or "becoming." It is what you are that matters ultimately. Faith and works cannot be separated. If both are real, one does not appear without the other. In Matthew, Mark and Luke there are many more passages which speak as if a person is saved by works in contrast to the very few passages (primarily in John) which would seem to indicate that a profession of faith in Jesus is enough. The whole tenure of the teachings of Jesus lean overwhelmingly towards the importance of works for one's salvation, however repugnant that might seem to some.

> Not everyone who says to me, "Lord, Lord, will enter the kingdom of heaven, but he who *does the will* of my Father who is in heaven." (Matthew 8:21) (italics mine).

This seems to say that there are some who "talk" about their belief in Jesus, when it may only be a self-righteous show; whereas, instead, those who find salvation will be the persons who, because their faith is real, do God's work. Something very akin to salvation by works seems to be foremost in Jesus' teachings.

Yet the literal interpretation some Christians have placed upon the need to believe in Jesus in order to have salvation has created a divisive church and an elitist company of Christians. However painful the idea is for a conservative, God's love is great, and it includes salvation for non-Christians. It may even be great enough to include salvation for the elitist Christians who believe that non-Christians are lost.

The literalists—conservatives and fundamentalists—are the Pharisees of today! This is precisely why Jesus was upset with these religious leaders of his day. They took the law literally. They were the ones who were zealous in preserving the law down to the finest letter. They were devout and were meticulous in obeying God's rules. Such a literal approach to the law made them blind to the spirit of the law. For those who are not shocked at strong, crude language, it would be worth reading and pondering what Jesus said about these literalists. My modesty prevents me from using the kind of language Jesus used in his condemnation of the conservatives and fundamentalists (Pharisees) of his day. I can give you only the references: Matthew 23:13-36, Mark 7:1-13, and Mark 12:38-40 are some fine samples of the castigation. That the Pharisees strained out gnats and swallowed camels (Matthew 23:24) is among the "nice" things Jesus said about them.

Woe to those who take everything in the Bible literally—if in fact they actually do. They are not giving much credit to the Bible and those who wrote it. The writers may have been wrong at times, but they were not stupid. Yet the literalists demean the writers by viewing them as simply two-dimensional persons with little intelligence or imagination! The writers and the ideas expressed in scripture usually have more depth and more meaning than just the superficial appraisal made by the literalists.

As I said before, it is a shame conservative and fundamentalists insist on taking certain passages literally, when they, for their convenience, have passages they prefer to take figuratively. Nobody takes the Bible literally!

NOTES:

[1] Geddes MacGregor, The Bible in the Making (New York: J. B. Lippincott Company, 1959), pp. 309-310.

5. Big Fish Stories Aren't Lies

Everyone knows the story of Jonah and the whale. Those who know the story better than the rest of us remind us that it was not a whale, but a big fish. But how many believe the story? Is the book of Jonah fact or fiction? A majority of Christians at this point in time may accept Jonah as fiction. Being fiction does not make the story false or a lie. It is simply a story that uses a certain medium to convey truth. In this case the story of Jonah is like a parable in that it is trying to tell us something about the nature of God and God's will for people. It isn't necessary that the book be actual history in order to make known truths about God. In fact, insisting that the book be actual history is in a way to belittle its author who had a very creative imagination and who used an exciting art form as a vehicle for conveying theology. Such insistence does not flatter the reader much, either.

God sends Jonah to Nineveh, the capital of Assyria, an enemy of Israel, to warn all the people that God is going to punish them. The book was written about 350 B.C., but Assyria was the wicked enemy about 400 years before this time. Nineveh is described in the book as being such a big city that it would take three days to walk through it (Jonah 3:3)—somewhat of an exaggeration. Jonah preaches his sermon and, to his surprise, successfully converts the entire city, a success unparalleled before or since. Moses, Isaiah, Jeremiah, Paul, and even Jesus could not boast of such a reception. Despite the author's use of literary license, the book of Jonah reveals interesting truths about human nature as well as about the greatness of God's love. Jonah is not only unhappy that all of the people were saved, strange as this seems, but he also bemoans the death of a plant.

Then God says,

"You pity the plant, for which you did not labor, nor did you make it grow, which came into being in a night, and perished in a night. And should I not pity Nineveh, that great city, in which there are more than a hundred and twenty thousand persons who do not know their right hand from their left, and also much cattle?" (Jonah 4:10-11).

That God also cares for the animals is a nice touch.

Sometimes I wonder if the literalist really sees beyond the simple story and is able to appreciate the deeper truths in the message or the beauty in the medium. With the track record of the literalists being what it is, they probably wouldn't be nearly as happy as God was over the wholesale salvation of these wicked masses. As a matter of fact, find yourself a literalist and he or she will undoubtedly quickly tell you that nowhere in the book of Jonah does it say those folks were saved. Yes, here we yet sit like Jonah under the shade of the plant.

I repeat that the fact that the book of Jonah is fiction in no way makes it a lie or makes it false. The Bible uses many kinds of literature to tell its stories. The Old Testament is much richer in its variety of literary forms than the New. Handicapped as the literalist is in her or his lack of appreciation of the various kinds of literature, and given the figurative nature of so much of the material, her or his understanding has such a narrow focus that the outcome of her or his interpretation is often painful and tends to stretch one's credulousness. As we mentioned previously, their beliefs about God often make God into a tyrant and make God's love seem inferior to that of human beings.

Such a narrow interpretation of scripture has been responsible for driving many persons away from the Christian faith. Many well-educated persons have found much of Christian dogma too unpalatable. That such a void exists between some "intellectuals" and the Christian faith is recognized to such an extent that some conservative and evangelical Christians are very suspicious of anything that smacks of education. Although I expect to receive significant criticism (possibly from both ends of the theological spectrum) for saying it, still I will assert that there is a recognizable inclination (with many exceptions of course) for Christians of a conservative or fundamental bent, in a very general way, to be less educated, and a corresponding tendency for Christians at the liberal or mainline end of the theological spectrum to be better educated. One should be able to detect a significance in the "kind" of education as well. Conservative-tending Christians suspect that education has a way of making a person doubt the Bible, thus undermining one's faith and leading one to atheism. For instance, education is suspected of fostering belief in evolution, and evolution is anathema for conservatives. Evolution (as we shall discuss in a later chapter) supposedly destroys belief in the creation stories of Genesis.

A good education should help a person to recognize and appreciate various kinds of literature along with the nature of figurative or stylistic language. And part of good Bible education should make us familiar with the variety of literature that the Bible encompasses. For example, from good Bible study one learns that some scripture is an attempt at history, some scripture is fiction of one sort or another, and other scripture comprises the whole spectrum of literary genre. In order to fully appreciate the values in our scripture, we find it necessary to be familiar with the different kinds of literature found in the Bible as well as how it came to be written. A short history of the latter will appear in a later chapter.

Can we pause for a parenthetical thought? It may sound, at times, as if I am inordinately hard on Christian conservatives. While there is substance to such an accusation, I would like to go on record that I have the deepest respect for many individual conservative Christians and some conservative denominations or churches. Perhaps more than any other branches of Christianity, the Quakers (or Friends), the Church of the Brethren, the Mennonites, and The Salvation Army have shown me what it really means to be a Christian. The rest of us could learn much from their understanding of what the love of God means in terms of human relationships and social service!

Now let's examine the different literary forms in the Bible.

As Jonah is generally recognized as fiction, there are many other such stories in our Bible. The famous story of the flood found in Genesis (chapters 6, 7 & 8) is another work of fiction, one that struggles with some critical theological ideas. Among other things, the flood story deals with the "why" of natural disasters. It tries to make some sense out of the problem of God allowing, or in this case causing, a disastrous natural tragedy. It seeks to explain why a good God would do such a terrible thing, or even allow it to happen. There must be good reasons, and the Genesis flood author thinks he or she has some adequate answers.

The flood story has its counterparts in the histories of several other cultures. Since the people of the Bible were supposed to have originated in the land of Babylon, it is not surprising that the Genesis flood story closely resembles the flood story found in an earlier Babylonian myth preserved in the Gilgamesh Epic.[1] We are told that such legends are found in the histories of almost every people.

Stories like the flood are called myths. A myth is a story not based on fact that grows up with the tradition of a culture in which imagination has preserved some ideas concerning the past. Myths may incorporate supernatural creatures or events and usually are set in a more primitive world view. Our Bible certainly has its share of myths, notable of which are the birth stories surrounding Jesus.

Matthew and Luke are the only gospels that have anything to say about the birth of Jesus. Mark and John ignore his birth. Paul has nothing to say about it, and even Jesus, himself, makes no reference to it. The birth myths preserved in Matthew and Luke are stories that grew up over the years as legends, similar to those stories concerning many other great persons that developed over time and were embellished in the process of being told and retold. George Washington's chopping down the cherry tree is such an example. Given the overwhelming universal recognition of Jesus, it would be most unusual for there not to have been any legends or myths regarding his life.

We have stories of the unborn baby, John the Baptist, leaping in his mother's womb when Mary, presumedly already pregnant with Jesus, enters the house (Luke 1:39-44), and wise men and shepherds being told of the birth of Jesus and coming and bringing gifts (Luke 2:8-20, Matthew 2:1-12). Angels appear to Joseph on three different occasions (Matthew 1:20, 2:13,19) regarding the birth of Jesus and the angel Gabriel visits Mary to tell her of the special circumstances of the birth (Luke 1:26-38). Angels also appear to the shepherds (Luke 2:8-13).

After all of this, a person wonders why no one later seems prepared for the ministry of Jesus! Mary "kept all these things, pondering them in her heart" (Luke 2:19). Then she seems to forget for there is confusion for the family when Jesus as a young boy is found in the Temple. His parents were "astonished" (Luke 2:48). Later after his ministry had begun, his family came on one occasion "to take charge of him" because the people thought that he had "gone mad" (Mark 3:21, 31-32). The question springs to mind, "Why weren't they prepared for extraordinary things to happen after such auspicious beginnings?"

Another question is equally intriguing, "How did all of these early events surrounding his birth ever become preserved for us?" The same question arises concerning his temptations (Matthew 4:1-11) and his struggle in Gethsemane just prior to his arrest (Luke 22:39-46). On these last two occasions he was alone except for the devil in the first instance and some disciples who were asleep at a distance in the second instance. How did the information concerning these experiences get into the record? Did Jesus tell someone? Was there someone there to overhear? Did God simply dictate the details to the authors of the gospels? Surely not the last option since God would not have made the mistakes nor allowed the discrepancies that appear in these stories that we noted earlier (chapter three).

Obviously it would go beyond proof to deny that God dictated these stories, or that through some other process they were preserved for us as actual history. It becomes a matter of one's personal beliefs. If we were to approach the matter using reason or logic, it seems more reasonable to understand that some of these stories are myths that have grown up surrounding the life of Jesus because of his legendary and heroic nature. It does not seem reasonable that, for many of us, our faith depends upon the historicity of some of these myth-like stories. The birth stories have nothing essential to do with the meaning of the historical Jesus. Their authenticity is not necessary to validate Jesus and all that he revealed to us through his life and teachings, nor the cross and resurrection experiences. These events should be recognized as historical and as having their own inherent worth. A faith that believes the birth stories necessarily need to be true, is a faith that is shaky at best and one that has missed out on the power of Jesus, his life and teachings.

The question, and a very legitimate question it is, that bothers everyone is, "If some part of this life of Jesus is not historic, but is instead a myth, then how can we rely on any of what we read about Jesus, or anything else in our Bible for that matter?" This concern about pulling a loose thread and having everything come unraveled—about where we stop when we begin questioning or doubting the historicity of scripture—deserves its own separate discussion in a later chapter.

Myths carry their own particular kind of truth. The temptation episode in the life of Jesus, if it is not literal fact, certainly has its value as a significant theological struggle that Jesus most likely experienced. Being a myth takes nothing away from the value of the ideas expressed. Much like some of the parables that Jesus told, the value is not in whether it is fact or fiction, but rather the value is in the message the story dramatizes. The "Good Samaritan" parable (Luke 10:25-37) is considered by most Christians as just that—a parable. There is always the chance that such an incident happened exactly as Jesus told it. However, the power and beauty of the message depends not on whether it is fact or fiction. As a story of fiction told by Jesus, it retains all of its value for us.

Along with myths and parables, the Bible also contains allegory. Indeed there is much allegory found in myths and parables. To allegorize is to relate a symbolic narrative in which the listener or reader is intended to understand another meaning behind a literal interpretation of the words.

Literalists do see the allegorical nature in portions of scripture. As mentioned earlier, conservatives and fundamentalists have made much fuss and commotion over the symbols found in the allegorical material of the books of Daniel, Ezekiel, and Revelation. Discussion of the nature of prophecy in connection with interpreting this kind of material also will be dealt with in its own separate chapter. That the visions of dragons and leopards with bears' feet (Revelation 12 & 13) certainly must be allegory, we can all agree. But what these symbols actually represent is probably still open for further investigation. The honest Bible student would probably have to say, "We do not know exactly what the symbols represent; most of them remain a mystery." Those persons with more reckless imaginations think they have unraveled the mysteries, and they are prepared to pontificate for our edification. Their literature is omnipresent and legion.

Understanding the other kinds of literature that make up our Bible will facilitate our interpretation by helping us get to the truth and meaning of what we read. For instance, we have in the book of Job what many think to be an outstanding play. Job is thought to be a drama and not history because of the very rhythmic nature of its style as well as the way the various characters speak in rotation, in a certain order, and in a very contrived manner. Thus Job is a play that deals with the theological issue that challenges us perhaps more than any other: "Why does God allow pain and suffering in our world?" As one can see, it does not really matter whether Job is fact or fiction. What matters is the theological struggle involving an issue that perplexes all of us, and its attempt at finding some adequate answers.

Is there nothing "real" in our Bible; is there no fact or history? Yes, there is much history. It begins with the record of the Hebrew people and their settling of the "Holy Land" (a term apparently only used once in the Old Testament: Zechariah 2:12). This history starts with the twelfth chapter of Genesis and the story of Abram. Portions of history continue throughout the Old Testament, through the gospels, and the book of Acts.

Scholars tell us of an "oral tradition" involved in the preservation of our Bible history. It is suggested that much of the material was passed only in spoken word from person to person, and from generation to generation before being written down. Mark, the first written gospel, seems to have a composition date in the neighborhood of the 60's A.D., about 30-some odd years after the life of Jesus. Matthew and Luke appear a little later, with John providing the last history of Jesus. While there might well have been some written recollections of a much earlier date than these writings, and most likely there was something, the differences found in the four accounts of the life and teachings of Jesus can be attributed, not only to style and the purpose of the author, but to a lapse of time between the events themselves and the written word.

When dealing with the historical portions of scripture, we are confronted with the dilemma of either accepting the fact that there are some inaccuracies and contradictions in the material or, as the literalists do, of having to do some creative imagining in order to bring some coherence to the story.

Another kind of literature found in our Bible, particularly in some of the earlier books, is ritual or law. Exodus, Leviticus, Numbers, and Deutronomy have a great many laws and rituals, some of which even make very good sense. Also there are some which are obviously archaic in their primitive cultural world view. Most Christians usually pass over these portions considering them to be very dry and boring. However, a casual browsing might amuse and pique one's interest. We will find some unusual ideas and practices, if indeed certain of these strange rituals were ever practiced. Something the reader might enjoy trying sometime is the ritual for the eradication of leprosy from her or his house and the subsequent purification of that house. This is not a case of the persons in the house having leprosy, but is in fact a case of the house having leprosy although some versions suggest that it is only mildew. This rite involves a sprig of hyssop, a red cord, a clay bowl, some cedar wood, and the dipping of a live bird into the blood of a bird just killed (Leviticus 14:48-53). Actually, one should more properly leave this ritual for the priest to preform.

However, it may be difficult to find a priest who specializes in this ritual today, but at least the Old Testament law and ritual can make interesting reading.

If the reader is curious about why God permits us to eat certain creatures but prohibits others from our diet (Leviticus 11:1-23), he or she can find an interesting, if not far-fetched, explanation in the apocryphal Gospel of Barnabas, chapter nine.

These laws and rituals grew out of cultural myths and confusion over some of the mysteries of life. Some of them are based simply on good practical common sense, and many of them might even manifest God's will as in the case of the Ten Commandments.

Many versions of our scripture use some form to indicate the differentiation between prose and poetry found in the original languages. Prose will be indicated by the common paragraph form, while some form of indentation similar to poems with which we are familiar will be used to denote poetry. This contrast can be seen in the books of Jeremiah and Lamentations, as well as many others. Tradition tells us both books were written by Jeremiah.

The book of Jeremiah has both forms, much of the book being written in paragraph form to indicate prose and some of the material showing varying degrees of indentation to indicate Hebrew poetry. Such literary arrangement is common among the prophets. The book of Lamentations, a book of five poems, is entirely poetry.

Hebrew poetry used such literary devices as meter and occasionally acrostic arrangement—wherein each line may start with a different letter of the alphabet in sequence, a feature which is totally lost in the translation into English. Quite often Hebrew poetry employs the characteristic of repetition.

In this latter case Hebrew poetry would state an idea and then repeat the same idea or expression in the next line, only using different words. Some examples are indicated as follows:

But ask the beasts, and they will teach you; the birds of the air,
and they will tell you; (Job 12:7)

O Lord, who shall sojourn in thy tent? Who shall dwell on thy
holy hill? (Psalm 15:1)

For the Lord is enraged against all the nations, and furious
against all their host, he has doomed them, has given them over
for slaughter. (Isaiah 34:2)

Herein lies the explanation of the "Mystery of the Two
Donkeys" posed earlier in chapter three of this book. Mark, Luke,
and John all have Jesus entering Jerusalem on "Palm Sunday"
riding on one animal. Matthew tells us clearly that Jesus came
riding on two donkeys (Matthew 21:1-7). Why the difference? It
was mentioned earlier that one of the central concerns of Matthew
was to prove that Jesus fulfilled all of the Old Testament prophecy
regarding the coming of a messiah. Matthew often relates some
incident in the life of Jesus to a quotation from the Old Testament
to indicate that Jesus fulfilled the prophecy. In the case of the two
donkeys, Matthew quotes what he thinks is an appropriate verse
regarding Jesus' triumphant entry to Jerusalem:

"Tell the daughter of Zion,
Behold, your king is coming to you,
humble, and mounted on an ass,
and on a colt, the foal of an ass." (Matthew 21:5)

Let us go to the Old Testament source:

Rejoice greatly, O daughter of Zion!
Shout aloud, O daughter of Jerusalem!
Lo, your king comes to you;
triumphant and victorious is he,
humble and riding on an ass,
on a colt the foal of an ass. (Zechariah 9:9)

Matthew did not have the reader's advantage of vast and scholarly
wisdom concerning Hebrew poetry. Apparently Matthew did not
understand their propensity for repetition. Zechariah was not talking about two animals as Matthew supposed, but rather was talking
about one animal in a multiple description. Matthew misunderstood, believing there were two animals involved. Consequently,

although, no doubt, the story came to him with reference to only one animal, he believed that Jesus would have fulfilled Old Testament statements concerning a messiah. Since he mistakenly thought that the Old Testament passage was making reference to two animals, he simply wrote a "corrected" version with the appropriate two animals. It would make no difference how awkward riding two donkeys simultaneously might be; that is just the way it had to be. Matthew could have used a handy Bible commentary.

While we are on the subject, Matthew's account of the death of Judas which contradicts the Acts' account (which we discussed in chapter three) could be attributed to Matthew's attempt to bring the story into line with Zechariah 11:12-13.

In regards to the aforementioned literary genre called poetry, another literary form in our Bible is the hymn or song, which could sometimes be called a prayer. The book of Psalms readily comes to mind. Psalms is a marvelous collection of poems with a strange contrast between words that were obviously highly inspired, and words that express the meaness of human nature—and often in the same psalm. Some believe David is the author of all of our psalms. However, the text suggests that while particular ones were composed by David since many of them begin with the words, "A Psalm of David" (Psalm 144), others may have had different composers. Psalm 82 and others begin with "A Psalm of Asaph." Psalm 72, for instance, begins, "A Psalm of Solomon."

Many of these prayers soar to heights of great religious thought. At other times human frailties appear in the form of petitions of anger and revenge. The same psalm may contain beautiful ideas and expressions, as well as some of the baser of human emotions.

> I will sing to the Lord as long as I live;
>> I will sing praise to my God while I have being.
>>> (note the poetic form of repetition)
> May my meditation be pleasing to him,
>> for I rejoice in the Lord.
> Let sinners be consumed from the earth,
>> and let the wicked be no more! (Psalm 104:33-35)

One of my favorite psalms (Psalm 139) contains this interesting contrast between the sublime and the small-minded:

O Lord, thou hast searched me and know me!

. . . and art acquainted with all my ways

. . . Such knowledge is too wonderful for me;

. . . How precious to me are thy thoughts, O God!

How vast is the sum of them!

If I would count them, they are more than the sand

. . . Search me, O God, and know my heart!

Try me and know my thoughts!

In the same psalm we find these words,

O that thou wouldst slay the wicked, O God,

. . . Do I not hate them that hate thee, O Lord?

And do I not loathe them that rise up against thee?

I hate them with perfect hatred; . . .

Proverbs and Ecclesiastes are examples of books containing a unique kind of literature referred to as wisdom literature. Some persons attribute both books to Solomon, and each book opens with references to the like. Tradition identified wisdom with Solomon; consequently, he was given credit for these books, but it is very unlikely that he composed much of the material.

This particular kind of literature is supposed to be wise or clever folk wisdom, pithy cliches, or platitudes. However, it would be an insult to attribute all of this work to God, as in "the word of God." As one might expect of "folk" wisdom, given its origins and nature, there is some very good advice mixed in with some very questionable suggestions. Some of the ideas that God would not be embarrassed to claim include:

For in vain is a net spread in the sight of any bird; (Proverbs 1:17)

Such are the ways of all who get gain by violence;
it takes away the life of its possessors. (Proverbs 1:19)

The way of a fool is right in his own eyes,
>   but a wise man listens to advice.
The vexation of a fool is known at once,
>   but the prudent man ignores an insult.

(Proverbs 12:15-16)

A soft answer turns away wrath,
>   but a harsh word stirs up anger.

(Proverbs 15:1)

Wine is a mocker, strong drink a brawler;
>   and whoever is led astray by it is not wise.

(Proverbs 20:1)

On the other hand, I am sure that God does not want to claim:
No ill befalls the righteous,
>   but the wicked are filled with trouble.

(Proverbs 12:21)

since this is not the way the world is run! The Bible in several places challenges this kind of theology. For example, we find this contradiction to the above quoted proverb in the book of Job:
Why do the wicked live, reach old age,
>   and grow mighty in power?
Their houses are safe from fear,
>   and no rod of God is upon them.
They spend their days in prosperity,
>   and in peace they go down to Sheol.

(Job 21:7,9,13)

There is other "wisdom" found in Ecclesiastes that I am sure God does not claim as it is full of pessimism and bitterness. The author disparages life and almost everything about life. One cannot be honest with this book and at the same time gloss over its pessimism and depression pretending they do not exist.

One explanation that is sometimes offered is that the pessimism of the book may represent Solomon saying that he has experienced life from the perspective of extreme wealth and materialism and has found it all less than satisfactory—wealth does not bring happiness. Such an approach does not salvage this book. Sometimes we must admit that it just is not God's word. Some of the passages reveal emotions and behavior totally inappropriate for a Christian. There can be no question the author of Ecclesiastes is a very bitter person.

In a similar vein we have to read some of Jeremiah's work as an inappropriate outburst of emotion uncharacteristic of a great religious leader, even though it was certainly provoked by much stress and suffering (Jeremiah 20:7-12,14-18).

We need to be more honest with our scripture and allow it to always speak for itself as it actually is. The selection we may be reading at any given moment may not be "God's word." It may be an exaggerated myth, someone's mistaken notion of what God is like or what God wants, an error, or simply poor advice. We have to know what kind of literature we are reading. Only then can we know how to understand what is being said and be able to know how it should be interpreted.

Before leaving this subject, a word should be said about a literary device called anthropomorphism. Anthropomorphism is the act of ascribing human characteristics to non-human things. In the case of scripture, it is most often used in relationship to our ideas about God, though there are other instances such as the talking serpent (Genesis 3:1) and Balaam's donkey (Numbers 22:28-30).

Anthropomorphic thinking and conversation about God is not just a literary device. It is difficult to approach the idea of a creative power or spirit that is invisible and everywhere at once because our minds are so accustomed to reflecting upon this limited physical world. If we add the dimension of "personal" to this mysterious spirit, it becomes much easier and only natural to wax anthropomorphic, and to envision God as human-like. Sometimes for convenience, but more often because of a tradition that has prejudiced our thinking, we refer to God as "He." Although we know better, we yet maintain a childlike concept of God as an elderly, caucasian male (probably as do many people of color) with long, white hair and beard, wearing robe and sandals.

"He" is certainly not overweight, and may or may not wear wear glasses.

Such anthropomorphism is not lost on many of the authors of the Bible. It has been used throughout scripture as a literary device. From the opening chapter, God is given human traits in the creation stories. God culminates "His" work on the seventh day by "resting" (Genesis 2:2). God is pictured as liking to walk in the garden during the cool of the day (Genesis 3:8). Few of us actually take all of the anthropomorphic references about God literally: that God needs the rainbow as a reminder of the covenant God made (Genesis 9:12-16), or that God needs to have details written down in a book in order to remember all the wicked things we have done (Malachi 3:16, Revelation 20:11-12), although "He" may find it necessary in the case of some of us more prolific sinners.

Most Christians are mature enough in their faith to get beyond a simple, literal understanding of scripture and are able to recognize the various kinds of literature and literary devices that call for a figurative interpretation. As one Jewish scholar put it:

> The Bible, and indeed the Talmud too, abound in many anthropomorphisms, some of which offend modern sensibilities. The purpose of the Torah was to instruct men. It therefore had to speak in the language of men. Since language grows out of the experience and thought of men, it cannot transcend human experience and thought. The anthropomorphisms are never regarded as anything but figures of speech.[2]

As I said earlier, the literalist does not give the scripture writers much credit for intelligence and imagination in the use of the poetic or the pictorial. Similarly, the literalist has suppressed her or his own intelligence and imagination in her or his failure to recognize depth and sublties of the figurative literary devices used in the marvelous variety of literature and styles of our Bible. The honest approach to scripture is to allow the Bible to breathe and let it speak in its own language, if that be poetry, myth, and, even on occasions, error.

Big fish stories are not lies. They may not be history or fact, but they often contain great theological truths.

NOTES:

[1] The Interpreter's Bible, Volumn 1. (New York: Abingdon Press, 1951), pp. 536-537.

[2] Morris Adler, The World of the Talmud. (New York: Schocken Books, 1963), p. 90.

6. Nobody Takes It Seriously Anyway

I remember seeing a short test concerning the Bible. It was a very elementary test involving the simplest of Bible knowledge. The purpose probably was intended to show that, while we revere the Bible as "the word of God," most Christians spend very little time reading it. For a large per cent of Christians, the extent of their exposure to the Bible consists of the brief span of time their minister or other persons devote to reading to them from the pulpit on those Sunday mornings when they are attending worship services.

I have often given short Bible tests to members of churches I have served and have been dumbfounded at their lack of knowledge of the simplest facts. Oftentimes they could not place the books in their proper "testament." For example, they would place Hebrews and Acts in the Old Testament while putting Psalms and Genesis in the New Testament. This may have been an indictment against me as their pastor and teacher, as much as it was an indictment against them. Perhaps I did not do an adequate job of helping them to become familiar with scripture, nor did I stimulate their interest enough that they became better Bible students. Anyone reading her or his Bible for only five minutes just one day a week ought to know where to turn to find the four gospels, at the least. But I digress.

I want to share with you the brief test I came across not long ago in order that you might test your Bible knowledge. How much do you know regarding the most elementary facts pertaining to some of the best-known stories in your Bible? Answer these simple questions, please. Don't peek at the answers that are given below, and when you have finished, put your head down on your desk and wait for further instructions.

1. How many wise men visited the baby Jesus?
2. What fruit did Eve tempt Adam to eat in the garden?
3. What swallowed Jonah?
4. How many of each kind of creature did Noah take on the ark?

That wasn't so hard, now was it? Now it is time to grade yourself. If your answers were:

1. Three
2. Apple,
3. Whale
4. Two

join the vast majority of persons who also answered all of the answers incorrectly. You don't believe those are wrong answers? Well, you may be partially right. There may have been three wise men; the fruit may have been an apple; and the big fish perhaps was a whale. However, there is no way of knowing for certain because the Bible is not that specific. You may check out the right answers by looking up the following references:

1. Matthew 2:1-11 (we probably assume there were three persons because there were three gifts: gold, frankincense, and myrrh).

2. Genesis 2:8-3:13 (we have always believed it to be an apple because that is how artists and literature have portrayed it and because it seems to be the fruit that comes to mind more often than any other when the word "fruit" is mentioned).

3. Jonah 1:17-2:10 (a "large fish" brings the whale to mind immediately).

4. Genesis 7:2-3.

If you have trouble locating these books, and your minister can't find them for you, your Bible may contain a table of contents in the front.

Again, my contention that many Christians do not take their Bible seriously is borne out by the fact that many Christians read their Bible so seldom that they basically are not familiar with its contents.

Much furor is raised over the effort to keep prayer and Bible reading out of the public schools. One reason for this separation of church and state is to avoid giving any one religion special preference because it happens to be the religion of the majority. Certainly Christians would never want to promote their faith by unfair special privilege, using state property and funds. Some of those same persons who are adamant about including Bible reading in the public school curriculum may be some of the same persons who don't really take the Bible seriously enough to spend time reading and getting acquainted with it at home. Obviously, there would also be many good Bible students who think we must have required Bible reading in the schools. Bible students they may be; sensitive to other religions they are not.

The fact remains that too many Christians, while talking about the sacredness of "God's word," the "Holy Bible," still do not bother to read the book. If it is all we claim it to be, why don't we spend more time reading it? There may be a myriad of answers, such as—we are lazy, we think that we will be "saved" anyway, we think we know enough about "being good" already (after all, we know how many wise men there were and how many of each creature Noah took into the ark), we intend to get around to it one of these days, or, to be completely honest, others "need it worse than we do." But we still don't take it seriously.

Not using our Bibles is one way in which we do not take the Bible seriously. There is another very important way in which we ignore scripture: by not complying with or heeding its admonitions. Some scripture tells us how God wants us to live and what not to do, such as, "Thou shalt not _____," as well as what we should do, such as "Love one another" and "Feed the hungry." We pay the highest allegiance to the "Holy Bible" and place it upon a pedestal, and then with great care we ignore it or reject its teachings. Perhaps we should no longer seriously consider it as appropriate worship to slaughter animals, burn them, and sprinkle their blood on the altar—simply passing the offering plates on Sunday morning is much less messy. However, just as we ignore or reject certain of God's suggestions as no longer fashionable even though we were told that such laws and regulations would stand for ever (Leviticus 16:29, 23:41, 24:3, 24:8 to note a few examples), we also ignore or reject some Biblical ideas that probably are not meant to be considered optional.

The Old Testament tells us not to eat pigs. We say that today Simon says, "It is okay." Jesus also tells us in the New Testament some things we should and should not do. These we also "brush under the table." Given a choice, we would choose to take the admonition concerning pigs seriously rather than some of those difficult things Jesus taught.

It is convenient, and obviously more comfortable, to ignore what Jesus taught concerning wealth. Jesus was very hard on material possessions, insisting that there is danger in allowing possessions to become too important in our lives:

> Do not lay up for yourselves treasures on earth, where moth and rust consume and where thieves break in and steal, but lay up for yourselves treasures in heaven . . .

> For where your treasure is, there will your heart be also. . . .

> You cannot serve God and mammon. Therefore I tell you, do not be anxious about your life, what you shall eat or what you shall drink, nor about your body, what you shall put on. (Matthew 6:19-21,24-25).

I remind you of the story concerning the rich man who came to Jesus looking for eternal life (Luke 18:18-23). Even though the man apparently had been a very good person, Jesus felt he still lacked one very important thing in his life. He needed to give all that he had to the poor. That seems a little extreme to most of us. We take solace in the fact that the man was rich and we are not. Since most of us consider ourselves "middle class" and not at all rich (as do also some people who are very rich as I have been told), we cannot identify with this scriptural incident. We consider it irrelevant to our station in life. And though there are literally millions of persons in our world who are dying of hunger, we, after all, do not have all of our needs met either. It is not as though we ever waste, or spend foolishly, or have more than we need. Certainly Jesus could not have been thinking of us when he said to give everything to the poor. He instructed the rich man to give it all away, we say, because that person probably had some problem with wealth. We, of coarse, do not have a problem with wealth, excepting only that we think we need more. We should have such problems.

However, after using all of the rationalization at my imagination's disposal, I yet have that uneasy feeling that Jesus might also have been talking to you and me—at least to you for sure. He might not say "give everything," but I can imagine his telling us to give several times more than we presently do.

Almost everyone who reads these words has much too much, while at this very moment there are many who are dying because they have nothing. Jesus warned us:

> How hard it is for those who have riches to enter the kingdom of God! For it is easier for a camel to go through the eye of a needle than for a rich man to enter the kingdom of God. (Luke 19:24-25).

We must stop looking the other way. Our lives are too full of accessories and excuses. We eat too much and waste even more. We have far too much entertainment and comfort.

Jesus told a parable that should haunt us every day: a poor man named Lazarus lay outside the gate of a rich man (Luke 16:19-26). Clearly implied is that the rich man did not share enough with his poor neighbor. They both died; the rich man went to the bad place, and Lazarus went to heaven. The rich man suffered terrible torment for his sin of not caring for a person who was in great need.

This parable is not about heaven and hell, nor about rewards and punishments. It is about our having a social conscious. All people are God's children, making them all our sisters and brothers. And we are letting many of them die in torment while we enjoy too much of the world's resources.

Despite the fact that we would rather ignore what Jesus had to say concerning wealth and turn to more comfortable passages, such as, "The Lord is my shepherd. . .", the rest of the Bible agrees with Jesus on this issue: God cares for the poor and expects all of us to do the same. Amos speaks for most of the Old Testament concerning possessions and the poor. He condemns the rich as:

> . . .they sell the righteous for silver,
>   and the needy for a pair of shoes—
> they that trample the head of the poor
>   into the dust of the earth. . .
> Hear this word, you cows of Bashan,
>   who are in the mountain of Samaria,
> who oppress the poor, who crush the needy,
>   who say to their husbands, "Bring, that we might drink!". . .
> Woe to those who lie upon beds of ivory,
>   and stretch themselves upon their couches. . .
> who drink wine in bowls,
>   and anoint themselves with the finest oils,
>   but are not grieved over the ruin of Joseph!
> Therefore they shall now be the
>   first of those to go into exile. . .
>
> (Amos 2:6-7, 4:1, 6:4, 6-7).

You ask, "What's your point?" I lost control there for a moment and went to preaching. The foregoing was not intended to be a sermon on wealth. I meant only to illustrate one significant way in which we do not take Jesus seriously. It is illustrative only because, in fact, for we ignore Jesus on many issues.

Let's examine a second issue. The Old Testament tells us to "love your neighbor as yourself" (Leviticus 19:18), and:

> If your enemy is hungry, give him bread to eat; and if he is thirsty, give him water to drink. . . (Proverbs 25:21)

However, since the Old Testament has seriously compromised itself on this theological point with far too many contradictory examples, we must look to the New Testament for a clear message of pacifism. Jesus tells us to do more than just love neighbors; we must love our "enemies and pray for those who persecute" us (Matthew 5:44). Paul echoes Jesus' teachings with precision concerning love and pacifism. Romans 12:14-21 parallels Matthew 5:38-48 so meticulously. We must:

> Bless those who persecute you; bless and do not curse them. Repay no one evil for evil. . .Beloved, never avenge yourselves. . .No, if your enemy is hungry, feed him; if he is thirsty, give him drink. . .Do not be overcome by evil, but overcome evil with good. (Romans 12:14,17,19-21)

There can be no question but that Jesus taught pacifism: "Turn the other cheek" and "Go the second mile" (Matthew 5:39,41),

> Put your sword back into its place; for all who take the sword will perish by the sword. (Matthew 26:52)

> Jesus answered, "My kingship is not of this world; if my kingship were of this world, my servants would fight. . . " (John 18:36)

Pacifism is central to the teachings of Jesus. Jesus made it very clear that pacifism is the only way for Christians.

Even Reinhold Neibuhr, no pacifist himself and a chief spokesperson for Christianity earlier in this century, "readily admits the pacifism of Jesus."[1] As G. H. C. Macgregor concurs,

> . . .there can be no question that the teaching of Jesus, if taken at its face value, is uncompromisingly pacifist. Niebuhr has no patience with those Christian theologians and ecclesiastics who still seek to discover loopholes through which war may be actually brought within the pale of Christian ethics and blessed in the name of the Prince of Peace.[2]

It is ironic and unfortunate that the high ethical calling of Christianity—pacifism, which places the values and principles of Christianity high above most of the other religions—is the very thing we choose to either ignore or deny about our faith. On this issue we find it very difficult to take our Bible seriously. We labor assiduously at the task of finding grounds for interpreting the teachings of Jesus in a more palatable manner. One such way is to focus upon very simple facts instead of significant theological ideas.

Once upon a time long ago, a clergy person asked me in front of a large group what I thought about the fifth Commandment. I had no idea, and still don't, as to which one is the fifth (although at that moment I wanted to plead the fifth). He smiled at my embarrassment in what I thought was a malicious way. He knew the Commandments by their appropriate numbers. As he smiled in a pleased way, I realized that it was useless to try to explain that it was more important to know what the Commandments were all about than it was to know their proper numerical order. I had been had.

For too many Christians, knowing certain facts about the Bible is all that matters, such as being able to name all of Joseph's brothers (Joseph of the Old Testament) or recite the "gifts" and "fruits" of the spirit as if the lists were clearly delineated separate entities instead of just general descriptions. Memorizing lists deprioritizes more important matters such as working through the Bible's serious ethical issues and other great ideas. We should ask ourselves what are the most important values to be found in our Bible because those are probably the very items which we are not taking seriously.

Certain "evangelical" and "conservative" churches are very critical of the "mainline" and "liberal" churches for not preaching the whole gospel. For the past twenty years or more, the liberal churches have been concerned over a trend toward a decrease in membership while some of the conservative churches have experienced an increase in membership. This trend of persons gravitating from one persuasion towards another in cases where that is actually happening is often blamed on the mainline churches' failure to preach the full gospel. Consequently, we have seen the emergence of very popular and rapidly growing conservative churches which are purported to be preaching the "full gospel." Actually, I always assumed that the "full gospel" is, in fact, offensive to people and might tend to drive certain persons away rather than attract them. Preaching about certain of Jesus' teachings can be very unpopular. It should have a strong tendency to upset those Christians who are not yet ready for the "meat":

> But I, brethren, could not address you as spiritual men, but as men of the flesh, as babes in Christ. I fed you with milk, not solid food; for you were not ready for it; and even yet you are not ready, for you are still of the flesh. (I Corinthians 3:1-3)

Old Testament folks found the message of the prophets very disagreeable. Offended by what they heard, they were less than kind to the prophets. Jesus offended enough persons that it cost him his life. Tradition tells us all of his followers continued to offend people with the "full gospel" and suffered for it. Paul boasts about his suffering due to the unpopular things he had to say (II Corinthians 11:16-33).

I seriously suspect that the gospel is still offensive to a large number of people today and when it is preached in the comfortable, nice, amicable middle-class churches, there will be an exodus of some significance by persons in search of the "pat-you-on-the-back-and-make-you-feel-good" kind of churches that are growing by leaps and bounds. Don't be caught standing in the doorways and get trampled.

Where the "full gospel" is actually preached, some persons are going to be offended. Of course, do not think that the reverse is true: that because the message is offensive, it must necessarily be the gospel. However, wherever we find a successful, rapidly growing church filled with congenial, happy Christians, we might want to snoop around to see if perhaps some part of the gospel is being ignored or denied so as not to upset anyone. Which churches are taking the Bible seriously today?

There are many minor points that would be interesting to explore regarding this idea of taking our Bible seriously. Has the ban really been lifted from eating pork? What about worship on the Sabbath? Is it the seventh day or the first day of the week, or does it matter? Are the "Ten Commandments" the only Old Testament laws applicable for Christians today? Are all of the other Jewish laws no longer in force, and if not, what is the difference? Does it have anything to do with Jesus seemingly implying that keeping "The Ten" was necessary when he spoke with the rich man in the incident mentioned above (Luke 18:18-22), or is it for other reasons?

In regards to certain suggestions found in the New Testament, is it really better if a person doesn't marry (I Corinthians 7:1, 8, 26-27), or should we marry (I Corinthians 7:2, 9)? What about the confusing scripture which reads, "From now on, let those who have wives live as though they had none?" (I Corinthians 7:29) Or should we just skip over the seventh chapter altogether?

The questions continue on. Is the man really the head of the woman, should a woman, but not a man, wear a veil or hat in church, and should a woman have long hair but not a man (I Corinthians 11:1-16)? If we Christians should speak in tongues (I Corinthians 14:4-5), why are there so very, very few who do? Are women really not supposed to be ministers (I Corinthians 14:34-35)?

There are so many frightening questions to answer if we try to take the Bible seriously. Do you have satisfactory answers to these and the many other difficult questions we find in scripture? Some persons think they do, and this is frightening in itself.

Even the Bible does not take itself seriously at times. There is no question that the Old Testament mandates death for persons who have committed adultery. Yet we read where Rahab, the prostitute, (Joshua 2) was not only spared execution, but was treated with special care and presumedly with God's blessings (Joshua 6:17,25). And we worry about discrimination and inequalities in our judicial systems today.

David not only commits adultery with Bathsheba, the wife of a man named Uriah, but finally decides to have Uriah killed in order to keep Bathsheba permanently (II Samuel 11). David, of course, is too important of a figure to be executed, or even imprisoned, although he doesn't escape punishment entirely. Like the wealthy and influential of today, David received a reprimand. That isn't entirely true; there was additional punishment such as losing a child, losing some of his wives, and general trouble in his administration (II Samuel 12:10-14). Notice, however, that most of the suffering fell upon other members in the family.

Either capital punishment didn't apply to kings and other leading citizens such as, Rahab, the prostitute, or else the Old Testament Law wasn't taken very seriously.

There is an intriguing case in the Old Testament concerning another law—the law that mediums and persons who consult with dead people should also be put to death (Leviticus 20:27). Our story unfolds with the death of Samuel, the prophet who anointed kings. At about that same time, Saul decides to enforce the law just alluded to from the book of Leviticus concerning mediums. Despite the fact that the law dictated that mediums should be stoned to death, Saul, bless his lenient heart, only runs them out of the country (I Samuel 28:3). Not having all of them killed turns out to be fortuitous because only about four verses later, he is terrified about an upcoming battle with the Philistines, one with which God doesn't seem willing to help. Saul calls for the services of a medium. Saul wants to talk with his old, but very dead friend Samuel to ask his advice. Through the talents of the medium, Samuel returns from the dead and visits with Saul (I Samuel 28:4-15).

Not wanting to spoil the story for you by telling you the ending, I simply want to ask some interesting questions. Many conservatives and liberals alike today do not believe in mediums. Was this lady really a medium? Is this another example wherein certain miraculous things can happen in the Bible world but cannot happen in real life today? Did it really happen then? Did Samuel do wrong in "coming back"? Did God somehow participate in this event? Isn't somebody guilty of not taking the Bible seriously when the law was so conveniently ignored in this situation? Somebody should be punished and we hope we can watch.

I made the assertion that many of us Christians do not take our Bible seriously. We don't bother to read it with expectation as if we believe it is the "Word of God." Many don't bother to read it at all.

But most important of all, we don't take seriously the critical, and uncomfortable, teachings of Jesus regarding significant ethical living: for example, we just go on busily killing each other and letting other people starve to death.

NOTES:

[1] Rufus M. Jones, ed., The Church, the Gospel and War. (New York: Garland Publishing, Inc., 1971), p. 51.

[2] G. H. C. Macgregor, The New Testament Basis of Pacifism and the Relevance of an impossible ideal. (Nyack, New York: Fellowship Publications, 1960), p. 127.

7. Who Said It Was Perfect?

The Bible, I am told, is more widely read, studied, and written about than any other book and is consequently a constant best-seller, all of which makes me wonder why I wrote this book. What more could be said? No doubt, it has all been said and said much better already. It is a best-seller, probably because of what is believed about it, and what is believed about it is that it is the *perfect* word of God. If you have read this far, you now know that many persons believe that there are errors and contradictions in the Bible as well as ideas that are absolutely antithetical to our perception of a loving and good God. However, a good many lay-persons, and more clergy-types than God would care to have, still believe in the inerrancy (the perfection) of the Old and New Testaments to the extent that they are ready to embrace some crazy notions about God and the kind of conduct God desires of us. If we are ever to allow the "truth to make us free," we have to get beyond this stiflingly narrow perspective and into a serious search for the real heart of God's Word that lives somewhere in the Bible.

But who said it was perfect anyway? Were do we get the idea that this book is somehow set apart from all other books in an almost magical way?

William Jennings Bryan, in his book In His Image, declared that the Bible was written either by men or by God. If written by men, there was no reason for us to believe any of it. If written by God, then every word of it was trustworthy.[1]

The phrase, "no reason for us to believe any of it" if it was written by people, has interesting ramifications. Does that mean that anything written by human beings is not trustworthy and cannot be believed (including Bryan's own words)? No, Bryan is suggesting that books written by people, without God's help (how do we know whom God has helped?), may or may not be true. The all-important question is, "How can we know?" The only answer is that the written word will have to reveal its intrinsic worth by its witness to truth as measured by consistency with common sense and reality. Ultimately, each one of us has to be the judge of that. We can explore more of this in the fifteenth chapter.

As eminent as Bryan is, with his Scopes "monkey trial" fame and all, it will take more than his word to authenticate the infallibility of scripture. There are two possibilities: either scripture itself pronounces its own status of perfection or some persons or council of exalted authority has said so—or both. In either case, a familiarity with how our Bible came to be would be helpful. Such is the nature of the discussion of the next chapter.

Some persons believe that there are passages within scripture that make the claim of inerrancy for the whole of the Bible at once. I'm sure that several such passages readily spring to your mind, the first of which might be:

> You shall not add to the word which I command you, nor take
> from it. . . (Deuteronomy 4:2)

Is this telling us that the inerrancy of God's word must be preserved with extreme care? If it is, it certainly comes with exalted authority for it purports to be a passage given by God to Moses. However, the context clearly implies that it refers only to the law or commandments of the Old Testament and to nothing else. Likewise, Jesus is referring to the Old Testament law and prophets when he says,

> Whoever then relaxes one of the least of these commandments
> and teaches men so, shall be called least in the kingdom of
> heaven. (Matthew 5:19)

Interestingly enough, despite the fact that Jesus says,

> Think not that I have come to abolish the law and prophets; I
> have come not to abolish them but to fulfill them. (Matthew
> 5:17)

Jesus immediately proceeds to make explicit and definite changes in those laws by quoting them and then suggesting different ideas in their stead. For example:

> You have heard that it was said to the men of old, "You shall not kill; and whoever kills shall be liable to judgment." But I say to you that every one who is angry with his brother shall be liable to judgment. . . (Matthew 5:21-22)

This is not so much a change in God's law as an expansion on it in order to give a greater meaning than that contained in the Old Testament. He continues to quote the Old Testament:

> You have heard that it was said, "You shall not commit adultery." But I say to you that every one who looks at a woman lustfully has already committed adultery. . . (Matthew 5:27-28)

Again, Jesus is merely expanding our understanding of God's will in contrast to the limited Old Testament vision. But then he begins to suggest greater change in the law:

> It was also said, "Whoever divorces his wife, let him give her a certificate of divorce." But I say to you that every one who divorces his wife, except on the ground of unchastity, makes her an adulteress. . . (Matthew 5:31-32).

It is clear that Jesus made a change in what the Old Testament law said about the nature of divorce. He tells us that God's will regarding marriage and divorce is to be understood in a very different way.

Next, Jesus quotes Old Testament policy concerning the nature of oath-taking, but then tells us not to take an oath at all (Matthew 5:33-34).

What follows these examples are two radical changes in Old Testament law and theology:

> You have heard that it was said, "An eye for an eye and a tooth for a tooth." But I say to you, Do not resist one who is evil. But if anyone strikes you on the right cheek, turn to him the other also. . . (Matthew 5:38-39)

You have heard that it was said, "You shall love your neighbor
and hate your enemy." But I say to you, Love your enemies. . .
(Matthew 5:43-44)

Yes, Jesus dared to change the Bible.

Were you about to quote the following passage?
Jesus answered them, "Is it not written in your law, 'I said, you
are gods'? If he called them gods to whom the word of God
came (and scripture cannot be broken). . ." (John 10:34-35)

What does Jesus mean by saying, "scripture cannot be broken."
First, Jesus is referring again to the Old Testament, specifically
Psalm 82:6, wherein God is enigmatically calling people "gods."
There is nothing wrong with suggesting that, while Jesus clearly
made changes in Old Testament teachings, he could also say that
when and wherever the Old Testament does reveal the nature of
God, or God's will for us, it is an eternal truth. But if you would
like to make a case that Jesus is saying that *all* Old Testament
passages are true forever, then I remind you that you should have
had your children stoned to death when they disobeyed you
(Deuteronomy 21:18-21), or that you should stone to death anyone
who curses God (Leviticus 24:15-16).

Let us look at two parallel passages regarding the status of
scripture:

All scripture is inspired by God. . . (II Timothy 3:16)

. . . no prophecy of scripture is a matter of one's own
interpretation, because no prophecy ever came by the impulse of
man, but men moved by the Holy Spirit spoke from God. (II
Peter 1:20-21).

Having an understanding of how the Bible grew up over long
periods of time, book by book, one realizes that the phrase,
"Scripture is inspired," here means only the Old Testament. At the
time when these words in the Timothy and Peter letters were
written, there was no New Testament nor any notion of scripture
yet beyond that of the Old Testament. One could argue that such
references were prophetic and actually referred to something that

did not exist yet, a whole Bible of sixty-six books. However such an idea would have been utterly unintelligible to those for whom II Peter and II Timothy were written, and it most certainly would qualify as an anachronism. The readers of II Peter and II Timothy would understand the reference only in application to the Old Testament. However, the words themselves do not claim inerrancy, but simply tell us that "some scripture" (we *cannot know* for sure which portions) are "profitable for teaching, for reproof, for correction, and for training in righteousness" in order that we might be "equipped for every good work" (II Timothy 3:16-17).

But what does it mean that scripture is inspired? For some it means that God dictated to people whose sole involvement in the process was to be little automatons simply recording what God told them. But we know that didn't happen, because then there would be no errors in scripture. No one would want to attribute to God the silly notions, contradictions, strangeness, and mistakes found in the Bible. There is no question but that all of those reflect the handiwork of human beings who are very human. Much closer to the truth is to say that many of the writers were influenced by the spirit of God and were thus able to capture some of the essence of the truth of God. Some scripture is inspired in this way, while there is scripture that we have to confess is not inspired at all—some scripture that God would even like to see expunged from the Bible. Each Christian actually makes choices about those passages that she or he thinks is inspired; for example, passages one keeps going back to for guidance and inspiration time after time. We could say that those sections are inspired not only because the writers were tuned in to the truth of God, but also because they are passages that inspire the readers.

If II Timothy were actually making the claim that scripture was inspired by God, we would be caught in the web of the circular argument again. Are we to believe that scripture is inspired by God only on the basis that the book makes the claim? Do we believe everything we read without making some other comparison for evaluation? If Charles Dickens had written somewhere in his novel, *Our Mutual Friend*, that "this work is inspired by God," would that be sufficient for us to believe that it actually and unquestionably was inspired by God? Why then are those words any more reliable when found in II Timothy, if they were meant to refer to II Timothy itself?

In many cases it is not the writing that is inspired so much as it is the persons who are being written about. One could say that it is Jesus who is inspired by God and not Matthew who records only what he has heard about Jesus.

The two passages just mentioned, II Peter and II Timothy, are making reference to the Old Testament when they refer to "scripture" because neither book was, itself, considered scripture until much later, and then only after much dissension and debate. On the other hand, the following passage from Revelation,

> I warn every one who hears the words of the prophecy of this book: if any one adds to them, God will add to him the plagues described in this book, and if any one takes away from the words of the book of this prophecy, God will take away his share in the tree of life and in the holy city, which are described in this book. (Revelation 22:18-19)

refer to, and only to, the book of Revelation and to none of the other sixty-five books in the Bible. The words, "this book," could not mean the sixty-six books of the Bible as a whole because, we repeat, at the point in time when Revelation was written, there was no Bible as we know it today, no New Testament, nor any unanimity on which books would be included in the Bible or the New Testament.

These words, appearing as they do at the end of Revelation and consequently, as well as coincidentally, at the end of the Bible in its more common order of books, have caused many Christians to interpret them as a sort of benediction for the entire Bible as well as some kind of pronouncement concerning the importance of scripture. They see it as a curse placed on any who dare tamper with it, a curse similar to that placed on the mummy's tomb. But there is no claim to inerrancy or infallibility for the Bible as a whole nor even just the book of Revelation in those closing words.

No word can be found that pronounces such perfection for the Bible within the book itself, and the various books of the Bible were gathered together in final form so many years after the writing of any individual book that no single passage could intelligibly be referring to the entire Bible.

The first suggestion was that scripture was perfect because it makes the claim itself. We find, in fact, that it makes no such claim, and even if it did, how valid would such a claim be? No logician could ever accept such a circular argument. The argument runs as follows: How do we know that scripture is perfect as well as the word of God? Because the scripture says so. But how can we believe what scripture says? Because it is the perfect word of God. But how can we know that? Because it says so.

We are forced to go outside of scripture for any designation regarding its status. It remains for some one person or for some council or group to decide what scripture is and tell us. Then we must be willing to accept that individual's or group's authority on the matter. But what good is the word of any group or individual pronouncing the Bible to be infallible when the Bible record is filled with errors and inconsistencies? To take the word of any outside authority that the Bible is infallible would be to do so in the face of insurmountable evidence to the contrary—the evidence of the Bible itself!

If we look to some authority figure or council for confirmation that the book is perfect, we are only diminishing its credibility. At the same time we would need to substantiate the validity of the outside source in terms of its expertise in the matter. In other words, we have to ask by what authority that particular individual or group comes by the power to pronounce infallibility. This only puts us on the road of the infinite regress argument.

To be honest, we must acknowledge that the church (whoever that may be) has never given us a consistent, unanimous, or definitive statement as to in what sense the Bible is the revelation of God. In the most appropriate sense then, we are left as individual Christians to select those sections of scripture that edify and inspire us, and then to relegate to a lesser status those passages that lack significant meaning or that, in fact, are harmful in their suggestions. As dangerous as this seems, and it does have its danger, it is the only way to the truth of God. It becomes obvious that some sort of measuring device—some reliable way of discriminating—will be necessary to know and separate the wheat from the chaff. That secret will be unveiled in chapter fifteen.

NOTES:

[1] L. Harold DeWolf, The Case for Theology in Liberal Perspective. (Philadelphia: The Westminster Press, 1959), p. 46.

8. If The Stork Didn't Bring It . . .

So few lay people have any real perspective on just how the Bible came to be. At some point in a child's education, we assume the child should cultivate a deeper understanding of how the Easter Bunny does her job, have a greater acquaintance with Santa Claus, and have greater appreciation for the work of the Stork. It might be safe to assume that most six-year-old children know more about the Stork, the Easter Bunny, and Santa Claus than most adults do about the origins of the Bible.

The Bible was not brought down from heaven by elves, and God did not personally dictate each word to people who took careful notation. We know that human beings wrote all of our scripture and that those people were sometimes upset, angry, intelligent, loving, prejudiced, inspired, gifted, poetic, and some-times very primitive in their world view. Our scripture was written as letters, records, songs, history, myth, and even as bigoted propaganda. The more we know about the creation of our scripture, the better will be our appreciation and understanding of its truth and value for our own personal lives. Like any subject of history, we will never remember very much of the details—specific dates and facts—after we have become acquainted with them. Neverthe-less, we can have an overall accurate and general impression of the process of the coming together of the material of our Bible which will enhance our pursuit and understanding of its meanings.

The Bible is not very helpful concerning dates of composition, and it is only somewhat better in identifying some of its authors. From various items of internal evidence such as references to events that have been dated with some degree of accuracy in other historical records outside of Biblical material, scholars have been able to place a semblance of chronological order to the books along with some approximate dates.

Most scholars make much of an oral tradition that existed prior to the advent of keeping written records. Apparently people did much better at remembering things that happened and were able to pass that information along to later generations by word of mouth without the metamorphosis that plagues our oral discourse today. The written word was sparse, and those who could read it anyway were fewer in number. Necessarily, this heightened speaking and listening skills making any oral history more reliable than we could imagine it would be today. Both Old and New Testaments, we are told, may have had a significant period of oral history prior to any written works. An illustration of the power of oral transcription is the way a new joke will be remembered and transverse the country by word of mouth only.

Be what it may, this high regard for oral tradition reliability cannot justify our considering the stories that purport to be history of a very early age as being very dependable as factual history goes. Some persons may have had remarkable memories, but when it came to remembering what God did on the third or fourth day of creation, no one's memory is that good. These early stories, such as Creation, The Garden, Cain and Able, The Flood, and The Tower of Babel, are myths. These stories, like "why the snake has no legs" (Genesis 3:1-15), rank alongside Uncle Remus' story of "Why Brother Bear Has No Tail," except that while Uncle Remus is only telling amusing stories, the Biblical myths are trying to give some explanation of why things are the way they are (not so much as to why snakes are without legs as to why there is sin and death in our world and similar issues), and we must remember they were told from a very primitive world point of view.

No one believes the Tower of Babel account is an explanation of how our world developed a variety of languages (Genesis 11:1-9). On the other hand, the two creation stories and the Garden of Eden account of sin, while being myths, do carry some great theological truths.

Any semblance of history does not really get under way until apparently oral tradition remembered an Abram (Abraham) and some legendary events attributed to him beginning with the twelfth chapter of Genesis. Abraham would have lived around 2000 B.C.

He didn't know that, of course, since he wasn't using our calendar. Even with our calendars, Bible scholars find it impossible to extrapolate any dates for these early events that can be agreed upon.

None of these early personages like Abraham, Isaac, Jacob, and Moses are the subject of any careful biographical material. The earliest written material found in scripture probably was an early written form of some laws and ritual, possibly some "commandments" attributed to Moses. This was followed by a little early poetry and some written narratives gleaned from oral preservation that probably took on written form during the 1200's and 1100's and 1000's B.C. After the appearance of the settled nation and the Temple, from about 1000 B.C. on, some Temple records and histories were kept.

Scholars feel that the first written book in our Bible that had anywhere near the form as we know it today was the book of Amos, coincidently written by a man named Amos, about 750 B.C. Shortly after, other prophets appeared on the scene who also left written records for us: Isaiah, Hosea, and Micah in the late 700's, and Zephaniah, Jeremiah, Nahum, and Habakkuk in the 600's. Some records and bits of history began to take shape over this period, and some of the law in Deuteronomy was in circulation. These were the first books of the Old Testament; however, we cannot be sure of their original form. Books like Amos, Isaiah, and Zechariah, according to Bible students, could represent the work of two or more persons living many years apart in time. The last few chapters of Amos could come from the mid to late 500's, two hundred plus years after the first part of Amos.

Scholars think they even see possibly three authors for the book of Isaiah. One outstanding Old Testament professor suggests this as a possibility: The original Isaiah wrote in the late 700's, while an anonymous writer in the mid-500's wrote chapters 40 through 66 (though subsequent scholars think chapters 56 through 66 represent still a third person and a later period of time) which were then, at a later point in time, copied onto the blank space at the end of the original Isaiah scroll, only later to be mistakenly identified as belonging to Isaiah.[1]

Those who are purportedly "in the know" tell us that there are other books that either have material in them that was written by someone other than the original author or are books that an anonymous author has written under the name of a well-known person. For example, some scholars believe that, although I and II Timothy and Titus make the claim that Paul wrote these letters, Paul did not write them. We are told that it was not uncommon for persons to pass off their own writing under names of other persons who were much better known. This was not frowned upon in that day of relaxed copyright laws as it is in our own.

It is important for us to remember that persons who wrote the books now contained in the Bible did not know that they were writing the Bible. They had no intention of writing any Bible. They were simply responding to the current contingencies whether it was writing a letter to answer some question that arose, trying to record some meaningful events or ideas, giving expression in a prayer or hymn to feelings of deep emotion, or trying to organize laws and ritual for ethical living and religious worship. In the beginning they did not have any notion of what we call scripture, nor did most of them have any inclination to see their work in the light that we view it today.

Little by little, written materials accumulated until books like Ecclesiastes, Daniel, Psalms, and Proverbs were organized into a more finished form between 200 and 100 B.C. There was no "Old Testament" as we know it for Jesus to read as an authenticated scripture. Certain chapters of Deuteronomy (probably 5-26, 28) were canonized (declared as scripture) by a prophetess, Huldah (lucky for us she lived before Paul's time), in 621 B.C. (II Kings 22). This was the first "Bible." Next, the first five books of the Old Testament (the Pentateuch) were canonized around 400 B.C.

There still existed other works and manuscripts for which the Jews had great respect, some books more than others. Official pronouncement of what we know to be the Old Testament took place about sixty years after the time of Jesus at the Council of Jamnia in 90 A.D.

We are told that the New Testament began with the letters of Paul. In about 50 A.D. Paul is believed to have written a letter to the Thessalonians, a community where he had started a church, this letter being the first in a series of letters written by Paul to various religious communities until about the year 60.

Scholars believe that somewhere around 65 A.D. the Gospel of Mark was set down by Mark, the early missionary partner of Paul and Barnabas. This would have been some thirty years after Jesus. Again we are told that a strong oral tradition circulated concerning the life and teachings of Jesus until Mark's work. But this does not rule out the possibility that there were written fragments or notes from a much earlier time that preserved some of the events and teachings.

Between about ten and fifteen years later, the gospels of Matthew and Luke were written. They relied heavily upon Mark, thereby giving the descriptive name of "synoptic gospels" to the three books. The gospel of John is later still, perhaps fifteen or twenty years after Matthew and Luke. Luke, the physician who wrote Luke, also wrote Acts, the book that gives us the history of the early church immediately following the time of Jesus. Revelation, written by one of the Johns, and Hebrews were written after 90 A.D. along with a few other books. Some New Testament books might have been written as late as 120 or after, notably I and II Timothy and Titus.

But when did our New Testament finally become official canon (scripture) with the twenty-seven books we recognize today? It seems that many years passed before there was any unanimity concerning which books should be "in" and which ones should be "out." Some local churches accepted certain books—some gospels, some of Paul's letters, and some other books—while other churches accepted an entirely different list of books they felt were important. For many years there was no "official" New Testament. Each local church had its own list of valuable writings and at that time may not have had any thoughts concerning any of them being "scripture." Perhaps the issue has never been officially settled yet! Harold DeWolf tells us:

Indeed, the canon never was fixed by a general council, unless one is willing so to designate the Roman Council of Trent. The extent of the canon still differs considerably in the various branches of Christendom. It was historically established for most Protestants by the Westminster Assembly of 1643 and the Swiss Declaration of Faith in 1675.[2]

The "canon" in this quote denotes the New Testament. The Council of Trent was called in 1542 and met from 1545, off and on, until 1563. Other authorities assign the completion of the canon to a time about 400.[3] Jerome translated the New Testament into Latin in 388. His translation of both Old and New Testaments is known as the *Vulgate*. His New Testament listed the twenty-seven books that most Christians accept as New Testament today.

Most people today do not appreciate the struggle that surrounded the issue of which books should be included and which should not. It turns out that determination of what was scripture or the word of God came about through "committee vote" and/or popular appeal long after the books had been written. There never was unanimous agreement by any churches or church councils on the canon list. There exist books that were left out, much to the dismay of many Christians, and there are books in the Bible that some persons adamantly felt should not be there. The latter only survived "the cut" after long and heated debate. What are some of these books that someone decided you would not have in your Bible, and which are the books in our present Bible that were approved only after much protest?

The "almost Bible" books, those left out, (they will be discussed in a later chapter) include what is called the Apocrypha (not to be confused with the apocalyptic books of our Bible such as Revelation, Daniel, and Ezekiel discussed briefly in chapter 5). These are the fifteen books (depending on whose counting, as they are grouped differently at times) that are found in the Roman Catholic versions of the Bible. Protestants are beginning to notice these books appearing in their Bible more often. They include I and II Esdras, Tobit, Judith, Additions to the book of Esther,

Wisdom of Solomon, Ecclesiasticus (sometimes called Sirach, or Wisdom of Jesus the Son of Sirach [not to be confused with Ecclesiastes in our Bible]), Baruch, Jeremiah, The Prayer of Azariah and the Song of the Three Young Men (which forms part of chapter 3 of Daniel in our Bible), Susanna (which can be chapter 13 of our Daniel), Bel and the Dragon (which can be chapter 14 of our Daniel), The Prayer of Manasseh, and finally I and II Maccabees. Roman Catholics accept these fifteen books as having the same inspired authority as any of the books of the Old and New Testaments.[4] Jerome's *Vulgate*, mentioned earlier, included these books thereby giving veneration to their status.

These books were written for the most part during the period between the Old and New Testaments, just prior to the time of Jesus. They make for both inspired and interesting reading. We are told that Christopher Columbus became inspired to take his voyages of discovery because of a passage found in one of these books, II Esdras.[5]

I believe that the Roman Catholic concept of purgatory comes from references in I or II Maccabees with perhaps some feeble support from I Corinthians 3:11-15 and Matthew 5:26. While support for a purgatory from scripture, whether in the apocrypha or otherwise, is very questionable, I like the theology that eliminates an immediate assignment to a heaven or a hell, and allows some "second chances," if this is what purgatory is all about.

There are other books that did not "make the cut." Such books as The Shepherd of Hermas, Revelation of Peter, Epistle of Barnabas, Gospel of Thomas, The Teachings of the Apostles, Epistle to the Laodiceans, and I and II Clement received strong support from some of the great leaders of the early church, but to no avail for they were censored by committee vote. This does not exhaust the list. But aren't you curious to know what those works contain and how valuable they are?

One might think the books that made it, the sixty-six we accept as our Bible today, were admitted to the canon with a happy unanimity. That is not so. Some of our Bible books were challenged and admitted only after much resistance and stubborn debate—some more than others, of course. You wonder which of our Bible books nearly did not become scripture? The list includes Ecclesiastes (considered very questionable), Song of Songs, Daniel, Hebrews, James, Revelation, II Peter, and Jude. Martin Luther, as everyone knows, did not like the book of James (personally, one of my favorite books) and no doubt would have removed it from the Bible. Remember the earlier quotation in this book concerning how John Wesley felt about certain passages from the Psalms.

As frightening as the suggestion may seem to some readers, a Christian must take the critical posture in Bible reading of selecting the "good" material and discarding the "bad." This is the mark of a thinking and discriminating reader—one who is more apt to find the greatest value in her or his Bible. In other words, each Christian will become a committee of one creating his or her own little canon by selecting those passages in scripture that are the most meaningful and inspirational.

Now that we have the canon closed, or nearly so, how was the Bible handled and preserved through the ages to become the book that each one of us now spends two or three hours each day assiduously pouring over? (We will reserve for a later chapter a look at the various translations.)

To begin with, there are no original manuscripts, unless you, the reader, have a hidden copy somewhere. If so, bring it out and become an instant millionaire. We have only copies of copies. Until the well-known discovery of the Dead Sea Scrolls in 1947, the oldest manuscripts dated from the fourth century A.D. And there are literally thousands of manuscripts, but many are only fragments. Finding the Dead Sea Scrolls provided us with copies that are much closer to the originals. They may date to a time even before Jesus. They do not include all of the Old Testament, but only portions: all of Isaiah, some of Habakkuk, some Psalms, and some works not found in the Bible. A few more fragments of Genesis, Leviticus, Deuteronomy, and other books were found later, and there is always the possibility that other ancient manuscripts will be found some day that will bring us even closer to the originals.

The obvious importance of finding earlier copies is that they should, generally, be more accurate, for the manuscripts we have now do not always agree. Scholars often have to choose from among different manuscripts the one which they believe might be closer to the original, perhaps using the context for consistency. Good translations of the Bible will have numerous footnotes that indicate the problems that translators faced. It would be of interest for the reader to look for those notes in a translation that has them in order to become acquainted with the many possible variations in the words and phrases extant. For example, you might encounter along the bottom of a page in your Bible words like "One ancient translation:" or "Some translations:". These notes will then be followed by another version of the text. Scholars, then, had to choose which wording to use. Other footnotes might say "Hebrew uncertain." or "Probable text:".

As more comes to be understood concerning the language as used during different periods of time—for we know that the meanings of words change through use over the years—scholars will be able to more closely capture the meaning of the Hebrew or Greek they are reading as it was used in the time period in which it was written. Archaeology's continued search is invaluable in this regard.

Scholars are aware of errors that crept into the manuscripts over the centuries because of mistakes by the copyists. Sometimes a copier would make a note concerning the text in the margin, and a later copier would insert it into the text assuming it to be part of the original that the earlier copier had mistakenly almost omitted.[6]

Examples of differences in the extant manuscripts have been preserved in some translation or versions. In the manuscripts most used by scholars, the gospel of Mark ends with the eighth verse of chapter sixteen. However, you probably have a version of the Bible which has an additional number of verses (9 through 20) not found in earlier manuscripts. This ending to Mark is found in later manuscripts and may have been added sometime during the second century A.D. There is even yet another two verses found in later manuscripts and positioned at the end of Mark in some versions.

Many very early manuscripts do not have that beautiful passage where Jesus is confronted with persons bringing a woman caught in adultery to be stoned (John 8:1-11). It is a beautiful passage of forgiveness and love. You remember the words, "Let him who is without sin among you be the first to throw a stone at her." Think how much poorer we would be without this great story. Yet many of the early manuscripts do not include it, and some that do place it in other positions: after John 7:36, after John 21:24, and after Luke 21:38.

Knowing now what we do about how our Bible came to be written and preserved for us should caution us about how we do our interpreting of scripture. Of course, under no circumstances should we ever lift a passage out of its context to be used as a maxim or a "proof." A more realistic appreciation of how our Bible developed should teach us to look for consistencies, look for the overall spirit or meaning of the passage, and to always be prepared to test out the ideas or theology for logic as well as compatibility with the Christian Faith as a whole.

Knowing that the stork did not bring the Bible and that God did not just send it down from heaven should dispel some of the magic we believe about the book. It is a very real book (collection of books) written by very real people, mistakes and all.

NOTES:

[1] Robert H. Pfeiffer, Introduction to the Old Testament. (New York: Harper & Brothers Publishers, 1948), p. 415.

[2] L. Harold DeWolf, A Theology of the Living Church. (New York: Harper & Brothers Publishers, 1960), p. 80.

[3] Williston Walker, A History of the Christian Church. (New York: Charles Scribner's Sons, 1959), p. 60.

[4] Roy L. Smith, Know Your Bible Series: Number 1—How Your Bible Grew Up. (New York: Abingdon Press, 1955), p.

[5] Bruce M. Metzger, An Introduction to The Apocrypha. (New York: Oxford University Press, 1957), p. viii.

[6] Geddes MacGregor, The Bible in the Making. (Philadelphia: J. B. Lippincott Company, 1959), p. 24.

9. Can You Squeeze a Dinosaur Into Your Bible?

You may remember the story of the librarian who encountered a monkey sitting at a table in the library one day. Noticing two books lying open on the table before the monkey, one being Darwin's *The Origin of Species* and the other being the Bible turned to Genesis, the librarian inquired of the monkey, "What are you doing?" The monkey replied, "I'm trying to figure out whether I am my brother's keeper or my keeper's brother."

Why does science have so little respect for religion? That question may seem unfairly skewed. Obviously in all of the major religions of the world there would be found eminent scientists who were faithful adherents, and one could not begin to count the number of scientists who are believing Christians. Unfortunately, however, there are too many scientists who look askance at the Christian faith as well as religion in general. I think it is fair to say that there has been an uneasy, even at times a hostile, relationship between theology and science. It seems there might be a propensity for science to make either a "believer" out of a person or an agnostic. Some say there are no true atheists; only agnostics (I understand an atheist is one who definitely does not believe there is a God or supernatural force, while an agnostic simply says, "I don't know if there is or not.")

To say that science has a tendency to make either a believer or an agnostic out of a person may not seem like a very significant statement. What else is there besides these two alternatives? The thought I am trying to express is that science has a way of forcing the issue. Some persons may not have a well-thought-through philosophy until science dramatizes the issues and causes those individuals to be confronted by the major questions of life including the ultimate question, "How does it all begin, and is someone or something of a supernatural power involved?" A significant exposure to science may influence a person who may never previously have seriously thought through her or his stance to become more reflective about this question to the extent that she or he decides, "Yes, there is a God" or "No, there is not a God."

The reasons for this may be that a scientist is a theologian, whether the scientist likes it or not! And a theologian or anyone seriously committed to a religious faith must be a scientist! In either case, the one without the other is a very inadequate discipline.

Scientists are theologians because they are investigating God's world and are consequently investigating God. As one views this from a Christian perspective, God created all that exists. Therefore, anyone who studies any aspect of our environment, our world, or our universe necessarily studies the handiwork of God, and thus is studying God. To use a popular analogy, anyone who takes a watch apart immediately becomes acquainted with certain characteristics of the watchmaker. The watchmaker is very mechanically adept and certainly very clever. The watchmaker has some elementary grasp of the metaphysics of time: how it progresses, how it can be measured, and how something as abstract as time can have different intricate interrelated increments. The watchmaker has very good reasons for determining the change of time and understands communications, and therefore must be, to a significant degree, personal.

Likewise, the scientist examines all of the little gears and levers of this giant clock called the universe and comes to know something about the universe maker, God. Various sciences reveal the natural laws and the structure of all things and explore certain unexplainable mysteries. For the scientist, either the universe has always existed or else it had a beginning (the theory that it had a beginning most often nowdays takes the form of a "big bang" where there was nothing and then, poof, there is something—a sort of explosion that brings everything into existence). In either case, no matter how scientists argue each possibility, either alternative remains a seeming impossibility: the universe could not always have existed, neither could it have just arrived on the scene out of sheer nothingness. A theory involving a stork and a delivery seems more plausible.

Scientists really have nothing better to replace the notion of a supreme supernatural being who is creating and organizing matter and natural laws, not to mention spiritual laws such as love and honesty. Thus from the Christian perspective, the scientist is studying all about God. This makes the scientist a theologian with a speciality in nature.

On the other hand, every theologian, as well as every person who is serious about his or her faith or religious quest, must of necessity be a scientist to some degree. In the infancy and early decades of the development of science, in fact, many scientists happened to be theologians or religious leaders—and not just coincidently. This is a natural marriage. One who worships a supernatural being or power and believes that power to be the force or mystery behind the creation of all that is should, consequently, be drawn by curiosity to want to know more and more about this universe which God has created. Any worship, study and meditation of God must naturally draw one to an inquisitiveness and an appreciation concerning nature: the wonder of flowers, clouds, animals, insects, atoms, rocks, and stars. How could anyone who has become sensitive to God help but become excited about nature and the universe? It should be as elementary as a person after a long, hot desert hike desiring a cold drink. Either one is led from ideas about God to the wonders of God's creation, or one must be led from the marvels of our world directly to the mystery of God. Cosmology (study of the origin, processes, and structure of our universe) screams out God, while at the same time religion leads us irresistibly to nature.

But the two don't get along. We may think we have gotten beyond the controversy whereby science sometimes views religion as primitive or childlike and too conservative or narrow to accept the progress of modern discovery and whereby religion fears that science is undermining faith with ideas that go contrary to scripture. But we have not resolved our differences. There is still a decided number of Christians who have unsettling nightmares concerning evolution. What seems like a natural—a beautiful union between theology and science—is in reality still oftentimes a relationship of mutual disrespect.

The problem probably stems partly from the fact that the Bible is captured by the scientific worldview of the day in which it was written. The earth was flat and surrounded by water. There was even water overhead; it was kept from spilling down upon us except for an occasional rain or snow by a vault called the "firmament" in which were placed the sun, moon, and stars (Genesis 1:6, 7, 14-17). The drawing indicates the popular concept of the universe during much of early history and during Biblical times.

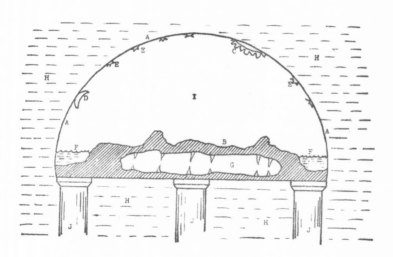

THE WORLD IN BIBLE TIMES

A	The Firmament	F	Oceans and Seas
B	Earth	G	Sheol, the abode of the dead
C	Sun	H	Water
D	Moon	I	Air or Sky
E	Stars	J	Pillars holding up the world

Through the use of the telescope Galileo, in the early 1600's, provided evidence for another model of the universe, described by Copernicus in the mid 1500's, wherein the earth was not flat and not the center of the universe. This contradicted the Biblical model and thereby challenged the truth of scripture. The church became unhappy, and Pope Urban ordered Galileo to appear before the Inquisition where he was threatened with torture if he did not recant.[1] The church has an uncomfortable history of saying, "My mind is made up, don't confuse me with the facts."

Related to our perception of the structure of our universe is the notion held by some Christians that heaven was up in the sky somewhere. This notion was based perhaps on the ascension of Jesus or our concept of the appearance of angels from the sky, and there was no way we were going to successfully send spaceships out towards the stars. Some Christians believed that it would be blasphemy to even try. God wouldn't allow us to come close to heaven with spacecraft.

An example of the Bible being trapped in the scientific world-view of the day is the Biblical understanding of illness as being caused by the presence of demons within us. The writers of the Gospels, in recording the healing works of Jesus, understood through the science of their day that disease and other problems could be caused by the influence of demons, and demons could even invade the person (Luke 8:2,26-33). There was no other way to interpret any miraculous healing than that demons had been exorcised. Modern science be darned—some persons still believe disease can be caused by demons today.

The hottest debate between science and religion has been and remains the conflict between "creationism" as found in Genesis and some form or concept of an evolutionary process. There is still a large contingent of Christians today who find the idea of evolution abhorrent, and even at this moment the battle rages over what the text books should be allowed to say. It is a shame that such a narrow and simplistically literal approach to scripture has imprisoned so great a number of conservative Christians today in a sixteenth century world. We are determined not to learn from history. Science brings us marvelous new revelations about our universe such as the staggering information that our galaxies have been developing over a period of billions of years and that life has unfolded on earth through the fascinating process of over millions of years of evolution. And all the while the church must be brought (very slowly) kicking and screaming into the present age. Those who simply will not give up the outmoded primitive world view—and they unfortunately make up too large of a contingent—cause problems for themselves and others with their too simplistic view of the Bible.

Genesis has two different marvelous myths concerning creation that come from two different periods of history. Both are very poetic, beautiful and pregnant with great religious truths and surprising scientific accuracy. Christians with a fundamentalist bent have not given the authors of these two myths credit for any depth, but instead interpret the creation stories as if they were written by third graders.

The first creation myth runs from Genesis 1:1 to 2:4a and apparently comes from a period in the northern kingdom's (Israel's) history when they were using the name "Elohim" for God perhaps in the neighborhood of 750 B.C. The second creation myth (conservatives would see only one creation story and certainly wouldn't recognize any differences between the two even if the stories jumped up and bit them) begins with Genesis 2:4b and runs through the end of the second chapter. This second story is probably southern kingdom (Judah) in origin, dating from about 850 B.C. At this point in time the name for God was "Yahweh." It is more likely the history of both stories, as they have come down to us through separate channels, actually date from even earlier times. Many versions of our Bibles, such as The King James and The Revised Standard among others, have preserved with indicators the different historic periods of the two stories for us. For example, when we are reading the first story (1:1-2:4a), the word "God" is used to indicate the historic use of "Elohim" while in the second story (2:4b-2:25) the term "Lord God" is used to connote that "Yahweh" is the Hebrew word being used. In this way many versions have indicated the two separate creation myths.

When one is alerted to the presence of two stories of creation instead of just one as is ordinarily assumed, a person quickly begins to see the differences between the two. In the first myth God creates the sea creatures and then the birds on the fifth day (Note that, anachronistically, God didn't get around to creating "days" until the fourth day) after having created the vegetation on the third day. Be advised that the order of events except for the creation of days and seasons follows closely what science tells us. We come to the sixth day, and God starts making the other animals. After making all the other creatures, God finally makes people last.

However, the second myth tells us that God made a person (the male first—clearly indicating that God is a male?) (2:7) and then, deciding that the person needed companionship, made all of the other little creatures and brought them around for the person to name (2:18-19). Because they could not speak English, the animals, it was quickly perceived, were not going to be good company (their original purpose) for the person, which consequently resulted in God's needing to create a second person, a female. In the first story, animals were clearly created before people; in the second story a person is clearly created before the animals. The conservative will quickly cry, "Wait a minute. You're taking the creation story too literally." Interesting turn of events, wouldn't you say?

If one allows a somewhat more liberal·interpretation of the term "day," the Genesis ideas match up rather well with science's theories of creation, remembering, of course, that Genesis is not really interested in science, but religious truths instead. Many mainline Christians would see the creation stories more in accord with modern scientific views by simply understanding the word "day" in the first creation myth to mean a long period of time. It could even be millions of years if we were to understand "day" in the same sense, for example, as when we say "in this day and age," we clearly are indicating a much longer period of time. There is no doubt that the earlier writers probably did not have a concept of millions of years involved in creation's process, but there is no reason for not allowing them to be bright enough folks to imagine that there were long periods of time involved.

On the other hand, given the nature of a myth, there is nothing wrong with supposing they meant an actual "day." We need only to remember that they were without the benefit of any scientific knowledge of our world.

Evolution remains one of the biggest threats to the conservative mind. While James Ussher, bishop of Armagh, Ireland, in the seventeenth century, was able to calculate the date of creation using the ages of the patriarchs as found in the fifth chapter of Genesis as being in late October in the year 4004 B.C.[2], science began to suspect about 200 years ago that creation was a rather lengthy process. In the 1700's Kant speculated on the possibility of apes becoming human beings, and Goethe wrote about the "metamorphosis of plants."[3] In the 1800's, Spencer talked about evolution before Darwin and Wallace developed their theories.[4] Today, among practical scientists, some kind of evolutionary process for the universe, the earth, and life on earth is a matter of fact; only the details need to be worked out. The discrepancies among current theories of evolution are minor and certainly of no threat to the basic idea that the history of the universe and our planet was an extremely long one involving slow change and development. To eliminate an evolutionary process, one would take the heart and soul out of such sciences as astronomy, geology, paleontology, biology, botany, anthropology, etc. These disciplines base their work upon the concept that there has been a history of long, slow change that must be measured in millions, and in the case of astronomy, billions, of years. The alternative is that God simply created everything in mid-stride; while this is not impossible, it seems a bit bizarre.

For example, the elimination of evolution in the case of geology would mean that God created the earth very much as we find it today with dinosaur bones buried in the ground as if they had lived and died some time in the past when in actually there really were no dinosaurs—only bones. There is no room for dinosaurs in the Bible. There seems to be a place for dragons, but not dinosaurs. But even God sometimes has a hard time telling the two apart. To be truthful, probably even the more conservative

Christians don't take the dragon in Revelation 12 as literal, but instead see it as symbolic in a way that is similar to many of the other creatures in Revelation. Still there is no room for dinosaurs in the scriptures. The thought that they might have perished during the flood because Noah couldn't get specimens of such large and fierce creatures on board the ark doesn't really fit the scheme of things. We either have God making the planet with bones of dinosaurs, which never lived, already buried in the ground undergoing the process of radioactive decay which in turn is already in a stage of advanced progress through which scientists are able to do radiometric dating, or we have evolution. Which is it to be? In the modern, yet time-worn expression, I say, "Get real!"

The same applies to the vast ages advanced by astronomy. These are our choices: either the universe is billions of years old or God made everything to seem to be that old when it is not.

One of our closest galaxies, an island of stars grouped together in space similar to our own personal group of stars, the Milky Way, is named Andromeda, and it is so far away from us that it takes light, traveling at about 186,000 miles a second, about two million years to get here. If everything was created in 4004 B.C., give or take a few days, there is hardly enough time for the light from Andromeda to have reached us. This would mean God needed to have created everything including the light from the many distant objects in our universe at a stage of being almost here. The diagram shows that it would be necessary to create the universe with the light rays or waves already having traveled most of the way between galaxies, analogous to creating everything, including somewhere an apple in mid-fall from a tree, in progress at the moment of creation. "Not impossible," you say, but rather an awkward scenario.

It is more complicated than one supposes—quite complicated, in·fact. The universe under such a theory was created with light from the stars in other galaxies in mid-travel from those galaxies to other points in the universe, including planet earth, while never actually ever having left those galaxies, and yet bringing us alleged evidence of a history those galaxies never had.

Diagram of Starlight if Creation took place at 4004 BC:

(We must pretend we are living in the year known by Christian standards as 1993 AD. The scale of star to earth to distances may be found to be mildly distorted.)

S   A star 20,000 light years from earth

E   Earth

A   A continuous light ray that has traveled 5997 years since creation originating from the star and is still only one third of the distance to earth at this moment.

B   A void of no light rays in the line of sight

C   Another continuous light ray that started 5997 years ago (at the moment of creation) at point x which is one third of the distance between earth and the star. The ray or star beam of light had (has) no source except God igniting it at point x continuously until such time as star beam A travels across void B and reaches point x to take over. Then God can stop igniting beam or ray C.

(I have simplified the situation by leaving out such additional complexities* as accounting for lateral and other kinds of movement earth and the star might be engaged in relative to each other. We can only assume that God either had an adequate grasp of the technical mechanics involved in such a situation or else God consulted Carl Sagan concerning the matter.)

*(For example: such complexities would include the fact that the light from the star—ray C—probably arrived before this year which would necessitate moving point x much closer to earth or perhaps it could mean that the ray of starlight C was created already stretching from point x to earth at that moment in 4004 BC. Turn your imagination loose on other possibilities.)

Common sense dictates an evolutionary scenario as more practical. Evolution is the process of creation that is still going on around us all of the time. Each individual human being begins as a simple cell developing slowly through all the stages of growth, tracing the evolutionary process (including a stage with a tail, I'm told), and is finally born to continue the slow evolutionary process to adulthood and old age, if lucky. This unfolding of life, as well as the processes of inorganic change going on around us constantly, simply mirrors the method of creation—or is, in fact, creation in progress.

For those whose faith cannot survive in an evolutionary world or in a world that modern science has described for us, and who propose that the myths of creation in Genesis are literal, the world of the Bible is totally unlike our own world. The Bible tells of a world where the unconventional and magical are happenstance and quite alien to our present experience. This conservative picture of two different worlds makes the Bible seem quite unreal. If the Bible-world is viewed as dissimilar to our own, is it any wonder that we don't take Jesus's teachings very seriously.

In the same vein, doesn't it strike us as very strange that the world view of our scriptures is so limited in its knowledge of geography (that North America existed), astronomy, and even history of other contemporary cultures (such as China), not to mention it's ignorance of the future (but that is another chapter)? Wouldn't the Bible, if it were as perfect as our more conservative sisters and brothers claim, be less tied to such an archaic world view? The Bible is very much a creation of its own time frame with severely limited scientific understanding. You would think this would raise some red flags regarding its dimensions.

Our faith should be able to grow in the light of the revelations that science brings us regarding the wonders of God's world. The miracles of science (to name a few: the fields of medicine, space exploration, and machine calculation) reveal only the greatness of God. Why then do we go on clinging to such childlike ideas of a conservative's make-believe world view? Science has only expanded my concepts of God's greatness and strengthened my faith. Fear and narrow-mindedness, not science, are the culprits that undermine truth and faith. Newton did not think that scientific theories diminished the role of God. For him, science was a form of worship, and the real miracle is existence itself.[5]

Scientists are primarily theologians; and a person of faith must necessarily be, if not a scientist, at least a person insatiably curious about all of God's creation.

NOTES:

1   John Herman Randall, Jr., The Making of the Modern Mind. (New York: Columbia University Press, 1976), p. 235.

2   Timothy Ferris, Coming of Age in the Milky Way. (New York: William Morrow & Company, 1988), p. 220.

3   Will Durant, The Story of Philosophy. (New York: Simon & Schuster, 1961), p. 267.

4   Ibid.

5   Ferris, p. 122.

10. Is There Any Future In It?

Is the Bible a crystal ball? Indeed, one would tend to think so since central to the conservative faith is the theme that our scriptures are telling us all about eschatology—the last days, the "second coming," the "rapture," etc. Conservative preaching places the second coming of Jesus as the main focus, far above any other concern. Yet with a brief but adequate study of the Bible and some common sense, one should quickly see that the second coming should be a negligible topic at best. However, evangelical preachers have always been obsessed with this idea of making their sermons full of sound and fury signifying nothing. So much concern and energy have been wasted on this hollow doctrine.

This kind of preaching is very egocentric; its appeal is narrow and selfish. The message is, "Get yourself saved—like me!"—an appeal to one's own self-interest. In contrast, most mainline preaching tends to be directed towards others with messages concerning how we need to be more loving and kind and be servants in the world.

Evangelical preaching places its emphasis on "getting yourself saved" from a sense of urgency that Jesus will return any minute. I have sensed little remorse for the lost—those who don't make it—in this kind of preaching. I once asked a conservative how heaven could really be heaven for her if her parents or other loved ones did not make it, but instead were condemned to a hell of some kind for eternity. Her answer was that God simply makes us forget them. Somehow I had always hoped that God would be at least as compassionate as we are.

It is interesting that conservatives are severe in their condemnation of fortune tellers, mediums, and psychics when in reality they, the conservatives, use the Bible in exactly the same fashion. The Bible, for them, becomes a book of fortune telling;

they are able to read all of the signs hidden in the pages which tell us when this second coming of Jesus will take place.

But this is only one way in which the Bible is understood to predict the future. Perhaps there are three kinds of predictions in the scriptures that we should examine. It is believed that:

A. The prophets of the Old Testament foretold historic events that were presently to come to pass,

B. The Old Testament foretold the first coming of Jesus,

C. The whole Bible foretells the second coming or the last days.

We can examine each of these in turn.

A. There was a period of prophecy during Old Testament times which began near the time of 750 B.C. and extended for many years, in which some of the great people such as Isaiah, Amos, Jeremiah, Hosea and Ezekiel lived. These persons seemed to be able to tell their fellow citizens that in the near future God was going to send another nation against them to conquer them and carry them off as punishment for their disobedience to God. That is about the extent of their "predictions." After all, they weren't really concerned about the future so much as the present (their present, not ours). Theirs was a message of social concerns aimed at current events. They were called by God to pronounce judgment upon their fellow citizens, condemning unrighteousness and injustices, and saying that because they were a nation of sinners, God would have to punish them. For the most part, that punishment would be in the form of one of their neighbors, usually Babylon or Assyria, descending upon them in warfare, destroying and carrying off people into captivity. In one instance some scholars believe that Jeremiah in his early preaching was predicting that the people who were to be the instrument of God bringing war and destruction upon Judah was the Scythians. Since there is no evidence that the Scythians ever attacked Jerusalem, either the scholars were wrong in thinking Jeremiah meant the Scythians, or else Jeremiah was wrong in his prediction. We all know who gets the nod in this mistake.

Hordes of Scythians did appear on the horizon in 626 B.C. and were seen as a threat to Judah. Jeremiah knew of the wickedness of his country and also believed that God would find a way to punish his country for its sinfulness. Old Testament theology was saturated with the belief that whatever happened was God's will. When another country attacked, it did so because God had a reason for its doing so. If the Scythians were going to level Judah, Jeremiah could easily interpret it as divine punishment. God was using the Scythians only as the instrument for this judgment (Jeremiah 4:5-31, 5:15-17, 6:22-26).

Zephaniah (1:4-8, 14-18, 3:1-5) is believed to have preached the same doom for Judah at the hands of the Scythians. For those who persist in thinking that passages such as 1:7 ("For the day of the Lord is at hand"), and 1:14 ("The great day of the Lord is near, near and hastening fast") refer to "the end," the latter days, etc., we will return to such thoughts shortly.

As we mentioned, the assault on Judah by the Scythians never "militarialized" because they were bought off with a bribe by Psamtich I of Egypt and went home.

The major prophets, as we said, were concerned, not with the future but the immorality of their present:

"What do you mean by crushing my people,
　by grinding the face of the poor?"
　　says the Lord God of hosts. (Isaiah 3:15)

Woe to those who go down to Egypt for help
　and rely on horses,
who trust in chariots because they are many
　and in horsemen because they are very strong
but do not look to the Holy One of Israel or
　consult the Lord! (Isaiah 31:1)

Will you steal, murder, commit adultery, swear falsely, burn incense to Baal, and go after other gods that you have not known, and then come and stand before me in this house, which is called by my name, and say, "We are delivered!"—only to go on doing all these abominations? (Jeremiah 7:9-10)

Jeremiah was a pacifist and got himself into a great deal of trouble by preaching this doctrine when his country later found itself in the middle of war with Babylon.

> And to this people you shall say: "Thus says the Lord: Behold, I set before you the way of life and the way of death. He who stays in this city shall die by the sword, by famine, and by pestilence; but he who goes out and surrenders to the Chaldeans who are besieging you shall live and shall have his life as a prize of war. (Jeremiah 21:8-9)

He preached surrender and submission to the enemy.

> To Zedekiah king of Judah I spoke in like manner: "Bring your necks under the yoke of the king of Babylon, and serve him and his people, and live." (Jeremiah 27:12)

And the hawks responded:

> Then the princes said to the king, "Let this man be put to death, for he is weakening the hands of the soldiers who are left in this city, and the hands of all the people, by speaking such words to them. For this man is not seeking the welfare of this people, but their harm." (Jeremiah 38:4)

Central in the preaching of every prophet was concern for justice, righteous living, and ethical conduct on the part of individuals as well as the nation—not the foretelling of future events:

> You eat the fat, you clothe yourselves with the wool, you slaughter the fatlings; but you do not feed the sheep. The weak you have not strengthened, the sick you have not healed, the crippled you have not bound up, the strayed you have not brought back, the lost you have not sought, and with force and harshness you have ruled them. (Ezekiel 34:3-4)

> You have plowed iniquity, you have reaped injustice,
>   you have eaten the fruit of lies
> Because you have trusted in your chariots
>   and in the multitude of your warriors.
>   (Hosea 10:13)

> Thus says the Lord:
> "For three transgressions of Israel, and for four,
>   I will not revoke the punishment;
> because they sell the righteous for silver,
>   and the needy for a pair of shoes—
> they that trample the head of the poor into the dust of the earth,
>   and turn aside the way of the afflicted. . ."
>   (Amos 2:6-7a)

"Hear this word, you cows of Bashan,
   who are in the mountain of Samaria,
who oppress the poor, who crush the needy,
   who say to their husbands, 'Bring,
that we may drink!'"   (Amos 4:1)

But let justice roll down like waters,
   and righteousness like an ever-flowing stream.   (Amos 5:24)

He has showed you, O man, what is good;
   and what does the Lord require of you
but to do justice, and to love kindness,
   and walk humbly with your God?   (Micah 6:8)

One of the most powerful witnesses made by an Old Testament prophet came from Nathan two to three centuries before the advent of the writing prophets. II Samuel 12 records the daring confrontation that Nathan had with King David when the prophet accused David of having one of his soldiers Uriah killed in order that David could steal his wife Bathsheba. That is what Old Testament prophecy is all about, and that is Old Testament prophecy at its best.

Honesty, justice, peace, proper ethical conduct—these are the concerns of the prophets rather than predicting secrets of the future. The only extent to which the prophets were concerned with the future was in a very general way (the very near future in relationship to their lifetime): God would punish the people and the nation for their sins. Yet there was always hope that one day things would again be prosperous and peaceful as they believed it to have been under King David some 300 or 500 years earlier. The punishment:

Therefore thus says the Lord God:
   "An adversary shall surround the land,
and bring down your defenses from you,
   and your strongholds shall be plundered."   (Amos 3:11)

The hope:

"In that day I will raise up
   the booth of David that has fallen
and repair its breaches, and raise up its ruins,
   and rebuild it as in the days of old. . ."

"Behold, the days are coming," says the Lord,
   "when the plowman shall overtake the reaper

and the treader of grapes him who sows the seed;
   the mountains shall drip sweet wine,
and all the hills shall flow with it.
   I will restore the fortunes of my people Israel,
and they shall rebuild the ruined cities and inhabit them;
   they shall plant vineyards and drink their wine,
and they shall make gardens and eat their fruit."

(Amos 9:11,13-14)

We have looked at the first possibility of the Bible foretelling the future, that of the prophets predicting some specific events relevant to their own times, and found that they were not concerned with fortune telling. Instead they majored in moral pronouncements. However, many Christians believe they can read into some Old Testament passages a clear indication that God had communicated to the writers some of the events surrounding the coming of Jesus. They believe that specific passages clearly refer to this event.

So we will now turn our attention to this second way in which it is believed the Bible becomes a crystal ball.

B. Concerning the Old Testament's ability to forecast the life of Jesus, as well as some events surrounding his life, there may be four possibilities. First, some of the passages indicate that persons of faith in the Old Testament had some vague hopes for a Messiah, even if not one quite like Jesus. Second, later biographers of Jesus, such as those responsible for the material in the four Gospels, make Jesus' life conform to what they considered to be predictions of Jesus found in the Old Testament. As unpalatable as this may seem to some, there could be significant evidence for this. Third, Jesus himself may have chosen to deliberately "fulfill" some of the Messianic expectations of the Jews. Finally, there is always the possibility of coincidence.

1. First, to what extent did the Old Testament envision the life of Jesus? Everyone knows that there had been a dream or hope of a Messiah for the Jewish people that developed during Old Testament times. The little land of Palestine had been the target of so much war and invasion, and the people were the victims of

much suffering over the centuries since they first occupied the land. It was logical to expect a theology of hope to develop and grow over time. Belief in a just and caring God did not allow for their suffering at the hands of neighboring nations to go unpunished and unrelieved notwithstanding the prophets' message that they deserved such punishment because of their apostasy. In times of distress, and particularly severe distress such as the events described in Lamentations, the people would cling to the hope that some day things had to be better. In addition, since the other nations were wicked, they must not go unpunished.

Along with the concept of a Messiah coming to their rescue, there grew up the idea that they were a chosen people with whom God had covenanted, and if God felt that way about them, then surely there was a future out there where things would be wonderful once again. Such a "golden age" at its best is described in passages from Isaiah:

> But be glad and rejoice for ever in that which I create; for behold, I create Jerusalem a rejoicing, and her people a joy.
>
> I will rejoice in Jerusalem, and be glad in my people; no more shall be heard in it the sound of weeping and the cry of distress.
>
> They shall build houses and inhabit them; they shall plant vineyards and eat their fruit.
>
> They shall not build and another inhabit; they shall not plant and another eat;
>
> The wolf and the lamb shall feed together, the lion shall eat straw like the ox; and dust shall be the serpent's food.
>
> They shall not hurt or destroy in all my holy mountain, says the Lord. (Isaiah 65:18-19, 21-22a, 25)

Also read the entire 35th chapter of Isaiah as well as verses 6-9 in the eleventh chapter for additional description of the "golden age." Wolves and lions cohabitating with lambs and oxen is a popular theme of many paintings, greeting cards, and needle point work because all of us have pain, fears, disappointments, and loneliness at times, and it is nice to have dreams of peace and comfort. Afterall, God had promised that some day things would be like this in the conversation God had with Abraham (Abram) in Genesis 12:1-3.

There is by no means any solid agreement in the Old Testament regarding the exact nature of that ideal kingdom which God would bring to pass, and even less agreement concerning what the Messiah would be like—the one who was to make it all happen.

David lived around 1000 B.C. and is credited with ushering in a time of peace and prosperity, which extended through the reign of his son Solomon. It was a peace like that of no other time in the history of these people outside of the Garden of Eden. It was therefore natural for King David to be the prototype of the Messiah in some of the Messianic theology, and most believed that it was very probable the Messiah would be a descendant of David.

> There shall come forth a shoot from the stump of Jesse, and a branch shall grow out of his roots.

> In that day the root of Jesse shall stand as an ensign to the peoples; him shall the nations seek, and his dwellings shall be glorious. (Isaiah 11:1, 10)

Jesse was David's father; the Bible often avoids being direct when indirect will do just as confusingly. Joseph and Mary, Jesus' parents, were descendants of David, a circumstance, we are told, that had something to do with Jesus being born in Bethlehem. For the purists, Mary had to be a relative of David also since Joseph was supposed not to be the biological father of Jesus.

At least two distinct views concerning how the Messiah would behave seemed to surface in Old Testament theology. Some thought he (it would have to be a man, of course) would come with power as a king—not as "king" in the post-Jesus sense of the word—throw off the yoke of whoever happened to be the current resident oppresser of Palestine, and restore national independence for the Jews along with all of the other good things of the kingdom. Others—not many, actually—had a vision that God's anointed would have to come as a gentle, kind, loving, peaceful person who, consistent with God's love, could not hurt anyone. He would, in fact, suffer harm and death himself rather than hurt another—in other words, he would be a pacifist.

Such an unorthodox theological concept of the Messiah as a "suffering servant" is best described by Isaiah and, to some degree, Psalm 22.

> Behold my servant, whom I uphold, my chosen, in whom my
> sole delights;
> I have put my Spirit upon him, he will bring forth justice to the
> nations.
> He will not cry or lift up his voice, or make it heard in the street;
> a bruised reed he will not break, and a dimly burning wick he
> will not quench;
> he will faithfully bring forth justice. (Isaiah 42:1-3)

> He was despised and rejected by men; a man of sorrows, and
> acquainted with grief;

> Surely he has borne our griefs and carried our sorrows;
> yet we esteemed him stricken, smitten by God, and afflicted.
> But he was wounded for our transgressions, he was bruised for
> our iniquities;
> upon him was the chastisement that made us whole, and with his
> stripes we are healed.
> All we like sheep have gone astray; we have turned every one to
> his own way;
> and the Lord has laid on him the iniquity of us all.
> He was oppressed, and he was afflicted, yet he opened not his
> mouth;

> (Isaiah 53:3a, 4-7a)

Here we have an excellent example of the Old Testament having an accurate vision of what God's person would be like. This comes about as close as the Old Testament ever does to "foreseeing" the coming of Jesus.

The Old Testament is dead wrong when it speaks of the Messiah coming with power similar to a conquering military hero, like David, to destroy all of the nation's enemies. But the vision of a "suffering servant" hits the mark very well. Other than this salient concept of a suffering servant found only in a few passages, the ability of the Old Testament to accurately predict the nature and character of Jesus is almost nil. This may be part of the reason why the Jews do not accept Jesus as fulfilling the role of the Messiah and believe the Messiah is yet to come.

2.   Next, I believe there are many instances in which the Gospels "write" the life of Jesus by making it conform to or "fulfill" specific Old Testament statements the writers believed were relevant. One might challenge my suggestions that the Old Testament only very generally and vaguely envisions anything like Jesus (with the exception of the "suffering servant" theology just cited) by pointing to passages that seem to identify Jesus with more precision, for example, such a popular passage as,

> Therefore the Lord himself will give you a sign. Behold a young
> woman shall conceive and bear a son, and shall call his name
> Immanuel. (Isaiah 7:14)

First, as mentioned in an earlier chapter of this book, Matthew was wrong to quote *almah* as exclusively a "virgin." To be more accurate, Matthew should have used the reference with the words "young woman" and not "virgin." To be even more accurate, Matthew should not have used the passage at all. However, Matthew had an ulterior motive which was to make the passage say what Matthew wanted it to say. We will examine that motive in a moment.

Secondly, the passage as it is used by Matthew and any other Christians predisposed to connect it with Jesus is lifted totally out of context. Read the historic setting in chapter 7 of Isaiah, and if you take it literally, you will understand that it applied to Ahaz's day and not to Jesus' day.

Thirdly, Jesus was not named "Immanuel." To say that it was intended only to invoke the "meaning" of the name "Immanuel" as applying to Jesus, and was not intending that Immanuel be Jesus' name is to ignore the fact the child was to be named Immanuel. It is interesting how conservatives will not take the Bible literally when it is convenient not to do so. This is a fine example of an occasion in which the New Testament simply appropriates material from the Old Testament and writes it into the story of Jesus to prove to the people that Jesus did in fact fulfill some Messianic hopes they might have had.

Another example concerns Judas and his relationship with Jesus. We read that Judas was paid thirty pieces of silver and that he threw them into the Temple (Matthew 27:3-5). No doubt these details in the story of Judas were suggested by Zechariah 11:12-13. Please read the entire eleventh chapter of Zechariah. It is not Judas, but Zechariah himself who is speaking poetically. By no stretch of our imaginations can the ideas of Zechariah eleven be associated with Judas. Judas is not mentioned, not even obliquely referred to. We, along with Matthew, have no right to associate this passage with the story of Judas unless we are playing games with the Bible. Matthew alone makes the connection; the other Gospel accounts do not. Matthew (26:14-15) identifies the value at thirty pieces of silver; the other Gospels (Mark 14:10-11 and Luke 22:3-6) do not. Matthew alone (27:3-5) tells of Judas throwing the money down in the Temple; the other Gospels say nothing of this. We remember that Matthew is the Gospel that is overly concerned about "proving" that Jesus fulfilled Old Testament hopes. Continually, Matthew quotes Old Testament passages usings the phrase, "But all this has taken place, that the scriptures of the prophets might be fulfilled" (Matthew 26:56a among many other instances).

And how reliable is Matthew on these details? Remember how in an earlier discussion it was shown how he got the details wrong in the donkey episode. Everyone else knows Jesus rides only one donkey as he enters Jerusalem. Matthew, because he does not understand Hebrew poetry, has Jesus riding on two donkeys at once in still another effort to make Jesus' life conform to any Old Testament passage he can find. And don't forget Matthew thinks Judas went out and hanged himself (27:5) while Acts (1:18) reports an entirely different kind of death for Judas.

Again, Matthew reads in Isaiah's description of the suffering servant that he was connected with a rich man in his death (53:9), and so Matthew (27:57) makes a point of Joseph of Arimathea being "rich." Mark (15:42-47), Luke (23:50-56), and John (19:38-42) make no mention of this Joseph fellow being rich.

Our Gospels are not being dishonest when they try to make the life of Jesus "fit" selected Old Testament passages or simply include in their accounts myths that grew up around the life of Jesus in the thirty or forty or so intervening years between his death and the writing of these four biographies. They do this because there is no doubt in their minds who Jesus was: he was the son of God. For Matthew that meant Jesus was the Messiah whom the Jews had long expected. Consequently, anything said about the Messiah (or that in any remote way could be so construed) in the Old Testament must have, in fact, actually happened in the life of Jesus, whether reported or not. If the Messiah was to be a descendant of David, then Jesus had to be a descendant of David. If "casting lots for his garments" (Psalm 22:18) is in anyway associated with a Messiah, then that must have happened to Jesus.

The Jews may be right. Jesus may not have been the Messiah for whom they were looking even though we Christians believe he was. Therefore, we must accept the fact that many passages of the Old Testament expressing expectations of a Messiah do not apply to Jesus, for example:

> For to us a child is born, to us a son is given;
> and the government will be upon his shoulder, and his name will
>   be called
> "Wonderful Counselor, Mighty God, Everlasting Father, Prince
>   of Peace."
> Of the increase of his government and of peace there will be no
>   end. . .
> with justice and with righteousness from this time forth and for
>   evermore.
>
> Isaiah 9:6-7)

No doubt these words describe a dream of the Messiah; however, as a description of Jesus, it is not wholly accurate. The government being upon his shoulder is somewhat shaky. The same is true of the reign of peace, justice, and righteousness forever.

It should be a little disconcerting, to say the least, that if the Old Testament, in some instances, is really describing the life of Jesus, that it is so vague and speaks entirely in terms too general. Why does it not ever name Jesus, name his parents, or give more specific details? After all, if the Old Testament is speaking specifically about Jesus, and if it is God's word, then shouldn't it be more clear and precise? *The Book of Mormon* speaks of "the resurrection of Christ" (Mosiah 15:21), and that "if Christ had not risen from the dead. . .that the grave should have no victory" and "death should nave no sting" (Mosiah 16:7). And this is purportedly from 140 years or so before the birth of Jesus. It tells us that "Jesus Christ shall come" (Alma 5:48) and that his mother's name will be "Mary" (Alma 7:10), and this is some 80 years before his birth. If *The Book of Mormon* can do that well, one would expect the Old Testament to do just as well.

(*The Book of Mormon* alleges it is the history, between about 600 B.C. and 400 A.D., of some of the descendants of the tribes of Israel who came to North America where Jesus appeared to them shortly after his resurrection in Jerusalem. Either historians and archaeologists have missed all the evidence of this extensive history of North America, or else the Mormon faith is based on the greatest religious hoax ever perpetuated. I notice that most historians are politely silent about it.)

I expect the Old Testament to do just as well at foretelling explicit details of the life of Jesus as *The Book of Mormon* thinks it does. Because it doesn't and because it is so obtuse on the subject, it would seem that the Old Testament, in fact, is not predicting Jesus. Conservative Christians no doubt will tell us that God only wanted to drop a few hints, and had good reasons for not being very clear concerning the matter; though I can't imagine what those reasons would be.

Regarding the Old Testament's prediction of the coming of Jesus, I have mentioned: 1. That at times the Old Testament religious leaders had a true glimpse of what a God-like person might be like, i.e. the "suffering servant." Otherwise, they had a misconception of God's messiah, one that was antithetical to Jesus (a conquering hero on a charging steed), or at other times they were simply vague on the image. 2. The New Testament writers very probably researched the Old Testament to find and incorporate into the life of Jesus passages that seemed applicable.

3. Now in addition, I would suggest that on occasions Jesus might have intentionally adopted certain Old Testament images to reveal to the people that he was laying claim to the Messiahship. Perhaps the Old Testament reference to the lowly act of riding on a donkey was not as much a prediction hitting the mark as it was simply Jesus deliberately choosing this kind of demonstration to impart a message to the people.

4. Finally, there is always the possibility of coincidence. Certain ideas can be found in the Old Testament that only coincidently and inadvertently have a parallel in the life of Jesus. Examples would include such passages as "Strike the shepherd, that the sheep may be scattered" (Zechariah 13:7) which may have no relationship to the life of Jesus. However, it is easy to notice a striking parallel, albeit one that is certainly not inordinately coincidental. While some of the descriptions from Psalm 22 may have been appropriated into the story of Jesus' life, others could easily have been interesting parallels.

Unfortunately, there is not enough room here to cite and examine each Old Testament reference purporting to be a fortune-telling of the life of Jesus. I have suggested four real possibilities that might explain the phenomenon. Now I repeat the questions raised by the discussion. Why is the Old Testament so vague on identifying Jesus? It could have used his name, his parents' names, or other conclusive facts that would leave no room for doubt as to whom it was referring. Why are there ideas about the Messiah found in the Old Testament that clearly do not by any stretch of the imagination apply to Jesus? Wouldn't God want us, or the people of that day, to be accurate in our understanding and our expectations concerning the matter? Or would God rather have mystery and confusion?—which brings us to the next thought.

C. No doubt the phemonon that seems so clearly to be an instance of the Bible foretelling the future is that in which the New Testament (and to a certain extent the Old Testament) apparently seems to predict the parousia—the second coming of Jesus. There is certainly much more excitement engendered by this idea. The way in which conservatives understand this issue is more than just casually relevant to our concern; however, when it comes to the Bible's predicting the second coming of Jesus, we must ask, "Is there really any future in it?"

The Old Testament speaks about "the day of the Lord," and perhaps someone will come to usher in such a day. That "day of the Lord" is going to be:

... darkness, and not light; as if a man fled from a lion, and a
    bear met him;
or went into his house and leaned with his hand against the wall,
    and a serpent bit him.
Is not the day of the Lord darkness, and not light, and gloom
    with no brightness in it? (Amos 5:18b-20)

That the day of the Lord is going to be terrible and frightening is a very common theme for the prophets:

The great day of the Lord is near, near and hastening fast;
the sound of the day of the Lord is bitter, the mighty man cries
    aloud there.
A day of wrath is that day, a day of distress and anguish,
    a day of ruin and devastation, a day of darkness and gloom,
    a day of clouds and thick darkness, (Zephaniah 1:14-15)

On the other hand, we read about the Golden Age:

> My people will abide in a peaceful habitation, in secure
> dwellings, and in quiet resting places. (Isaiah 32:18)

> No lion shall be there, nor shall any ravenous beast come upon
> it; (Isaiah 35:9a)

Perhaps there are two explanations. Either it is true that, for the bad people, the day of the Lord is going to be unpleasant, to say the least, while for the good people it will be a time of peace and joy—or there will be different periods of time in a complicated scenario of "last days" events. There will be a millennium of happiness with Christ followed by a time of woe and destruction. This is described in Revelations 20 to some extent: however, it is never made clear in the Old Testament as to the order of good times and bad times. Those who make it their hobby of searching for an eschatological time table in the Bible are able to hunt and peck out raptures and snatches and so forth by gathering little bits and pieces of information here and there along the way while ignoring anything that does not fit the pattern.

These eschatologists have elaborate labyrinths of a complex ordering of events. However these "last days" experts cannot agree among themselves. I confess it is all rather confusing to me. If the Bible is a crystal ball, one needs a crystal ball to decipher the crystal ball.

I also find confusing the difference between the "suffering servant" and the warring hero who is coming. Which one is the real Messiah? Are both descriptions accurate, with one referring to a first coming and the other to a second coming? Not likely.

An intriguing question keeps emerging: "Are we, in fact, just like the Jews, still waiting for the Messiah?" Sometimes I wonder if the life of Jesus had any significance; many Christians are too busy waiting for Jesus to come again and need to be reminded that he has already come.

You might ask how there could be any doubt that Jesus will come back as the New Testament seems to make it very clear as well as making it a major theme. Consequently, many Christians are busy reading their Bibles looking for clues as to when that second coming will be and trying to discover those signs in the events of modern history. They do this despite the fact that we're told not to look for signs and that we cannot know the time!

Then some of the scribes and Pharisees said to him, "Teacher, we wish to see a sign from you." But he answered them, "An evil and adulterous generation seeks for a sign; but no sign shall be given to it except the sign of the prophet Jonah. (Matthew 12:38-39)

This passage is repeated in the sixteenth chapter, verses one through four. In both instances my conservative friends may claim that the sign looked for was a miracle that would prove Jesus was the Messiah. If Jesus intended the sign to be a miracle, how could he say that no miracle would be given except the miracle of Jonah (Jesus' own death and resurrection) when, in fact, the Gospels record many miracles preformed by Jesus?

While Christians are busy with the task of finding in scriptures just when such a second coming will be, there is a total disregard of the fact that we are clearly told we cannot know such a time.

Watch therefore, for you do not know on what day your Lord is coming. (Matthew 24:42)

But of that day or that hour no one knows, not even the angels in heaven, nor the Son, but only the Father. Take heed, watch; for you do not know when the time will come.' (Mark 13:32-33)

As is usual, the conservatives with the literal minds tell us, "Yes, we may not ever know the 'day' or the 'hour,' but we are really closing in on the month."

So when they had come together, they asked him, "Lord, will you at this time restore the kingdom to Israel?" He said to them, "It is not for you to know times or seasons which the Father has fixed by his own authority." (Acts 1:6-7)

Christians seem to be wasting much time and energy researching and then preaching about "when" a second coming is going to be while Jesus said (1) in the first place we cannot know, and (2) that we must be ready all the time. Are we to be "good" or "accept Jesus" because the time is near? Is it not better that we be at our best at all times even if the "time" is not near? We should believe in the revelation of God which Jesus has given us and should try our best to live the moral, just, righteous, peaceful life regardless of when the "time" would come! When the "time" might come should be totally irrevelant to our relationship with God and our following Jesus. Our life must be on the right track even if there never will be a second coming.

However, if you think the second coming theme is needed in order to bring a sense of urgency about one's response to God and Jesus, we will examine this idea before we close this chapter.

All of the references to the nearness of the end and the imminent return of Jesus cause confusion and seem inappropriate for "God's word."

> For the day of the Lord is near upon all the nations. (Obadiah 1:15)

> . . .for the time is near. (Revelation 1:3)

Even from the teachings of Jesus we hear this theme:

> Truly, I say to you, this generation will not pass away till all these thing take place. (Matthew 24:34)

Was the Bible speaking to the people in the day in which these words were spoken or written? Did Jesus actually mean the persons he was speaking to at the moment? "Who are intended to hear these words?" is a very difficult question. If the words were for those living in the first century, they raise serious problems. Apparently what was described and expected did not happen. One could interpret these words concerning an early return as meaning that the resurrection itself was the second coming. Or perhaps whenever a person accepts Christ, the second coming happens for that person. But neither of these suggestions is very satisfactory for most Christians. While such suggestions may be attempts to resolve the problem of Jesus saying that he would return again very soon, it will not answer for all attendant events described as surrounding "the day of the Lord."

Since the words and acts of Jesus were written many years after Jesus' lifetime on earth, the most practical explanation is that the early church had many myths and stories of what Jesus said and did during his lifetime, some accurate and some apocryphal, and in choosing what they believed to be authentic, as well as consistent with the Old Testament view of the nearness of the day of the Lord (note Obadiah above), they simply included the erroneous sayings of Jesus that he was coming back soon. After all, a statement like, "This generation will not pass away," before this all was to happen seems unmistakenly clear. Either Jesus was simply mistaken in his knowledge or else these thoughts grew up later in the folklore of the church and were ultimately included in the final story. None of us want Jesus to be wrong, so that leaves the blame on the early church.

But that theory is certainly unacceptable for conservative Christians who, consequently, have another theory. Since it is too problematic for Jesus to have intended the idea of an early return to be for the persons to whom he was speaking at that moment in time, the theory goes, then the words must have been addressed to persons of a later time—like today perhaps.

This raises another problem. Those persons who were standing there with Jesus and heard him speak the words that he would soon return were misled into thinking he was speaking to them.

And they asked him, "Teacher, when will this be, and what will be the sign when this is about to take place?" (Luke 21:7)

It would certainly seem from the context that Jesus was speaking to those of his own day. We can read another parallel of the above Matthew (24:34) quotation in Luke:

Truly, I say to you, this generation will not pass away till all has taken place. (Luke 21:32)

Wouldn't they expect Jesus to come before some of them died or during their own lifetime? Unfortunately, they were misled as have been all who have subsequently read these passages and believed this theory during the intervening twenty centuries since. Jesus did say, ". . .but the end will not be at once." (Luke 21:9)

The myth of an early return must have been alive and well in Paul's day because he promulgates the doctrine in one of the earliest of his writings, I Thessalonians 5. But this began to cause trouble for the people at Thessalonica, the same trouble that has plagued persons down through the centuries. Thessalonians believed Jesus would soon return, and some of them decided to quit their jobs to wait for him. After all, there would be no need to have an income for the future when the "Lord's Day" was about to change that future into one in which money would be superfluous. (I wonder if those adventist Christians today who seriously believe the end is imminent still bother with "nest eggs," retirement funds or other investments for the future.) This necessitated Paul's having to write another letter about three months later to tell them that the "return" could be later than some might think and that it was no time to apply for unemployment (II Thessalonians 2:1-3 & 3:6-13).

Repeatedly throughout the interceding centuries people have been fooled into thinking that the words were intended for them and only them (somewhat of an egocentricity), and that everyone previously living should have ignored the words in the scripture pertaining to a second coming. And every generation has been wrong.

Why would God fool so many people through so many centuries if the theory were true that the words were meant for a later age? Is this some kind of cruel hoax?

The answer to that question lies in the theory of the "signs."

Conservative Christians believe that both Old and New Testaments are inundated with evidence or signs that point clearly to the "right age" when Jesus will really return. Countless generations and millions of Christians did not need to be fooled by the statements of an early return if they had only read the "signs" in scripture carefully as do those today who are smitten by some kind of adventism! Conservatives spend much time searching through scriptures picking out the key signs that reveal the true time, which of course is always "this generation." There are unlimited possibilities when one begins to read all of the symbols and cryptic statements in the Bible. The secret seems to be to pick out only those that apply to today and ignore the rest. If we're wrong and it ends up not to be today, then the next generation can go back and find some new "signs" that were ignored earlier but that seem appropriate now for their day.

The way these treasure hunters jump around in the Bible lifting out obscure passages to build a case for "our day" is at once amusing and sad. Does God really play games with us by hiding all kinds of clues randomly, helter-skelter throughout scripture? The famous quotation of Albert Einstein that "God does not play dice with the universe" should have some parallel meaning here. Surely, God does not play little math games and puzzles with us. Do we need a secret de-coder to solve the riddle of the date of the second coming? Is the purpose of scripture really to provide us with a scavenger hunt to see who can find all of the clues and finally piece together the answer of when the end will come? To put it in modern colloquialism, "Get real. Every generation until now has been wrong in interpreting the signs, but we now have it all figured out—riiiiight?"

There remain a few addition problems with this theory we've been discussing. First, it is a mystery to me to know when some passages of scripture are speaking to the people of the day in which they were written or when they are supposedly speaking to us today.

The great day of the Lord is near, near and hastening fast. (Zephaniah 1:14

For Gaza shall be deserted, and Ashkelon shall become a desolation;
Ashdod's people shall be driven out at noon, and Ekron shall be uprooted. (Zephaniah 2:4)

Is the first Zephaniah quotation definitely intended for us today? Is the second quotation using symbolic names to represent modern cities, or does it have meaning only for the day in which those words were spoken or written? How does one know when a passage is intended for the day in which it was written, or instead when it is intended for the day in which it is being read?

Another nagging problem, previously mentioned, is the question, "Why can't the word of God be more specific?" Why do supposedly futuristic passages use old Bible names and places and not the geographical names of places of today if in fact it is today that is intended? Didn't God know what the names of countries and cities would be today, back then?

> Therefore, wild beasts shall dwell with hyenas in Babylon, and ostriches shall dwell in her; she shall be peopled no more for ever, not inhabited for all generations. (Jeremiah 50:39)

This passage from Jeremiah must pertain to a future time since otherwise the prophecy would not be true because people have been living in Babylon (occupied at present, I think, by our friends, Iraq and Iran) since that time down to the present. If it is referring to today, why doesn't the word of God give the name of the people or nation existing there at this time, if we are in fact living in the "last days"? Why doesn't the Bible ever give any modern names such as Russia, the United States, or China, or the names of whatever countries are involved in the "prophecy? It would have eliminated the unfortunate misunderstanding by millions of Christians over the centuries. But then I lost control for just a moment: we are not supposed to know the time, are we?

One further problem is troubling: if God has a definite plan for the end of the world as we know it, complete with a time schedule that was carefully outlined and then cleverly and mischievously hidden in scripture, wouldn't this suggest the possibility of some kind of predestination? Even though Paul mentions predestination (Romans 8:29), most Christians today do not believe in it. Mainline theology maintains that we exercise free will which allows us to bring about the end of things just about any time we choose with a nuclear holocaust. Such a possibility could throw God way off the predestined eschatological schedule. It would not matter when such a holocaust would occur, there is bound to be some Christians at that current moment expounding the perennial "final days" theme making them inadvertently right. There is no escape; it seems we will have to reintroduce predestination into our theology.

In closing our discussion of this topic, I would repeat an earlier remark: the doctrine of the second coming or the last days is entirely irrelevant! Not only does it cause us to use the Bible as if it were a ouija board or a crystal ball, but worse than that, it seriously distorts the message of salvation! It promotes a theology of salvation by fear. "You had better get yourself saved because there may only be a few minutes left. Get on board before it's too late!" Think about it: it seems as if a committment under those circumstances could be seriously suspect. One could challenge the motive of one's accepting Christ because of the fear that there is not much time left as being superficial. One could almost be caught embracing Jesus or Christianity only for expediency.

(Parenthetically, if it is necessary to use fear to reach persons by telling them time is running out, then actually their own death is much more of a threat than the second coming of Jesus. Death has certainly been a more practical and relevant termination event for everyone living heretofore in the last nineteen centuries since Jesus than has been any threat concerning the second coming; and it seems it would remain so today.)

Besides seeming to be a knee-jerk, fear response, accepting Christ in order that we might be saved would appear to be a very self-centered reason. Real commitment should be a response to God's love by our love in return. We accept God because God loves us. We should want to follow God's ethical way for our life, not because of "what's in it for us"—the best deal in town—but because as loving, caring persons we also want to be just, moral, kind, honest persons. Commitment on this basis is real and significant. I will always wonder about those who are getting saved only to make sure they are "covering all the bases." Too often the evangelist's pitch seems to be an ego-centric message.

If one's commitment to Christ is out of love and not out of the expediency of "getting in" before it is too late, the second coming has no relevancy. We must get away from the interim theology of a "last days" ethic. Our commitment to Christ must not grow out of fear of living in the final days, but we must deal with Jesus as a lifetime commitment, not a stop-gap measure. A second coming should make no difference in our personal life whatsoever. We must be living the Christian life if Jesus comes tomorrow or never comes. In fact, I think Jesus probably said that very thing, that we must be found to be about the Christian business no matter what.

Then how do can explain those New Testament passages that seem so clearly to describe a parousia or the millennium? Dramatic instances like Revelations 20 that give us great cryptic detail are to be understood as beautiful poetic visions of hope for troubled times. They are extremely euphuistic and imagerial.

On the other hand, the only logical explanation of the many references to a second coming in the Gospels and in Paul is that they are later additions by the early church that grew up as myth surrounding this great man Jesus.

Even though conservatives will see nothing in this chapter except a fulfillment of the prophecy in II Peter 3:3-4, I maintain that the Bible cannot be used as a crystal ball.

11. The Cosmic Magician

My wife said, "It's too bad that people have to believe in magic in order to have a faith." The statement was made in connection with a discussion on miracles in the Bible. She's right, you know. For many people, the miracles in scripture literally have to be miracles. If they are not true miracles, the validity of all scripture is called into question. Not only is it believed that to question one element of scripture (such as miracles) is to in turn threaten all scripture, but also it is commonly held that miracles themselves validate the rest of scripture. It would be difficult for many persons to believe in God, Jesus, or Christianity if the miracles of scripture were vacuumed away.

On the other hand, and by the same principle, there are those persons who feel that they cannot accept the Christian faith because of the presence of miracles. They also feel that the many miracles found in scripture must be accepted at face value as part and parcel of Christianity, and since they cannot believe in the miracles, they feel obligated to discard the rest of the faith.

Isn't it possible to be a Christian and not believe in miracles? I think so. However the Bible abounds in miracles; how is it possible not to believe, and why wouldn't someone want to believe in them? Before examining these two questions, let's attempt a definition of "miracle."

People probably use the term "miracle" in at least two ways that are somewhat in accord with how the dictionary defines it. We normally think of a miracle as some happening or event that apparently seems to contradict or set aside the physical laws as we know them. An example would be to see an elephant levitated in midair with no visible means of support. If there is no "trick" behind it, such as magicians use, then the suspended elephant is breaking our laws of gravity—a miracle.

Often we use the term "miracle" in another fashion. It is used to connote a remarkable or wonderful event even though the incident does not violate any known physical laws. Countless times we have referred to the birth of a baby as a miracle. Our world is filled with such miracles: the wonders of nature, the joy of love, the beauty of certain scenes, or the glory of music.

And the Bible is filled with both kinds of miracles. Just as life is filled with so many of these latter definitions of miracles, so we would expect to find many wonderful, miracle events in our scriptures: people willing to be martyrs for their faith, the love and ethical teachings of Jesus, God's forgiveness, and much, much more. We have no problem with any of this second kind of miracle; we accept it, believe in it, and can dispense with any further discussion of it.

What about the other kind of miracle—the parting of the Red Sea, the virgin birth, the many healings, and other similarly "impossible" events? Is God a cosmic magician who steps into history once in awhile to perform a feat that is outside of the realm of the physical laws? Does God simply temporarily set aside the law as we know it in order to accomplish some divine purpose and then set the laws into motion again? That *appears* to be what happened during the Old and New Testament era. Miracles of the law-breaking kind or impossible events happened with regularity, whereas today and everyday since the last scriptures were written, we see a miracle void. It would seem as if the Bible world was an unreal or super-real world where God had a part in the daily events through direct intervention. In contrast, the world since Bible times is radically different. God seems to have stepped back and finally said, "No more miracles: you are on your own." Events that appear to defy physical laws do not seem to happen any more. Oh yes, there are claims of such miracles once in awhile, but their documentation or verification seems rather tenuous. Flying saucers and ghosts appear (no pun intended) to have more credible evidence than do miracles.

Occasionally, examples are given of modern miracles such as a person who did not make her or his plane flight, and when the plane crashed killing all persons on board, she or he saw her or his being spared as an act of God. God stepped into history and caused a person's taxi to arrive late at the airport, or whatever the intervention agent God happened to use, and thus saved his or her life. This must mean that God wanted that person to live and about 200 other people to be snuffed out. A better explanation is probably coincidence. How many times have other persons not made their plane flight because of some accident, change of plans, or other reason, and that flight did not crash? No doubt there must be a high percentage of air line flights wherein someone, for one reason or another, missed his or her plane making such an occurrence rather normal; therefore, when any plane crashes there is a likelihood that someone was saved by not being on the plane—hardly a miracle.

Automobile accidents in which a person survives despite the devastating appearance of the accident which would seem to dictate that no one could have survived are labeled as miracles. Yet in such situations there is no solid evidence that the person *had* to die. An honest conclusion has to be that there is not sufficient evidence to indicate that God intervened.

In the absence of any seriously authenticated miracles in our modern world, the implication is that Bible days and the present day are two radically different worlds. The Bible world appears as a very unreal time—a time full of persons and events with which it is difficult for us to identify.

The truth of the matter is that the Bible world was not essentially different (culture and scientific change aside) from our own world. It wasn't really a miraculous fairy-tale world. God didn't step into history and destroy Sodom and Gomorrah because they were wicked. Any calamitous demise for those cities, if it occurred, resulted from a natural disaster such as an earthquake along the Jordan—Dead Sea fault. Such a catastrophe would not only not have been caused directly by God, but would actually have been against God's wishes. It would have been only the natural laws of our world at work.

In the same vein, many Christians have been busy over the years looking for everyday explanations for many miraculous events in the Bible instead of accepting the miraculous explanation. They have been trying to explain many of the strange Biblical happenings by natural phenomena. People try to identify the star that appeared over Bethlehem with planets in conjunction with each other or with a bright star, or they believe it might have been a comet or a super nova. The Red Sea crossing is believed by some to be a crossing of the Lake of Reeds which is further north and more navigable for the two contrasting traverses, the successful Israel one and the unsuccessful Egyptian one. This is thought to be by a natural phenomenon. Some try to explain the Flood as due to stories arising out of local incidents rather than a world wide deluge. All this effort spent on trying to find "natural" explanations for the miraculous events in scripture indicate that we are, down deep, very uncomfortable with the idea that God steps into history and sets aside the physical laws momentarily to benefit some pet cause, as a result of which, if that were actually the case, God's favorite team, the Saint Louis Cardinals, would be World Series champions every year. Furthermore, there are those who still believe that God cares about which athletic team wins, and some who will pray for victory with God's help.

Miracles would make God's world very undependable. We believe that we can trust the physical laws by which the world operates, but if at certain points in time those laws are changed for some special occasion, we will never know what to expect. Now, we believe that when we jump from the top of a tall building, gravity will pull us down to certain injury or death, and God will not suspend the physical laws to save our life. Or do we?

Perhaps we do sometimes believe that God will somehow intervene via a miracle and save us because we feel we are different—more special than other persons. Did you ever hear of the "It-can't-happen-to-me" phenomenon? Highway fatality statistics don't really apply to us. In the back of our minds we know that we are different; it only happens to others, never to us. God will take care of us even if it takes a miracle. The cosmic magician will do a trick for our benefit.

If God does not bend or break natural laws on occasion to accomplish some divine purpose, how then does God get involved in history to work out the agenda—the heavenly plans for the world? I am guessing that God operates in this world only through the natural law system. The physical laws such as laws of motion and attraction and the spiritual laws of love and truth are all a part of creation. These laws are indispensably inherent to the world, and God is working through such laws in an ongoing creating and sustaining process in connection with all life, as well as all material and spiritual things. If God wants something done in history, God acts and speaks only through people and in respect of individual freedom. God can bring change in the coarse of the events of history only insofar as God can catch our ear or attention concerning the matter. Only as we are in tune with the laws of love and truth, as individuals, and seek to speak and act within those guidelines is the will of God ever able to find actuality in the events of time. In our freedom, we are allowed to ignore and thwart what would be God's will for our world as we create horrible devastation in war or allow millions of sisters and brothers to starve to death. If God were a God who intervened in our lives and times by setting aside natural laws in order to fulfill a divine will for this world, we certainly would not have the atrocities that history records, for it is inconceivable that it is God's will that millions should starve. Undoubtedly one of the truths of life is that the natural laws of the universe remain inviolate, making our world (as well as God) wholly dependable and thereby making human beings responsible and accountable.

What, then, are we to think of Biblical miracles? We should believe that God does not cause earthquakes or floods to teach us lessons or for any other purpose. In the same way God did not send fire down from heaven to consume an offering and vindicate Elijah in a contest with Baal prophets (I Kings 18), nor keep hungry lions from eating Daniel (Daniel 6), nor have a fish swallow Jonah (Jonah 1 & 2). As recounted in the fifth chapter of this book, myths have grown up around otherwise "normal" persons and events to glorify religious leaders or to explain history in terms of God's will.

Over long periods of oral historic tradition, stories attesting to the greatness of many of the Biblical personalities naturally grew up around their lives similar to the story of George Washington chopping down the cherry tree or the virgin births of Buddha and other famous non-Biblical persons. After a while those who were seeking to record biographical material circulating about these religious leaders had no way of knowing which stories were authentic and which were apocryphal, so they all get included.

An example of an apocryphal story is the one involving the miracles surrounding the birth of Jesus which were legends that gradually developed in later oral history and finally were added to Jesus' biography. They are not mentioned in Paul's letters which are much earlier than the Gospels, nor are they mentioned in the first Gospel which is Mark. Neither does Jesus make any reference to his supposedly miraculous birth, nor does the Gospel of John. Why would such a legend take shape? Some obvious, and some not so obvious, reasons come to mind; let me suggest at least three.

One way of validating our claim that Jesus was divine as well as human is to make God enter the picture at conception similar to the many other stories found in secular literature telling of gods and mortals joining in holy wedlock to produce offspring (or for that matter, the Biblical account in Genesis 6:1-4). God becomes the father (confirming our sexist suspicion that God is a man) rather than Joseph. However, if Jesus had divinity thrust upon him instead of receiving God's spirit later in his life by his own volition in responding to God, one could certainly question Jesus' freedom and thus his other human qualities. It would then be only a short jump to suggest that the rest of his life was determined for him and entirely beyond his control, and there are many, I am sure, who are not at all that uncomfortable with such a prospect.

I am suspicious that another motive for the development of a virgin birth origin for Jesus is the idea that such a birth would free him from inheriting the dreaded original sin. It also eliminates the nasty element of sex from the experience. (And to be on the really safe side it seemed necessary to go back one step further and have Mary be a product of an "immaculate conception"—the original "safe sex"—a post-Biblical thought). Some persons might be more offended by the sinfulness of the sex act itself then they are of original sin. A virgin birth eliminates the unsavory connection of the sex act with Jesus. It just might also communicate the idea to some persons that there is a stigma connected with sex. (Did someone really say, "Sex is dirty and you should save it for the one you love"?) Only a very narrow perspective makes a "virgin birth" necessary to achieve divinity or to escape the contamination of original sin.

Dare I suggest that another reason for a virgin birth theme might be anti-Semitism? We say Jesus was a Jew (because we cannot avoid it), but if God were his "father," it just might somehow take away his Jewishness for those with anti-Semitic problems, might it not? In my sheltered world I have never heard of this proposal before, but it must have surfaced before; if not, then it could be a thought for further exploration by someone. Return to chapter three of this book for further details on the miracle of the virgin birth.

Jesus' healing miracles are more complex and perhaps require more space than allowed in this discussion. Suffice it to say that if we are to remain consistent with the idea that there are no miracles that depart from natural laws—"Anyway that's my story and I'm sticking to it"—then any explanation of Jesus' healing must conform to a non-miraculous natural phenomenon format. Some healings could have been psychosomatic while others, including that ultimate healing, raising the dead, could be our old friends "myth" or "legend" again.

This topic brings us to the resurrection of Jesus himself. Can we blatantly deny miracles and still maintain that Jesus was raised from the dead?

For most Christians, the resurrection of Jesus is the heart and soul of the Christian Faith. Tamper with that and God will strike us down with lightning. The resurrection and the cross are inexorably linked together in people's minds. What happened on the cross is vital to our salvation according to most Christians. There on the cross Jesus did something that we don't fully understand: he made an atonement, paid for our sins, changed God's mind or bought off the devil—something, at least, that is supposed to guarantee our salvation when added to our profession of faith. But we will deal more with this very difficult issue later in the chapter concerning Paul.

For now, we are looking at the resurrection, and the resurrection is probably that which gives full credence to the cross event. For most Christians the resurrection proves the validity of the cross and all that happened on the cross. The resurrection is God's word to us that the message of our salvation is real and is physical evidence of eternal life. It would be most difficult to dismiss the resurrection as just another myth or legend with which we have deceived ourselves with a false hope of heaven, particularly since it is the most authenticated event surrounding Jesus' ministry and the inspiration of the whole Christian Church. It is necessary to ask what could possibly have transformed several frightened Palestinians, who fled at Jesus' arrest and who through the proxy of Peter denied even knowing Jesus, into courageous martyrs for the faith? This astounding turnaround attests to the wonder of some kind of resurrection experience for his followers. Discounting the resurrection leaves us with only Jesus as the greatest ethical teacher of all time and not much else. Granted, that is no small wonder in itself.

But the theory we are working with is that a miracle is God setting aside physical laws for a moment in history in order to take direct action to accomplish some purpose, and we said that God does not interrupt history in this way. God and God's creation, the universe, can be counted on to be dependable at all times. The question becomes: Is it possible to have a resurrection of Jesus and still not have a miracle? It would be a miracle, of course, in the sense that we say the birth of a baby is a miracle or the beauty of a sunset is a miracle, but not in the sense that it broke nature's rules. I believe that we can still have our resurrection and yet have it conform to nature's way or "business as usual" in the realm of known physical laws.

Without going into great detail, I am saying that there is much to be said for a spiritual, as opposed to a physical, resurrection. Jesus' appearing in a room mysteriously, much like a ghost (Luke 24:36-37), and his strange and sudden ghostlike disappearance from a dinner table in Emmaus (Luke 24:31) (not withstanding the physical contacts such as that in which Thomas touches his wounds [John 20:24-28]), imply some kind of spiritual quality about his resurrection. This whole world of ESP, prayer, and ghosts is of an incorporeal nature that could have some substance (no pun intended) to it, and may not be incompatible with physical and spiritual laws of our universe. In other words the existence of Jesus after death is a normal experience for human beings, and his appearance in this physical world may not be out of line with the way our universe is created. At least there are many persons around who think they have had similar experiences with "ghosts" themselves.

Paul tells us (I Corinthians 15:42-44) that the resurrection was spiritual and not physical. Remember that Paul who began writing Christian literature before the Gospels made their appearance, though he has much to say concerning the resurrection, never mentions an "empty grave."

The resurrection made a very powerful impression on Jesus' followers, enough so that they were transformed from confused and insecure folk into the stuff that saints are made of, and they started a religious movement that is unparalleled in human history. I contend that God never interferes with history except only as we are receptive to God's will and act accordingly. The only miracles are the wonders that are a natural part of life and existence, and they are consistent with the laws of the universe. Granted, we do not know all about our universe and its laws yet; however, I cannot believe that God chooses to interfere directly, particularly as often and as dramatically, as suggested in Biblical days and yet not in our, or any other, time.

Old and New Testament history is written with the theology that God caused events to unfold under a divine plan complete with attendant miracles. Unfortunately, so many of those miracles seem to be either unconscionably cruel (i.e., the destruction of so many persons by the hand of God in the Old Testament such as the Egyptian army in the Red Sea), or needlessly frivolous (i.e., walking on water), or the practice of an un God-like favoritism (rescuing some persons and not others).

Reliance on miracles today would seem to be a hopeless and randomly inconsistent practice. We have inconclusive evidence that any modern miracle has ever happened. The days of the Biblical events, except for changes brought about through human beings, are not really different from the time in which we are living.

As we consider the claim that miracles happen today (though unsubstantiated) and the fact that the followers of Jesus were supposed to not only heal but to also *raise the dead,*

> Heal the sick, raise the dead, cleanse lepers, cast out demons. (Matthew 10:8)

why are there no dead persons being revived today? Even the Mary Baker Eddy folks (Church of Christ, Scientist or Christian Science) should be able to pull off one of these once in a while.

God is not in the magic business. Rather, God and the universe are totally dependable and consistent. Anything that has appeared out of the ordinary soon becomes explainable in terms of known laws when more is known about the experience. Similarly, anything we haven't yet understood will eventually become reasonable and compatible with this world's laws given our ability to gather enough information. Everything from the strange performance of quantum physics to the presently unexplainable mysteries of quasars, we will discover, given our ability to find the answers, will conform to the natural laws of the universe.

12. Rated R: Must be 18 or Over to Read

Is your minister too embarrassed to tell you about the pornography in the Bible? Not necessarily. Depending entirely on one's perspective of course, I would suggest there is probably no pornography in scripture. Yet sometimes in a discussion concerning pornography—what is and what isn't—someone will suggest that the Bible contains occurrences of pornography.

This is not a chapter on pornography, its justification or condemnation, or censorship. This is a chapter seeking to answer the charge that the Bible contains pornographic material.

As suggested in the first paragraph, it is an extremely subjective topic. A standard dictionary might give pornography the definition of being "writings or pictures intended to arouse sexual desire." While photography was not "well developed" yet in Biblical times, I have noticed pictures in some Bibles, but by no stretch of our imaginations could they be construed as lustful. On the other hand, some of the writing might make some persons uncomfortable, but hardly aroused.

The first material that comes to mind, though it is hardly sexually stimulating, is the love poetry found in the Song of Songs or Song of Solomon. I think the average person would not find the descriptions in the Song of Songs any more objectionable than they would the nude paintings of Michelangelo or his famous statue of David. The love poetry in this book is believed by some to be representing God's love for Israel or perhaps God's love for all people. Regardless of whether they represent this or if they simply represent the literal interpretation of love expressed between a woman and a man, the words are not sexually exciting. But then, of course, I'm getting old.

> Your eyes are doves
>> behind your veil.
> Your hair is like a flock of goats,
>> moving down the slopes of Gilead.
> Your teeth are like a flock of shorn ewes . . .
> Your lips are like a scarlet thread,
>> and your mouth is lovely.
> Your cheeks are like halves of a pomegranate . . .
> Your two breasts are like two fawns,
>> twins of a gazelle,
> . . . I will hie me to the mountain of myrrh
>> and the hill of frankincense.

(from the fourth chapter)

> Your rounded thighs are like jewels,
>> the work of a master hand.
> Your navel is a rounded bowl
>> that never lacks mixed wine.
> Your belly is a heap of wheat,
>> encircled with lilies.

(from the seventh chapter)

And that's as risque as it gets. It doesn't seem very dangerous unless your loved one takes objection to your calling her hair a flock of goats. The imagery from such a bygone day is probably lost on us, and yet I am glad this poetry was included in the Bible. The Song of Songs has more than just literary merit I'm sure.

While they would not be called pornographic there are some unsavory passages in the Old Testament. One set of parallel stories found in Genesis are rather unpleasant in aspect and cast a shadow over two otherwise highly respected personalities.

Genesis 12 records a strange story early in Abraham's appearance on the Biblical scene, though he was not young at the time. Abram and Sarai, his wife, (before their name change) are driven into Egypt by a famine. Because Sarai is beautiful, Abram is afraid the Egyptians will kill him in order to take his wife. He asks Sarai to pose as his sister instead. The assumption is that Sarai may have become the king's mistress or wife with Abram's approval because he feared for his life (Genesis 12:17-19). God becomes angry over the situation, just as we do, and straightens out the mess. The king seems to have had standards just a little bit higher than Abram's, or perhaps he was upset over God's punishment. Despite the fact that women were considered little more than property in that day, we still feel it was a despicable thing for Abram to do.

History repeats itself, or as some scholars would have it, an event in Biblical times is sometimes mistakenly repeated on different occasions as if it were two different occurrences (as perhaps the different accounts of Jesus feeding the multitudes [Matthew 14:15-21 and 15:32-38]). Only nine pages later, Abraham, not having learned his lesson in Egypt, passes Sarah (notice they have adopted their aliases by this time) off yet a second time as his sister, this time to King Abimelech of Gerar. God steps in again to stop this charade (Genesis 20).

In Genesis 26 we find a third parallel, the story of how well Isaac learned this trick from his father Abraham. Again there is a famine in the country, and Isaac is in Gerar and tells King Abimelech that Rebekah is his sister and not his wife. This story, whether history or legend, probably happened only once or was originally told only once about one of the characters, but later was mistakenly understood to be several instances. It does not make us proud of whoever the perpetrator was.

Even more ugly are the parallel stories found in Genesis 19 and Judges 19. Genesis tells how the men of Sodom came to Lot's home asking Lot to send out the two men (angels, we're told) in order that the men of Sodom might have sex with them (19:5); and Lot, instead of sending out his guests, offers to send out his daughters that the men of Sodom may "do to them as you please" (19:8). Judges tells the parallel tale of a Levite staying with a host in Gibeah. Men of the town came to the house asking the host to send out the Levite that they might have sex with him. The Levite had a concubine with him and they sent her out and let the men rape her (19:18-30).

The words chosen for the telling of these stories, or any mentioning of sex in the Bible, are never explicit. Sexual intercourse is always referred to modestly as "he *knew* her" in The King James or Revised Standard Versions, although newer translations will use the phrase "sexual intercourse." But explicit details are never given. Scripture is intended to communicate for edification and not for titillation.

For example, Lot's daughters are worried about their biological clock ticking down and the preservation of the family name. They schemed to get their father drunk and then "We will lie with him"; and so each in turn "went in, and lay with" him (Genesis 19:30-36). The most detailed scripture ever becomes is seen when Onan, trying not to father a child with his brother's widow, "spilled the semen on the ground" (Genesis 38:1-9). Another example of the extent to which scripture goes, or doesn't go, in terms of explicit language and at the same time reveals how puritanical the writers were in that day, is lifted from the Law wherein there are many directions as to conduct of a sexual nature:

> When men fight with one another, and the wife of the one draws near to rescue her husband from the hand of him who is beating him, and puts out her hand and seizes him by the private parts, then you shall cut off her hand; your eye shall have no pity. (Deuteronomy 25:11-12).

It was a modest Victorian time, and the writers were not about to be lewd or ribald.

There is some nudity in scripture. God forgot to make clothes for Adam and Eve, and they heard God walking in the garden one evening, were embarrassed because they were naked and hid (Genesis 3:8-11). In another garden scene a young man fled naked more out of fear than modesty (Mark 14:51-52). Among other nude scenes is the classic Bible version of "the Emperor's New Clothes." King David dances semi-nude down the streets of town, and one of his wives, Michal, looks out the window, fails to see his "new clothes", and is disgusted (II Samuel 6:14-16).

There are many incidents in scripture that are "delicate" in their subject matter and that could lend themselves as plots for racy or spicy films, but they are always handled in ways that certainly could not be construed as in any way pornographic. Examples are Jacob's being deceived into sleeping with Leah instead of Rachel whom he thought he was getting for his wife (Genesis 29:15-25), or Rachel's giving her maid to her husband Jacob (Genesis 30:1-4), or Joseph's being threatened by his employer-master's wife to either have sex with her or be accused of attempted rape (Genesis 39:7-18 for those of you who want to find out if Joseph was strong or weak). In all matters of this nature, I think we will agree that the scripture writers handled the incidents with taste and in a way that could not be understood as arousing or stimulating.

Some of the above-cited incidents could well be described as obscene and atrocious—Abraham giving his wife to another man and telling him it is his sister or Lot willing to send his two daughters out to be abused by the men of Sodom—but they would not qualify as pornography. Whereas there is nothing in our scriptures that could be defined as sexually arousing and the Bible cannot be R. or X. rated for explicit sex, yet it might be so rated for violence.

People occasionally use "pornographic" and "obscene" interchangeably. The definition for "obscene" is "offensive to modesty or decency; lewd; disgusting; filthy; or repulsive." In this vein persons will describe as obscene anything that is violent or destructive to people, animals or environment. For instance, war is often described as obscene. Consistent with this definition for obscenity, there are many passages in the Bible that, because of the atrocity of their nature or because of the viciousness they attribute to God, would be labeled "obscene," but not "pornographic."

There are many examples in our Old Testament of tragic violence, and sometimes we are told it is God's will. Ehud, one of the judges, seemed to have been sent by God to assassinate the King of Moab, whom God had placed in power in the first place (Judges 3:12-21). God seems to have taken part in many of the slaughters according to the books of Joshua and Judges, as well as throughout the Old Testament period. Some of us would call it obscene to attribute such violence to God. The God that Jesus knew and revealed to us would not have intentionally destroyed the Egyptian army in the Red Sea or killed almost everyone on earth in a flood. There may be many things that constitute blasphemy, but attributing such violence to God is, no doubt, our worst blasphemy.

Gratefully, the New Testament is particularly devoid of the violence found in the Old Testament, and, with some few exceptions noted, its theology is that God is loving and forgiving and not vengeful. One of those exceptions is that particularly distasteful story found in Acts wherein it is implied that God struck down Sapphira and Ananias, a wife and husband, for lying and withholding personal property from the church (Acts 5:1-11).

As mentioned in chapter two of this book, the people of that day were grossly in error in believing that God was so cruel, as were also the writers who recorded such a belief in our scriptures. Such theology taints our beliefs still today as we justify war and the use of the death penalty. One of the main purposes for this book is to encourage persons to free themselves from the strong conditioning that, if it is in the Bible, it is God's will.

One final example of the obscene is the story of Jephthah who promises God that, if God helps him defeat the Ammonites, he will offer up as a burnt offering the first person who comes out of his home to meet him when he returns from battle. An obscene promise! God gives the Ammonites "into his hand." An obscene idea! Jephthah slaughters a great many of them in twenty cities. An obscene waste! After God supposedly gives him the victory, Jephthah returns home, and his only child, his daughter, comes out from the house as the first person to meet him. He kills her as a burnt offering to God to keep his promise (Judges 11:29-40). An obscene tragedy from beginning to end!

13. The Devil Didn't Make Me Write This Book

You know many of them: Jupiter, Diana, Venus, Neptune, Zeus, Pan, Apollo, Baal, Ra, Isis, Osiris, and many more. The world has known many gods and goddesses. "Primitive religions" abound with hierarchies of gods, goddesses, and god-related creatures with chief gods or goddesses and lesser ones: a god of the sun, a god of fertility (substitute "goddesses" wherever applicable), a god of the underworld—usually evil (we have given our god of the underworld the name of Satan), and so forth. This may be one of Christianity's definitions of a "primitive religion"—many gods. Yet Christianity, with its emphasis on only one god, nevertheless is in danger of having its own pantheon—a system of deities including even a hierarchy.

It is often noted that one of the elements differentiating Judaism and Christianity from other religions is that they profess belief in only one god, God. Judaism is credited with having been the first religion to suggest monotheism which was inherited by Christianity. But Christianity has been criticized at times, particularly by the Unitarians, of having a polytheistic faith.

Despite its claim of monotheism, Christianity confuses us with the notion of a trinity, three gods in one, plus a devil, angels, and some other little forest creatures like cherubim and seraphim. There are sufficient numbers of passages in the New Testament, and the Old Testament as well, that support such a pantheon.

Going back to near the beginning, we find that God, as understood by Old Testament folks, is worried that people will incorporate worship of other gods into the Hebrew Faith. In an effort to forestall such an eventuality God tells Moses:

"Say to the people of Israel, When you pass over the Jordan into the land of Canaan, then you shall drive out all the inhabitants of the land from before you, and destroy all their figured stones,

and destroy all their molten images, and demolish all their high
places. . . (Numbers 33:51-52)

Moses passes the message on:

The Lord your God himself will go over before you; he will
destroy these nations before you". . . . (Deuteronomy 31:3)

The only sure way to keep the pagan religions from corrupting
Israel was to destroy them all—the people and their religions.
However, the people did not keep God's word. But then neither did
God keep the promise to destroy the other nations. The pagan
nations continued to exist beside the people of Israel, and their
gods infiltrated Israelite worship:

And the people of Israel again did what was evil in the sight of
the Lord, and served the Baals and the Ashtaroth, the gods of
Syria, the gods of Sidon, the gods of Moab, the gods of the
Ammonites, and the gods of the Philistines; and they forsook the
Lord, and did not serve him. (Judges 10:6)

This became a regular occurrence throughout the Old
Testament, and we find the Jewish faith was greatly influenced by
outside forces. We know that the Hebrews borrowed many stories,
ideas and traditions for their culture and religion from other
nations.[1] The Old Testament law relied heavily on Hammurabi's
Code, (he was king of Babylon) which was written over 1000 years
before the Deuteronomic Code, as well as on Assyrian and Hittite
influences.[2] In fact the influence of the Canaanite religions on
Hebrew religion is very marked.[3]

In our pantheon of gods, the existence of the devil, god of the
underworld, and his (the devil is always designated a male)
colleagues of demons probably had their origins in other primitive
religions:

Demonology is the animism pertaining to malignant spirits
which primitive man accepted as originators of disaster, disease,
evil, etc. Its counterpart in Biblical literature is angelology,
which deals with spirits that bring good to men. Judaism,
surrounded by the animistic ideas of primitive people, absorbed
some of these from Assyria, Babylonia, Greece (Isa. 14:12, 27:1,
34:13), and developed a distinct crop of its own.[4]

Clearly, the idea of a devil in our scriptures, in those instances when it is not simply a symbol for evil, is part of that mythical material. The book of Revelation certainly has elevated this symbol of evil into a classical myth when it has an angel coming down from heaven to bind Satan with a chain, who is at this moment disguised as a dragon, for a thousand years (Revelation 20:2). This account even refers to that earlier significant religious myth, citing "that ancient serpent," as it alludes to the story of the source of evil and death in our world—Eve and the snake—found in Genesis. Yes, technically it is a serpent in Genesis, but we all know that it is a snake. These stories are true myths, not to be taken literally, but meant to symbolize some religious ideas about the force of good and evil in our world. They have their own particular value in their unique expression of theology. However, there are other myths that are totally spurious in value such as the mating of gods or heavenly creatures with humans to produce a race of giants (Genesis 6:1-4), or the reference of an archangel Michael struggling with the devil to see who gets the body of Moses (Jude 9).

As mature adults we should simply see Satan or the devil as our device for symbolizing "evil" which is as intangible and unpersonified as the idea of joy or pain. For example, when we are told that Satan incited David to take a census of Israel (I Chronicles 21:1), there was no such creature as a devil that tempted David to do wrong (had there been, the creature would have had to have been very busy in David's case). To put it simply, David had two related thoughts: "I should take a census" and "I should not take a census." He was swayed, not by Satan, but by his own motives and desires to make the wrong choice (though it is beyond me why a census would be evil). Scripture simply uses the cute figure of speech: "The devil made him do it." Well, maybe the primitive writer of I Chronicles believed the devil did do it. But we, as more mature persons who know there is no such thing as the devil, use it only as a cute expression or as the personification of evil. We know that the devil did not make David take the census. No, seriously, the devil did not make David take the census; it was

God. Among the many, many contradictions in scripture, we find the exact same story about David and the census in another book wherein we are told that it was God who actually told David to do it and not the devil after all (II Samual 24:1).

There is no doubt that we should understand references in scripture to the devil as either a simple, primitive belief on the part of the author, or as a very poetic presentation of the idea of evil and temptation. And in most cases I am inclined to think that the author or recorder was sharp enough to have been conferring anthropomorphic characteristics to the ideas of evil and temptation by using the symbol of Satan or a devil for dramatic effect. As noted, Genesis and Revelation are classic examples. As for other examples, the book of Job springs to mind. Most scholars recognize it as a work of fiction or a play rather than history, and Satan is just one of the characters much like Petruchio and Kate in my favorite Shakespeare play, *The Taming of the Shrew*.

Then we have the court room scene from one of Zechariah's dreams or visions:

> Then he showed me Joshua the high priest standing before the
> angel of the Lord, and Satan standing at his right hand to accuse
> him. And the Lord said to Satan, "The Lord rebuke you O
> Satan!. . ." Zechariah 3:1-2)

Here we note, and will comment on at greater length later, that scripture often seems to be confused as to whether it is God or one of God's angels in these visions. But clearly we have here a dramatization and not a historical event. The devil is a character in a dream.

One additional rendering of the poetic personification of evil is this sample from Isaiah that comes complete with its own clues as to its source in primitive religions:

> "How you are fallen from heaven,
>   O Day Star, son of Dawn!
> How you are cut down to the ground,
>   you who laid the nations low!
> You said in your heart,

'I will ascent to heaven;
Above the stars of God
    I will set my throne on high;
I will sit on the mount of assembly
    in the far north;. . .' "(Isaiah 14:12-13)

Here we find the source for a "fallen angel" in Canaanite mythological religion. *Day Star* and *Dawn* ("Helal" and "Shahar" in the Hebrew) are Canaanite deities while *mount of assembly* is the abode of the gods.[5]

Another example of myth with primitive origins in regard to the devil concept (with overtones of an origin for the atonement concept that we will discuss when we come to Paul in a later chapter) is the cultic practice at some early point in Hebrew history of placing the sins of the community upon a goat (hence our usage of "scapegoat") and sending it out into the desert as an offering for Azazel, a devil or evil spirit (Leviticus 16:7-10).

In a word, there is no such person or fallen angel as the Devil. (In the words of one small child to another child, "He's like Santa Claus, it's your dad.") Then who tempts us? Well, let's first discuss what place Satan had in Jesus' temptation experience.

In dealing with Jesus and his encounters with Satan, we must simply understand such references as euphuistic. Again we have a storyteller's way of dramatizing ideas for effect. Jesus being tempted by the devil is an excellent example of this. At the beginning of Jesus' ministry, we have the story told of his going out into the wilderness for a time of worship and reflection. We can understand Jesus' need to prepare himself for the formidable task ahead of him. There is no doubt that he spent his time in serious prayer struggling over many decisions. This intense struggle in prayer was repeated near the end of his life in Gethsemane Garden before his arrest. However, in this initial desert experience where he was formulating his plan for ministry, it is said that he had some conversation with the devil. The devil tries to lure Jesus away from his work by making Jesus offers that he couldn't refuse. But he did refuse. Jesus was hungry, and Satan tried to entice Jesus to end his fast with a miracle of turning stones into bread. He offered Jesus the kingdoms of the world if he would only worship the devil. Finally, he suggests that, if Jesus would only throw himself from the top of the temple, God would protect him from all harm. By the way, this is the order found in Luke (4:1-13). John does not mention the temptations. Mark (1:12-13) makes only a passing remark concerning them. The only other gospel to delineate the temptations is Matthew (4:1-11), and he does not agree with Luke as to the order of events. Matthew and Luke tell essentially the same story, but in Matthew the jumping off the temple top comes before the offer to become the world's richest person. I mention this fact that one of them, Matthew or Luke, got the details out of order for the sole purpose of disturbing the literalists one more time.

How were the temptation stories preserved for us? Only four probable possibilities come to mind. The devil could have remembered the incident and told someone later, except that the devil is nonprosonna or the little man who wasn't there. Jesus could have related the experience to others later—not entirely unlikely. God could have dictated the account to Matthew and Luke—only we earlier settled the issue that God did not dictate the scriptures. Or very probably, the story is a mythological account of a very real—albeit devil-less—struggle Jesus experienced at the beginning of his ministry. His temptations were normal enticements not unlike the kind each one of us faces periodically. Matthew and Luke have dramatized with pomp and flair to make very vivid for us a most significant struggle in Jesus' life.

In his conversations, Jesus has on occasion mentioned Satan, but I think it is always in the oriental style of exaggeration and embellishment. For example, some teachers of the law attack Jesus saying that he has Beelzebul in him (Mark 3:22-26). Jesus picks up the caricature and continues using Satan as the symbol of evil in his response.

Part of symbolic nature of the presentation of the power of evil and temptation in an anthropomorphic style is the various aliases used in scripture for the devil. Satan is called by many terms as in

John (12:31, 14:30, 16:11) where Jesus refers to "the ruler of this world." At one point it even sounds like Peter is the devil. Jesus, apparently frustrated with Peter, turns to him and says, "Get behind me, Satan! For you are not on the side of God, but of men" (Mark 8:31-33). Of course, Peter was not Satan, nor was there a demonic or satanic spirit in him. Jesus could just as well have said, "Peter, you are missing the whole point!"

While some of the earlier writers no doubt mistakenly believed in a devil or many devils, we would have to believe that Jesus was more in tune with reality and was using "Satan" and other references to a devil just about the way we do today when we say, "The devil made me do it." Jesus was speaking figuratively about the idea of evil and temptation. It is parallel to the way we talk about romantic love as Cupid or being struck by Cupid's bow.

Before moving on to angels, we should have a look into hell which is closely related to Satan and then perhaps try to answer the question of how we are tempted if there is no one to do it.

Sheol, the Old Testament counterpart of hell, is not a very well-developed entity, and this is, no doubt, one of the few areas where the Old Testament is superior to the New Testament. *Sheol* is a vague, shadowy abode of the dead. Other than the fact that it seems to be a place of separation from God, not much is known about it. The New Testament uses a bit more vivid description of hell, although far from complete. However, much of our dramatic imagery of hell that we carry around in our minds may come more from extra-Biblical sources such as John Milton's *Paradise Lost* and Dante Alighieri's *The Divine Comedy*. I think that Paul can hardly add anything new to the few descriptions of hell which are found in Revelation and several comments by Jesus.

Revelation gives us some peeks into hell with such pleasant contemplations as "tormented with fire and brimstone. . .for ever and ever; and they have no rest, day or night" (14:10-11), and "as for the cowardly, the faithless, the polluted, as for murderers, fornicators, sorcerers, idolaters, and all liars, their lot shall be in the lake that burns with fire and brimstone" (21:8). Certainly, burn the liars and sorcerers, but the cowardly, too? It would all seem quite cruel if we forgot for a moment that Revelation is very cryptic and full of strange visions. Like those found in the rest of Revelation these descriptions are figurative ones employed for dramatic effect rather than ones to be taken literally.

When we get too literal in our interpretation of scripture and our Jonathan Edwards style of preaching and thereby suggest that God is busy sending people, and some them not really that bad, into eternal punishment, we wonder why we need Satan; God seems to fill the role quite well. With all that we hear about God in the teachings of Jesus—loving us beyond our ability to even comprehend the wonder of that love, and forgiving us past any meriting—it is totally incongruent to imagine God sending persons into an eternal torment. Such belief certainly makes a monster out of God—a devil in his or her own right. With a god like that, who needs the devil? Such theology misses entirely the point of a passage such as:

> If you then, who are evil, know how to give good gifts to your children, how much more will your Father who is in heaven give good things to those who ask him! (Matthew 7:11)

What parent would condemn his or her child to torture, let alone eternally, for non-belief, sinning, or whatever reason for which you think a person is assigned to hell? If Jesus has revealed anything at all about God, is it not that God's love is far greater than ours?

Of course there must be some ramifications for my sins and not just in this life, but in the life after death. I will have to experience some remorse spiritually and mentally, or perhaps my punishment is to enter that spiritual heaven with a soul that is less than satisfactorily developed and find that I have a considerable amount of maturing yet to do in order to overcome my sin-stunted state and reach the more sublime levels of heavenly appreciation. Who knows? Can we safely say that the doctrine of annihilationism (the wicked soul eventually simply perishes) is not a satisfactory option either? I think we do know that there is no eternal torture in hell awaiting us, even for people who write books like this.

Roman Catholics, recognizing the problem here, have contrived their own unique solution to avoid the severity of hell. "Purgatory" and "limbo" (doctrines supposedly found, I was told, in one of the books of Maccabees, although I haven't seen anything convincing yet) take the pressure off to a considerable extent. And I commend the effort; their hearts are in the right place.

Perhaps when we die we simply all enter into a spiritual life with whatever spiritual equipment we have generated for ourselves and grow from there, but not without some remorse and repentance along the way.

But we must not ignore what Jesus said about hell. As we look at his main comments, I would have to say they easily appear to be metaphorical in nature—dramatic ways of emphasizing an idea.

An example of the use of exaggerated imagery is observed when Jesus is trying to impress upon us the preciousness of life including the life of little children. He claims that it is better for us to die than to lead one of them astray, and then follows this thought with the comment that, if our hand or eye causes us to sin, it is better to cut our hand off or pluck out our eye than to enter into hell (Mark 9:42-48). We all know there is no need to cut off a hand or foot; the hand, foot, or eye does not cause us to sin. It is our mind that is tempted and makes the decision to sin. Putting millstones around our necks and jumping into the sea or cutting off our hands are ways of speaking that Jesus used to be emphatic about the important consequences of our words and actions. Vivid imagery was used to heighten the dramatic effect. His description of hell that includes "Their worm does not die, and the fire is not quenched" is employed for effect.

Another fine example of the metaphoric is the sheep and goats analogy in the great judgment scene which includes "eternal fire" and "eternal punishment" (Matthew 25:31-46). This great parable is spoiled when one concentrates on the judgment instead of the central message which is serving: feeding the hungry, visiting the sick, and watering the thirsty.

Another beautiful parable that cannot be taken literally, one which includes the image of hell, is the story of the rich man and Lazarus (Luke 16:19-31). The rich man fails to care for the poor Lazarus in this lifetime, and after death when the rich man in his torment in *Hades* looks across the chasm and sees Lazarus with Abraham in what must be heaven, the rich man asks for relief. Anyone taking this description literally rather than symbolically must be myopic, indeed.

Hell is not always described as fire, which would of course connote light. Jesus also described it as "outer darkness; there men will weep and gnash their teeth" (Matthew 8:12). Will there be some kind of remorse, for all of us to some degree in the afterlife? Yes! Will it be some eternal hell of torment and punishment? Not unless God is a devil. Mature adults put Satan in the same category with Santa Claus and Easter Bunny—except Satan is not as nice! Those who believe Satan actually exists only help feed the dementia of the sick and troubled persons who would be Satanic cult worshipers.

If the Devil doesn't make us do it, who does? To be honest, we really don't need any help. We do very well in the tempting and sinning departments on our own. We regularly think about things we shouldn't think about or desire to do something that we shouldn't do.

> Let no one say, when he is tempted, "I am tempted by God"; for
> God cannot be tempted with evil and he himself tempts no one;
> but each person is tempted when he is lured and enticed by his
> own desire. (James 1:13-14)

No one puts ideas into our head. Perish the thought. When we sit down at the table to overeat, the devil did not put all that food before us, nor did the devil entertain us with gluttonous notions. We deserve all the credit; no need to pass off the responsibility to anyone else. The world is full of so many good things for us to desire. They are all around us. We have ample opportunities to choose wrong. If in a scenario with ten options, one is the best or right way, that makes the other nine choices less desirable alternatives and, thus in varying degrees, wrong.

Enter by the narrow gate; for the gate is wide and the way is easy, that leads to destruction, and those who enter by it are many. For the gate is narrow and the way is hard, that leads to life, and those who find it are few. (Matthew 7:13-14)

If there were a devil with all the power and talent we so generously acknowledge as his, we wouldn't stand a chance! But in that case, neither would we be responsible!

And no wonder, for even Satan disguises himself as an angel of light. (II Corinthians 11:14)

How could we ever be expected to know that it was the devil behind so masterly a disguise? I am always amused reading the apocryphal books when Satan is described as looking and acting exactly like a good angel:

After this Satan, the hater of all good, took the form of an angel, and with him two others, so that they looked like the three angels who had brought to Adam gold, incense, and myrrh. They passed before Adam and Eve while they were under the tree, and greeted Adam and Eve with fair words that were full of guile. But when Adam and Eve saw their comely mien, and heard their sweet speech, Adam rose, welcomed them, and brought them to Eve, and they remained all together; Adam's heart the while, being glad because he thought concerning them, that they were the same angels, who had brought him gold, incense, and myrrh. (I Adam and Eve 70:1-3)

There is no way that we could help but be fooled.

But fortunately, there is no devil to tempt us and no eternal punishment in hell. We have only ourselves to blame for our sin and we must not blaspheme God in crediting God with such creations. In doing so, Jesus' teaching about a great loving God is lost on us. But what about angels?

With a closer inspection regarding the references to angels, it seems that in many instances we are dealing with a literary device or an example of dramatic emphasis, similar to that concerning Satan. If there are angels we would have a very difficult time differentiating between our system of angels and the panoply of gods of many other "primitive" religions. Just what is the job description of an angel, and how does it differ from the many *gods and goddesses* of other faiths?

Perhaps they are just ghosts or the souls of persons who have died and gone to heaven similar to the spirits that mediums are able to conjure up for us. I call your attention once more to the return of the dead Samuel at the hands of a medium (I Samuel 28). Is this the stuff of which angels are made?

Confusing gods with angels, since we don't really know what we are dealing with, is not uncommon. There are Old Testament moments when it isn't clear if it is God or an angel who is on the scene. Gideon is visited by an "angel of the Lord" (Judges 6:11-27). At one moment it is an angel of the Lord and the next it is "the Lord"—back and forth. Which is it? Anyone reading the passage literally would not be satisfied with the words that introduce the event, "the Lord. . .", as coming from an angel of the Lord. Earlier, was it an angel or God that Jacob wrestled with (Genesis 32:24-30)? We are told it was God, but that is hardly possible unless it is strictly a spiritual struggle, in which case we would have a literalist's reminder that Jacob sustained an injury to his leg in the match.

Often angels are only part of a vision. Jacob dreams of a ladder to heaven with angels ascending and descending (Genesis 28:11-12). Daniel is having a similar vision about an encounter with one of God's messengers (Daniel 8:15-26). And no one is going to see anything but allegory in the strange visions in Revelation of angels and dragons (Revelation 12:7-12).

Jesus includes angels in his story about Lazarus (Luke 16:19-31) which is certainly only a literary device and a part of a parable. I believe that when Jesus uses the term, he is doing so for effect and not to be taken literally as in:

> "Just so, I tell you, there is joy before the angels of God over one
> sinner who repents." (Luke 15:10)

In an earlier chapter we dealt with the idea that the second coming of Jesus is misleading. It sounds as if it will happen during the lifetime of those Jesus is talking to. Just as many scholars suggest these passages are no doubt later additions by the early church rather than the actual words of Jesus such as:

"For whoever is ashamed of me and of my words in this adulterous and sinful generation, of him will the Son of man also be ashamed, when he comes in the glory of his Father with the holy angels." (Mark 8:38)

So the story of the angel announcing the birth of John the Baptist to his father, Zechariah, in the temple (Luke 1:8-19) belongs to the same folklore as the stories surrounding the birth of Jesus.

Angels and Satan are joined by other mythical characters such as cherubim and seraphim who are no doubt ideas that have slipped over from Egyptian, Babylonian, and Assyrian mythology. They are strange, winged creatures that smack of the legendary. As in the case of miracles, we ought to be suspicious when we read about the appearance of angels, the devil or cherubim in "Bible times," while we never see them today.

Finally, we have a problem with the trinity and the idea of "three gods in one." As noted, the Unitarians have a legitimate criticism concerning those Christians who use the trinity concept. If we profess belief in one God, then drop the silly and confusing reference to three gods. Don't even use the term *trinity* unless you delight in confusing people. What is being described is three ways in which God has been revealed to us: as creator of the universe, as revealed in the life and teaching of Jesus, and as personal experience in our own lives through worship and prayer. The "trinitarian formula,"

"Go therefore and make disciples of all nations, baptizing them in the name of the Father and of the Son and of the Holy Spirit. . ." (Matthew 28:19)

is a much later addition to the words of Jesus by the early church if ever I saw one. We have here an excellent example of Ockham's razor, i.e., the thesis that entities should not be multiplied beyond necessity. We should not complicate a situation when the simple will do.

NOTES:

[1] Walter G. Williams, <u>Archaeology In Biblical Research</u> (New York: Abingdon Press, 1965), p. 17.

[2] Madeleine S. Miller & J. Lane Miller, <u>Harper's Bible Dictionary</u> (New York: Harper & Brothers, 1959), p. 243.

[3] Nolan B. Harmon, ed., <u>The Interpreter's Bible, volume 1</u> (New York: Abingdon Press, 1952), p. 296.

[4] Miller, p. 136.

[5] <u>The Oxford Annotated Bible</u> (New York: Oxford University Press, 1965), footnotes on page 839.

14. Was It Written With You In Mind?

An old joke tells of a lady who was seeking guidance from the scriptures and was in the habit of simply opening her Bible to any spot at random and putting her finger down to see what God might be trying to tell her. One day following this procedure, her finger happened to land on Matthew 27:5 where she read ". . .and he went and hanged himself." Knowing that this had to be a mistake, she sought some other message from God in the same manner and this time her finger happen to land on Luke 10:37 where she read the phrase, "Go, and do likewise." She gave it one more try and turned to John 13:27 in her random search, and her eyes fell upon, "What you are going to do, do quickly."

That may not be humorous at all, but it comes close to some of the superstitious ways in which we approach scripture! We all agree that God's word is there even if we cannot agree on what "God's word" is, or what "God's word" means. We are in total agreement that we can find truth about God and what God wants us to do in the Bible. The major question is how do we find that truth? Persons who spend a great amount of time studying the scriptures, yea, even "professionals," cannot come close to agreeing on what they find there.

Was it written for us? Was it intended only for the people of the day in which it was written? Is it universally applicable for everyone in every age? It has been clear by now to the reader that the position of this book is that there are many ideas and ethical principles found in the Bible that are totally contrary to God's way. There are many errors and misconceptions. So we have two lines of inquiry. For whom was it written and how do we sort out the real truth from the error? The second question carries us over into the next chapter.

There can be no doubt that much of the Bible's contents is heavily influenced by the mores and values of the day in which it was written. Animal sacrifice, polygamy, and the general dominance of men over women are simple, quick examples of how the traditions of the time, though definitely contrary to God's will, yet found their way into scripture as practices supposedly recommended by God. We could then say there are many things that we must ignore as they were written for a culture much different than our own and written with a definite cultural bias. The fact that these kinds of passages were written from their own cultural perspective does not make them "right" even for their own time in history. For example, passages in the Old Testament concerning marriage and divorce, what or what not to eat, and what crimes warrant the use of capital punishment reflect the social conditions of a time anywhere from 2500 to 3000 years ago and were probably "wrong" in that day as well as today.

However, there are many passages in scripture in which someone sensitive to God's will did understand and was able to capture God's truth for us. Among many possibilities, these few quickly spring to mind:

> You shall not kill. You shall not commit adultery. You shall not
> steal. You shall not bear false witness against your neighbor.
> (Exodus 20:13-16)

Obviously some amplification is necessary in each case to clarify the issue; for example, if we are not to kill, where do we draw the line: people, animals, or plants? But, overall, who would argue that these laws do not represent God's will for us? In essence we can see there certainly are universal "rules" or ideas that apply to all times and all persons. Our problem is to find a way in which to help us sort the wheat from the chaff.

Before we continue further, it would be prudent to look at the erroneous ways we too often go about searching for the grain. It may be no secret to anyone that most of us at times form our convictions or values first and only then hunt around in scripture for support for these ideas. Either we have been conditioned to want to believe certain ideas, or our prejudices lead us to certain conclusions. Then, in order to validate our position, we begin our search in scripture for supporting material—passages that say what we want to hear. And if they do not conform to our satisfaction, we simply put our own special interpretation on them.

An example of this selective method concerns capital punishment. If we are for it, we just ignore Jesus and look to the Old Testament law where we will be clearly vindicated. An example of how we might creatively interpret and manipulate truth surfaces when we suggest that Jesus, by saying, "And you will hear of wars and rumors of wars. . ." (Matthew 24:6), implies that he endorsed war and the use of violence. Making the statement that we will see the ravages of cancer for many years to come does not mean we are in favor of such prospects.

When Paul said, "I have become all things to all men. . ." (I Corinthians 9:22), that is not a clue as to the approach we are permitted to take with the scriptures. Yet, the Bible has been used to justify slavery, racism, inquisitions, witch burning, capital punishment and many, many more unsavory practices. Such use of scriptural justification is not necessarily a distortion of Biblical material—scriptural support for such goofy ideas is probably there all right. The problem is to recognize what is truth and what is error. However, instead, we have been very happy at times to have found in scripture justification for our immoral behavior.

We must approach scripture with an honest heart and let God's word speak through the nonsense that exists in the Bible. This means finding some guidelines to organize our search that will reveal God's word.

Before looking at this secret to sorting out God's will, there is another little matter that did not seem to fit elsewhere, and perhaps it could be a parenthetical addendum to this question concerning for whom scripture was intended. It is the "chosen people" issue.

A major theme of the Old Testament is the idea that God chose the Hebrew nation for a special task. Some mean-spirited Christians claim that the Jews failed in that calling and so now Christians step in to inherit the position the Jews forfeited. Some not-quite-so-mean Christians will tell us that Israel to a large extent fulfilled its mission as God's chosen people, but that now

Christians become chosen people for a new and greater role. What do you make of the "chosen people" concept?

First of all, a question concerning who among the chosen people really were the chosen people seems in order. It is always assumed that it is the Israel nation who were chosen. And to the extent that they began to worship God and followed the covenant and law that was set before them as a nation, they became the people of God. Despite the fact that the Old Testament people theologically saw themselves relating with God as a nation more than as individual persons, it is always ultimately each individual who must respond to the call to covenant. It is each individual who must choose to be faithful, or not, to the call to follow God's will. It turns out that it was individuals—Abraham, Moses, Joshua, Rahab, Deborah, Ruth, Jeremiah, Isaiah—who answered the call while the masses simply followed along with differing degrees of success or failure—and usually more often than not, more of the latter than the former. The masses of common folk in the Old Testament do not have an impressive track record of accepting the challenge to be the chosen. Note, for example, the grumbling and complaining in the desert and the golden calf fiasco to name but two incidents. More credit should be given to the solitary individuals, the great religious leaders of the Old Testament. They were the ones who were "chosen" and responded.

But the larger question should be why were the Jews "chosen" in place of other nations? Probably the most likely answer is that they weren't! They became the chosen, partly by default, simply because they were the people who were more sensitive to God's presence while others who received the same call failed to listen. God is calling all peoples at all times; the Jews—their leaders, at least—responded. There can be no doubt that God has been and still is calling all individuals to covenant relationships, and calling many individuals for leadership rolls commensurate with their abilities and talents. Had any other nation (series of individuals) recognized God in the holy smoke or the burning bush or heard a still, small voice, who knows what other revelations would have surfaced. Early South American peoples or ancient Chinese might have given us prophetic words or some law from God had they only been tuned in to the right frequencies. In fact, they probably were and they probably did! Jews and Christians do not have a monopoly on awareness of God. Religious evidence from all cultures and areas of our globe reveals that God's truth found its way into the minds of all people. There are many other cultures that have "sacred" writings or religious literature. With just a little patience the reader can enjoy a brilliant discussion concerning this matter in a later chapter.

One could ask the question, "Why is there a greater concentration of encounters with God in the Bible than elsewhere?" One answer would be *momentum*. One experience builds upon another. One person opens the door with a small revelation of God. Another individual, benefiting from the wisdom or experience of a predecessor, is able to open the door a little wider with new experiences. Succeeding generations will build upon the religious revelations and experiences of God that their forefathers and foremothers have had. Those who have gone before have introduced them to a "God of Abraham, Isaac, and Jacob."

The whole process can be made analogous to the modern automobile. It was built by teams of persons over many years improving upon what came before without each new generation having to re-invent the wheel. Someone in a certain part of the world discovers or invents something. This is exhibit "A." Because of the existence of item "A" others can modify, improve, or add to item "A" to make exhibit "B" and so on to create "C" and "D", etc. No other persons in other parts of the world can arrive at anything quite like a "C" or a "D" until they too have finally begun with "A." It is a matter of momentum. A nation will be more likely to raise up an Amos or Isaiah if there have been the likes of a Moses, a Samuel, a Nathan appearing beforehand. This is part of the theory of the unfolding development of the Bible.

But back to the question, "Was it written for you?" The answers "yes" and "no" would seem to cover all the bases. Yes, God's truth has been received and shared in manageable portions through the history of our scriptures in a growing and progressive fashion. Unfortunately, but not unexpectedly, due to the human qualities of those who received and preserved an understanding of God for us, the truth has grown up with the weeds or chaff all along the way. God's truth is there for us amidst the errors and dead end paths. How to get at the golden grain of God's universal truth is our foremost concern. Unveiling that secret is the happy denouement of the next chapter. We can only let you read on past this point if you promise to tell everyone.

15. Getting Humpty Dumpty Together Again

Up to this point you might have the impression that so many unsettling charges have been made concerning the Bible that if there were any truth to them there isn't much left of this valuable book. Errors, contradictions, absurdities, and un-Godlike passages have been pointed out that cannot be denied. They are there—in the Bible. I didn't invent these problems. They exist. They have always been there. And because of them, Christians disagree theologically, sometimes violently. Churches and clergy of different denominations sometimes refuse to have anything to do with each other (not to discount the many instances of fine ecumenical cooperation).

Because of these very questionable passages, Christians have believed some ridiculous ideas and practiced very foolish things from excommunication to handling poisonous snakes to accepting war to slavery and racism to the denigration of the status of women, to name only a few.

Because of them many intelligent youth and adults have been driven from the Christian Faith because they cannot believe such absurdities or condone un-Christian Christian practice.

The problems exist even though we try our best to ignore them in hopes that they will go away or, at the least, hope that no one will notice!

What frightens all of us and causes your minister to cover up the skeletons are the prospects that once you begin to doubt, where do you stop doubting? If you can question the validity of an incident of scripture or consider it a myth or see it as a serious contradiction of what God really wants us to believe, then what can you trust? The is a real and vital concern! How can we restore order and find the truth in the Bible?

I feel the answer is simple, yet challenging: the source of truth and the source of our faith must be found in the life and teachings of Jesus—we might say the "spirit of Jesus!"

One of my seminary professors, Bruce Rahtjen, stated the idea in essence. In speaking about the Old Testament he said:

> . . .we find that it contains a great deal of material which is unacceptable in terms of our Christian faith. Christians must be very careful in using Old Testament material as a basis for preaching, or as a basis for a standard of morality.[1]

> . . .we must evaluate that meaning in terms of our Christian faith. That is to say, we must read the Old Testament christologically.[2]

I would pursue that idea a little further and say that we must read the entire Bible, Old and New Testaments and even the teachings of Jesus, in the light of our understanding of the "spirit of Jesus."

The idea is to become so absorbed in the life and teachings of Jesus through reading and re-reading the gospels repeatedly that that we understand the "spirit of Jesus" enough to be able to anticipate what is and what is not consistent with the "spirit of Jesus." "What would Jesus do?" is an old question that can never become antiquated! As Christians we must become so immersed in the way of Jesus that we can "feel" what is right. It means opening our lives more and more to God's love so that we become more and more loving ourselves.

I believe that it is very possible for each one of us to have a high degree of understanding of the "spirit of Jesus"—the spirit of God's love—and still have a very difficult time living that life and love. By becoming so familiar with the way of life that Jesus lived and taught, we can instinctively know where that kind of love and compassion would lead us concerning any decisions we have to make, and yet still lack the strength and courage to adequately live that way ourselves. In other words, it is possible to arrive at the place where we can know what is right and wrong and still have a difficult time practicing the Christian life.

We are Christians because we believe that Jesus has given us the complete revelation of God's way. There is nothing in other sacred writings that can begin to compare with the life and teachings of Jesus.

Because we are Christians and believe that Jesus revealed the ultimate truth, we must judge all other ideas, philosophies, religious teachings, and moral and ethical principles in the light of the "spirit of Jesus." This would include, as mentioned, the Old and New Testaments and, strange as it may seem, even the teachings of Jesus himself.

When we finally arrive at an understanding and full appreciation of that spirit of Jesus, then we may begin to make critical evaluation of all other doctrine or religious ideas. We have a yardstick with which to measure everything else, always asking the question, "Is this consistent with what Jesus taught and consequently with God's will?"

When we examine material from the Old Testament in contrast with what Jesus taught, there is much of which to be critical. Whole books such as Obadiah, Esther, and Nahum, when seen in the light of our Christian standard, are severely lacking in any redemptive value. Obadiah is a book that delights in the revenge over one of Israel's enemies, Edom. Edom was unkind, to say the least, to Israel in Israel's time of need, and so Obadiah predicts that God will wreck revenge (or already has) on Edom:

> But you should not have gloated
>   over the day of your brother
> in the day of his misfortune;
>   you should not have rejoiced over
> the people of Judah
>   in the day of their ruin;
> you should not have boasted
>   in the day of distress. (Obadiah 12)

We find no compassion, no "turn the other cheek," no Christian love in Obadiah for Edom. But then this is pre-Christian literature. Nahum is another book, like Obadiah, full of feelings of gleeful revenge over the fall of an enemy, Nineveh. Esther also is full of revenge and hate. (Nahum 3 & Esther 7 & 9)

Another example of un-Christlike theology or morality in the Old Testament is the story of Samson. Notwithstanding the fact that Samson is only a fictional character and not historical, this "hero" is a far cry from exemplifying any Christian virtues. Along with the other not-so-nice things Samson did in his life is the final act of revenge when he prays that God will grant him a return of enough strength to pull down a building upon his enemies, the Philistines, destroying them and himself in the process (Judges 16). That God would answer such a prayer, as the story indicates, is to attribute to God vicious and vengeful behavior—un-Christlike to say the least.

This is precisely what Christians must do: judge all acts and ideas in accordance with what we believe to be God's will as revealed in the "spirit of Jesus."

In chapter 17 we will apply this process to Paul and his theology. But what in the world could I have been thinking when I suggested that we even have to apply the teachings of Jesus to the teachings of Jesus in order to make sure they are right with God? That sounds like the most blatant of circular arguments—using Jesus to prove or test Jesus.

My point is that, when we take a passage out of context, or when we have a later addition to the text that may not be authentically Jesus, or when we do not understand a passage fully, or for other reasons, we begin to see that these isolated passages do not make sense or seem totally out of character with Jesus. Working only with bits and pieces, we can easily end up with an idea that seems to be totally inconsistent with Jesus.

Each of us has heard many times, and even repeated it ourselves, that one must be careful not to lift ideas or passages out of context, for thereby we run the risk of abusing or twisting the meaning. We must be careful that everything we attribute to Jesus meets the test of being consistent with all that Jesus taught us about the love of God! We shouldn't use single quotations unless we are confident that they are in character with Jesus.

For example, it doesn't seem at all like Jesus to curse a tree and make it die (Mark 11:12-14, 20-21), to tell his followers to buy swords (Luke 22:36), or that he really believed that God let him down (Mark 15:34).

If we are to test every theological idea and religious ethic found in scripture, as well as everything outside of scripture, with what is consistent with the spirit of Jesus, then we need to look at the individual things that Jesus said and did to see if they also pass the "Jesus test." I would like to cite some examples of things that Jesus said or did that seem out of character, and make some attempt at establishing ways in which we can solve such "problems" and yet maintain the integrity of Jesus' consistency.

There are several ways in which "problem" passages might be dealt with in order to make sense of what Jesus said or did:

1. Sometimes we need the right interpretation of the passage. We must ask what is Jesus intending to say or do.

2. The passage might be a later addition—something that Jesus never actually said or did.

3. It could be an exaggeration, a device used by Jesus to make a dramatic emphasis.

4. Or it may be a passage that we will simply have to admit we have yet to understand.

You may want to suggest other possibilities to this list.

There are plenty of examples of passages that seem out of character with Jesus. One day the mother and brothers of Jesus came to inquire after him while he was teaching a crowd of people. When they told him his family were there to see him, Jesus, in what seems like a rude remark, asked who his family was and immediately answered by saying that the crowd gathered there, or those who do God's will, is his family (Mark 3:31-35). Of course we realize that he was not being rude to his family, but simply teaching us that we are all sisters and brothers, children of God, and "members one of another."

On another occasion Jesus said,

Do not think that I have come to bring peace on earth; I have not come to bring peace, but a sword. For I have come to set a man against his father, and a daughter against her mother, and a daughter-in-law against her mother-in-law; . . . (Matthew 10:34-35)

Reading the next four verses will help us understand that Jesus does not intend to say that he came to deliberately upset persons or disrupt relationships. In fact, Jesus would admit that he came to bring peace and harmony among all peoples. What he is saying is that a possible by-product of following his teaching may lead to misunderstandings and disharmony. It is possible that when a person takes a stand for a principle that Jesus taught, that that person will alienate other individuals, perhaps even members of his own family.

To illustrate, imagine yourself hearing someone making racially derogatory comments. You are prompted to respond in some way in order to help that person understand that racial slurs are harmful, and thereby you risk making the person who made the insulting remarks angry at you. Our intent is ultimately to bring peace and harmony. But others are free to act in anger instead of love and understanding. We offered peace, but inadvertently "brought a sword."

Jesus is not saying that he came literally to cause trouble; he is saying that we must always do what we believe God wants us to do even though it may be unpopular or cause antagonism, or even when others may not understand or appreciate our efforts.

No matter if Ralph Waldo Emerson said that "foolish consistency is the hobgoblin of little minds," consistency is important, and we never expect Jesus to say or do anything that is contrary to the love ethic he taught concerning God and God's will for us.

A passage that has led to serious problems because some Christians are unable to discern exactly the real intent of what Jesus is saying is the comment that Jesus makes concerning revealing another person's faults to the church (Matthew 18:15-

17). The misunderstanding of this passage has literally led to law suits between church folks. Thoughtless pastors have revealed church members' "sins" (occasionally those that have been shared with the pastor in the confidence of a counseling situation) from the pulpit to the congregation on Sunday morning. Only God knows and shudders over how many times this has happened because someone could not understand the spirit of the passage from the eighteenth chapter of Matthew. Such a passage must be approached with a strong dose of compassion or we could destroy someone's life! It is an excellent example of the need to test the teachings of Jesus in microcosm by the teachings of Jesus in macrocosm.

In the first place, one might note the word translated as *church* in this passage and wonder if this passage represents an addition made by the church long after the time of Jesus and is in fact not an authentic statement made by Jesus. I believe this to be the case.

Nevertheless, one should pay careful attention to the opening comment in which Jesus says, "If your brother sins against *you* . . ." One should also ask the question, "Does it involve situations in which the problem is already common knowledge to the entire church?"

Finally, we should all know that there are better ways of working through a problem then through public humiliation and shame. If I as a pastor broadcast a church member's sins to the entire church, or even to one other person, then who, in turn, will reveal my sins? Shakespeare, or someone, said something about only those without sins could cast stones. It seems only fair that when a minister reveals the secret sins of a church member, the minister should have her or his sins made public, also.

There is the interesting incident where Jesus seems very rude to a Canaanite woman (Matthew 15:21-28). He first seems to say he will not help her because his ministry is only to the Jews (certainly not in character), and then, I think, he calls her a "dog." I suppose one could say that Jesus was "setting up" a situation he could use to teach an idea. Jesus does finally minister to the woman implying either that he changed his mind or that his comments may have had some meaning as yet not clearly deciphered by us. If we have the words that Jesus spoke recorded verbatim, was he baiting the people with an expression of their own prejudices (she was not of the chosen and washed) before he shatters their delusion by finally showing compassion to the woman and telling how great was her faith? Who knows?

Then we have exaggeration for dramatic effect: camels passing through needle's eyes (it is not necessary to suggest as some do that the needle's eye is a small door in a wall, or, getting real goofy, imply it could be done by hypodermic needle after liquification of the poor camel in a blender) (Matthew 19:24); moving mountains through prayer and faith (Matthew 21:21-22); or suggesting that the dead can bury the dead (Luke 9:59-60). Perhaps these are all Oriental hyperbolic teaching devices for emphasis.

One final example will suffice. Jesus never ever sent demons into a herd of pigs (Luke 8:26-33) and destroyed the poor animals by having them jump into the lake and drown. Come on, friends. If Jesus were going to perform a miracle, he could do a better one than that. This is just an unfortunate legend that finally found its way into the text at some point by an indiscriminating scribe.

For those readers who would enjoy some challenging home-work, try struggling with Matthew 20:1-16, Mark 11:12-14, 20-24, Luke 8:9, or Luke 16:1-9!

The wonder of it all is that, despite differences in the Gospels, the presence of errors and later unfortunate additions, and passages that are difficult to comprehend, etc., the real Jesus is clearly discernible. When we read and reread Jesus until we know Jesus, the "spirit of Jesus" is unquestionably clear and consistently compassionate. When we approach the Gospels with honest and open minds, the great love of God in Jesus will clearly be revealed to us—compassion for enemies, forgiveness, sacrifice—as no other religion has been able to reveal.

It then becomes a matter of extrapolating from that "spirit of Jesus." If we are frustrated that Jesus did not speak explicitly to specific issues we face today—drugs, safe driving, abortion, etc.—

we need only to apply the nature of Jesus to each choice we have to make and ask, "What would Jesus really do?"

Some issues will be resolved only after serious study. For example, what would Jesus do about the issue of drugs today? He would do precisely what he did just before being nailed to the cross (Mark 15:23): he would refuse to use alcohol and other harmful drugs and expect us to do the same. Jesus would say the Christian cannot use non-prescribed drugs including alcohol, perhaps the most dangerous drug of all. Jesus would never without serious cause do anything to harm his mind or body and would expect us to act accordingly.

A perceptive reader will quickly point out that Jesus apparently drank wine, served it at his last meal with his friends and recommended that we commemorate the event with our use of wine, and even changed water into wine at a wedding. If Jesus ever takes the time to read the Gospel of John, he will assuredly be disappointed and shocked to learn that a "water-to-wine" fabrication was unfortunately included in his biography.

But how can we account for his use of wine? It seems totally out of character with his compassion for persons, the need to be at our best and sharpest, and the importance of taking good care of our minds and bodies. I find consolation in the fine scholarly work of William Patton and his book, *Bible Wines or Laws of Fermentation And Wines of The Ancients*. Patton makes a case in his book that *wine* in scripture includes non-intoxicating beverages or grape juice, as well as intoxicating drinks. The only way we can tell which kind of drink is being referenced in any Biblical passage is by use of the word in the context, which is often very clear.

If I understand the real nature of Jesus—his compassion for people and respect for our minds and bodies—I have no doubt that the *wine* Jesus was always associated with was harmless grape juice. Jesus was well-versed in the Old Testament where we read:

Wine is a mocker, strong drink a brawler; and whoever is led astray by it is not wise. (Proverbs 20:1)

Who has woe? Who has sorrow?
  Who has strife? Who has complaining?
Who has wounds without cause?
  Who has redness of eyes?
Those who tarry long over wine,
  those who go to try mixed wine.
Do not look at wine when it is red,
  when it sparkles in the cup
    and goes down smoothly.
At the last it bites like a serpent,
  and stings like a an adder. (Proverbs 23:29-32)

Jesus never would have imbibed himself, nor recommended intoxicating wine for others. This example is one of the reasons why clergy persons need to research these sorts of things and share them with their congregation.

As we become thoroughly acquainted with Jesus, our most dramatic impression will be that the highest ideal to which God calls us through the life and teachings of Jesus is the ultimate ethic of pacifism. Being able to love an enemy would seem to be the ultimate act of love—the perfect love of God. This is what Jesus taught. There can be no question about it, and it is this ethic by which we must measure our thoughts, words and deeds.

From the cross Jesus was able to say, "Father, forgive them; for they know not what they do" (Luke 23:34). Love that Jesus talks about is an active good will towards another. We may have difficulty even liking those who have offended us, but a Christian loves her or his enemies by desiring only good for those persons, treating every person in the best way she or he knows how. Pacifism is what elevates the Christian ethic above other religions.

This then is the ultimate measuring stick for all other ethics, religions, and philosophic ideas: if they are consistent with this highest kind of love that Jesus revealed—the love that can even forgive enemies and honestly desire only good for them, then we know that this is God's way. This is the "spirit of Jesus" that we hold up to judge our choices and actions, as well as all religious ideas.

Many ministers will vehemently deny that Jesus taught pacifism, and they will be wrong. To deny it is to be guilty of reading into the teachings of Jesus only what we want to find there rather than accepting what Jesus actually taught.

I repeat what I said earlier, one of the most influential theologians for the greater part of this century, Reinhold Niebuhr, did not think that pacifism was practical or acceptable for Christians today. Despite the fact he was not a pacifist, yet he was honest enough with Jesus to confess that Jesus preached pacifism. As Rufus Jones tell us,

> Niebuhr—perhaps the ablest and most influential of the Christian opponents of pacifism—readily admits the pacifism of Jesus.[3]

G. H. C. Macgregor concurs,

> . . . there can be no question that the teaching of Jesus, if taken at its face value, is uncompromisingly pacifist. Niebuhr has no patience with those Christian theologians and ecclesiastics who still seek to discover loopholes through which war may be actually brought within the pale of Christian ethics and blessed in the name of the Prince of Peace. . .[4]

But, as mentioned previously, Niebuhr thought Jesus' teaching was not practical for us. In his own words,

> Jesus thus made demands upon the human spirit, which no finite man can fulfill. . .[5]

> The ethical demands made by Jesus are incapable of fulfillment in the present existence of man.[6]

I am overwhelmingly convinced that Niebuhr is right that Jesus taught pacifism, but I cannot accept his assessment that those teachings are not practical for us. We need only to recall the witness of the many early Christian martyrs who were able to live this ethic, as well as the many Christians of every century, and even into this century, who were able to practice this ethic even under the oppression of a Hitler.

Jesus' ethical teachings are practical, and we must accept them as our goal. If Niebuhr were right and they are not practical, then we have nothing! In such a situation Christianity offers us nothing ethically superior to other faiths.

A partial test of how honest we might be in accurately interpreting what Jesus said is to ask ourselves if we like what we read. If we find ourselves happily agreeing with Jesus' ideas, there is the possibility we have tampered with or twisted their meaning until we are comfortable with them. If, on the other hand, we find ourselves uncomfortable with what we believe Jesus said and we don't like the challenge of his ethics of love and sacrifice, there are strong suspicions we have been honest in our understanding of Jesus. Obviously, the fact that we do not want to accept what we are reading as the truth *will not* always be an indicator that we are honest in our interpretation. What it does indicate is that we have not interpreted Jesus' teachings in such a way as to make them say that which satisfies us because of our own prejudices.

The discussion to this point raises a concern over the place of *reason* and the place of *faith* in our approach to scriptures. We will deal with this issue in the next chapter. In the remainder of this chapter it would be wise to ask ourselves who was this Jesus, what was important about his life, and what is the "good news" he brought us?

Christians say that Jesus was both human and divine. Human we can understand; some of us "are one." It is important that Jesus be human and not just spiritual as the Gnostics (an early Christian "heresy" that helped formulate much of early Christian doctrine as the church tried to organize its position against the sect's teaching) believed.

Jesus needed to be human in order to validate his suffering and death on the cross. If he were unable to feel pain and fear death (note his anguish in the garden after the last supper, Luke 22:39-44) then going to the cross was not the sacrifice it is signified as being. Jesus needed to be human in order that he might feel temptation which gives greater meaning to his decision to give his life in ministry for us. Jesus needed to be human in order that he might live what he taught—practice what he preached—giving us example and inspiration. Jesus needed to be human in order that he will be real for us. If it were God doing these things, then the life of Jesus is shifted to another dimension and entirely out of our experience; in which case Niebhur could be right: some of the Christian life and ethic would be justifiably impractical for us.

Jesus seems to have emphasized his own humanity. Invariably he uses the term "son of man" (Matthew 12:8, Mark 9:9, Luke 22:9, John 13:31) in disproportionate deference to any reference of being the Son of God or the Messiah. We sometimes make the mistake of talking about "worshiping Jesus" when what Jesus intends is for us to worship only God and not him; Jesus only points us to God. No doubt this is what lies behind the interesting exchange between Jesus and the ruler who came inquiring of Jesus,

> And a ruler asked him, "Good Teacher, what shall I do to inherit
> eternal life?" And Jesus said to him, "Why do you call me good?
> No one is good but God alone." (Luke 19:18-19)

It is hard to ignore his words at this point. He seems to be stressing his humanity.

Other passages seem to have Jesus claiming for himself a more divine role. Jesus appears to acquiesce to Peter's calling him "Christ, the Son of the living God" (Matthew 16:16). However, in this instance Jesus initiates the conversation with another reference to himself as the son of man (16:13). He then proceeds to use the word church (16:18) which again raises suspicions that this could be an addition much later than the time of Jesus. Finally, he certainly did have some conviction of his being close enough to God to be able to reveal God's truth to us.

The Gospel of John makes more of Jesus' divinity than the other three gospels:

> Do you not believe that I am in the Father and the Father in me?
> The words that I say to you I do not speak on my own authority;
> but the Father who dwells in me does his works. (John 14:10)

What does it mean that Jesus was divine? As God's creatures, most persons might accept the idea that the spark of the divine or the spirit of God is present in some varying degree in all of us. We are God's creation, and we have an awareness of God's presence within us. One definition of the divinity of Jesus could be that he had much more of the presence of God within him than anyone else ever had. He certainly was able to reveal more of God's truth than anyone else ever has and was able to live a life more consistent with his teachings—as far as we can tell—than anyone else ever has. The remarkable, even astounding, fact is that the power, the perfection, the marvelous revelation of God, this incomparably highest of ethical standards, all survive the perils of an apparent long oral tradition, as well as the differing perspective of those who wrote the Gospels, and survived with such overwhelming clarity and consistently.

Jesus, though human like us, was able to open his life to the spirit of God to a great extent far exceeding what we might think possible for a human being. But it was all Jesus' response. God would never coerce or control any person, including Jesus, in order to accomplish a purpose no matter how significant that purpose might be. We are free to say "yes" or "no" to God at all times, and so was Jesus. But whatever our own particular theology concerning the subject of the divinity of Jesus, there remains a mystery about God's presence and revelation that we cannot fully comprehend.

What is important about Jesus? The birth stories make interesting and attractive myth. The miracles stories are unfortunate and onerous except for whatever *natural* power there is in prayer and faith healing, psychosomatic or otherwise. But the things that matter about Jesus is his life—the witness he made by practicing what he preached, his teaching and ethical values, the cross, and the resurrection. The resurrection was dealt with in an earlier chapter, and the meaning of the cross will be discussed in a later chapter.

The "good news" is that God loves us and forgives us and that the soul lives on after this life—all ideas which are subjects of many, many books.

Again, the secret is to get to know Jesus. We must spend considerable time reading through his life and teachings until we know the "spirit of Jesus." It is the only way we will find the answers to the age-old question we need to continually ask, "What would Jesus do?" It is our only standard by which to measure all other Biblical ideas in order that we might sift out the truth and eliminate the errors.

NOTES:

[1] Bruce D. Rahtjen, Scripture and Social Action (New York: Abingdon Press, 1966), p. 12.

[2] Ibid., p. 17.

[3] Rufus M. Jones, ed., The Church, the Gospel and War, New York: Garland Publishing, Inc., 1971), p. 51.

[4] G. H. C. Macgregor, The New Testament Basis of Pacifism and the Relevance of an Impossible Ideal (Nyack, New York: Fellowship Publications, 1960), p. 127.

[5] Reinhold Neibuhr, An Interpretation of Christian Ethics (New York: The Seabury Press, 1979). p. 75.

[6] Ibid., p. 35.

16. So, Do You Have To Be Smart To Be A Christian?

However unreasonable the reader has found this book, and however illogical the support of the ideas expressed therein seem, it remains true that I place much more emphasis on the use of reason in all matters of religion, and certainly in the interpretation of the Bible, than most readers would care to do. Most persons are prone to say that we must trust more to faith; we shouldn't be questioning scripture but instead accepting it literally as we find it.

I can't believe that God's way involves any contradictions or inconsistencies. Ignoring for the moment any claims of process theology, God does not change (Malachi 3:6, at least one thing the Old Testament got right). God's will for our ethical behavior remains constant. God does not want us to lie, kill, cheat, or steal, (the examples raised by "situation ethics" are never violations of God's *law*; they simply illustrate that sometimes two ideals are in conflict—for example a person might have to lie or steal in order to preserve a life—but these situations are always rare occasions.).

God does not want us to kill animals as an act of worship today just as God never wanted anyone to do so at any point in history including Old Testament times. God's spiritual laws are consistent, logical and reasonable so that we may make sense of what is right and wrong and make our decisions intelligently. We are often told that God's way of doing things is so far above our level of comprehending that it will not necessarily make sense to us; we just have to accept it: "God has a reason" for what happens and we are not expected to understand. That is not true. First, to say that we simply do not understand God's reasons is to admit that we actually have no answers to some very embarrassing theological problems. Secondly, that brand of theology is associated with the idea that God controls everything that happens, a concept that is ridiculous. The Old Testament is permeated with this kind of thinking:

Does evil befall a city, unless the Lord has done it? (Amos 3:6b)

That the answer to this question is "yes" is obviously implied in Amos as well as most of the Old Testament and, sadly enough, also in the theology of too many Christians. God is responsible for many terrible and cruel things, we are told, and God's reasons are not for us to understand. Nonsense!

God's physical and spiritual laws for the universe make sense, and we can use our reason to comprehend them. Our ability to reason is a special gift from God. Just as we use our minds to discover a cure for some terrible disease or to send a space probe to the planet Neptune, God intended that we use logic and reason to make sense of moral or theological issues. God does not communicate with us as the book of Jonah, for example, would have us believe. When Jonah's shipmates want to know who is responsible for the storm, they cast lots (draw straws). Supposedly God speaks through this act of chance to indicate that Jonah is the suspect (Jonah 1:7-8). If God's will for our ethical conduct cannot be discerned through reason, then perhaps we should make our important moral decisions by just tossing a coin because the alternative—the one we most often use now—is to accept word-for-word passages from scripture without questioning their logic, their humanity, or their compassion. For example, the Old Testament repeatedly tells us that the use of capital punishment is God's will. We are even given special situations in which it is appropriate. To be satisfied with this conclusion is blind faith— blind and stupid faith Our reason leads us to the teachings of Jesus, and our logic deduces from those teachings that God does not want us to commit acts of violence and revenge as the Old Testament would have us do. There is a place for faith. After accepting whatever evidence is available for the existence of God, eternal existence for us after death, and other similar issues, beyond that we must trust to our faith. God would never have us place faith in the absurd or unreasonable when it runs contrary to all that Jesus taught. There is much evidence that Jesus condemned all use of capital punishment. For example, we have the story of the woman caught in adultery (John 8:1-11) though it is not found in many early manuscripts. The story was found in some copies of John and even Luke, but our compilers decided not to include it in the translations of Luke. We are very fortunate that it was finally preserved for us. Some teachers of the Law and Pharisees brought a woman to Jesus that she might be stoned to death. All of us know the denouement of this story. Jesus in fact repealed the Old Testament Law and in doing so revealed for us the fact that capital punishment is wrong. It is not God's will.

But it is not enough to only quote isolated passages (despite the inordinate number of times I have already done so myself in this book) to decide an issue. Remember, the secret is always to ask the question, "Is it compatible with the spirit of Jesus?" And in order to do that, we have to familiarize ourselves with the total picture of Jesus and the love he revealed. As we apply this method, we quickly see reason reveals that capital punishment is incompatible with Jesus' teachings.

We must use reason. We have nothing else! The alternative is to read and believe a passage which tells us we can handle dangerous snakes and drink poison and not be harmed (Mark 16:18, a passage which some early manuscripts do not have. Fortunately, Matthew, Luke and John saw fit to omit such a crazy idea.) Most Christians are intelligent enough to use reason concerning such passages.

Some die-hards may still insist there are some of God's laws that remain outside the pale of human logic. I grant that the universe holds many mysteries for us. There is more about the spiritual and physical universe that we don't know or understand as of now then there is that we do know and understand. However, when it is a matter of what our ethical conduct should be and what God is like and how God relates to our world, past and present, there is precious little that would seem not to conform to our reason and logic. God's way is reasonable and makes sense; otherwise, we are rather helpless in making moral decisions.

However, some of the teachings of Jesus do seem to defy logic. Will the meek inherit the earth? Should we repeatedly forgive? Are we to give more of our material wealth to the poor than we are presently giving?

When some idea seems difficult to digest or seems impractical, it is only so because we may be in our theological infancy. We are not yet ready for the meat; we still have to diet on milk for a while (I Corinthians 3:2). However, when we explore the matter rationally and logically or when we become acclimatized to God's way, it will all make sense.

For example, pacifism seems totally impractical, foolish, and unreasonable. And yet, when we spend enough time exploring all of the arguments, we find that it makes far more sense than any other alternative. It is only a matter of becoming acquainted with the entire line of reasoning, as well as the historical record. History has given us abundant evidence of the success of pacifism even under the worst of conditions. Most of us are just ignorant of these examples. When one begins to examine the different lines of reasoning and logic concerning this issue, all avenues point to pacifism as the only answer.

Relying upon our cognitive powers to sort out answers to scriptural questions brings its own immanent danger—our bias. We begin to read into scripture what we want to find (as if we didn't all do that already). Any time we are allowed to take liberties using our own subjective judgment to compare ideas in seeking out those that are consistent with what we know of Jesus, our prejudices get in the way. In order to eliminate as much of our own subjectivism as possible, there are steps we can take.

1. We can pray that we will be open to truth and simply not rearrange our own biases. 2. We can continue to become more familiar with Jesus by reading and rereading his life and teaching. 3. We can make concerted efforts to understand fairly both sides of the discussion on any question. 4. We can ask ourselves if we are always accepting the position that we like or feel comfortable with, or if we are capable of accepting some ideas and positions that we do not like. Looking over our track record concerning this last suggestion will give us some clues as to our openness or closed-mindedness regarding ideas.

If we don't think and use reason, if we don't compare and make judgments (always with the danger of allowing our prejudices to color our conclusions) as we work through our theology regarding the many contrasting beliefs found in scripture, the alternative may be far worse—accepting some very sordid theological ideas because we find them in the Bible and we assume they must be true.

An example of unfortunate theology that has ample scriptural support is the idea that God causes everything that happens. Parents lose a child in a car accident and blame God: "Why does God do these things?" You can find numerous Biblical passages that espouse this sort of theology. No matter how cruel it may make God seem, people will believe such an idea partly because it is substantiated somewhere in scripture.

There are just too many unsavory ideas in the Old and New Testaments to confuse us unless we use our judgment to separate the wheat from the chaff. One final example comes from the last book in our Old Testament:

> Will man rob God? Yet you are robbing me. . . In your tithes and offerings. . . Bring the full tithes into the storehouse, that there may be food in my house; and thereby put me to the test, says the Lord of hosts, if I will not open the windows of heaven for you and pour down for you an overflowing blessing. (Malachi 3:8-10)

It is quite easy for this passage to leave the impression that God can be bought. We might assume that we can buy God's blessings by giving money to the church—perhaps a not-too-uncommon theology of many Christians today.

For many Christians, thinking and reason in matters of faith are anathema. It is feared that thought, reason, logic, and too much education are a dangerous business. It will erode and undermine our faith and belief in scripture. It will cause us to doubt and develop perverted ideas about our Bible.

I believe that truth—certainly God's truth in scripture—can stand the test of the most penetrating scrutiny. Where there are errors or weaknesses, the probing questioning of reason and logic will clean up truth. Cobwebs of untruth will be brushed away to allow the gleam of truth to shine more radiantly. I believe that, where God's word is found in scripture, it will only be enhanced and brightened by intelligent and honest challenges. No one really ever wants to cover up or ignore misconceptions, contradictions, or errors—the ostrich approach to problems. Let reason, logic, common sense, and education help us clean up our act.

There have been many sects, many still exist today, who have a phobia concerning education. They believe that education will bring doubts that will destroy scripture. Some of them prefer not to have their ministers educated. That would be dangerous. Religious bodies have even passed ordinances prohibiting the education of their clergy.

Is it possible ever to rely too heavily on reason when interpreting scripture? I say, "Perish the thought."

With all of this emphasis on thinking and reason and the importance of education and logic in matters of faith and Biblical interpretation, you may well ask, "Does a person have to be smart to be a Christian?" It is an intriguing question with very compli-cated possibilities. At times it sounds as if it is a difficult task to arrive at the Biblically appropriate position concerning certain moral issues (abortion, euthanasia, etc.); and that is true. However, I believe that God has created a world where it is possible for even slow persons like myself to arrive at the knowledge of what is right and wrong without necessarily relying on others to give me the answers.

Permit me to reiterate the central thought of the previous chapter: when we are prepared to thoroughly immerse ourselves in the love of God revealed in the life and teachings of Jesus by familiarizing ourselves with repeated study of the Gospels, sincerely wanting to know Jesus instead of satisfying a preconceived agenda of our own prejudices, we will develop a "smarts" of the heart! We will come to have an impression of what is right for us. A *feeling* for the "spirit of Jesus" or the love of God will shepherd us. For it to happen, we must come with openness, sincerity, honesty, prayer, determination, love, humbleness, and all of those other good things:

> The fear of the Lord is the beginning of wisdom. . . (Proverbs 9:10a) ("fear of" = love and reverence for).

> Ask, and it will be given you; seek, and you will find; knock, and it will be opened to you. (Matthew 7:7)

17. The Man Who Made Jesus Turn Over In His Grave

Is it just me or do other persons also get the impression that too many Christians say they accept Jesus, but in reality we find them almost exclusively quoting Paul to support their conservative theology? They find themselves forced to look into Paul's writings for confirmation of ideas that could never be found in the teachings of Jesus. There is no question about the greatness of Paul. The problem is that Paul's weaknesses are usually glossed over (except for those persons who would exploit those tangential thoughts in support of questionable theological positions) as we pretend that they don't exist. Worse yet, we sometimes try to "interpret" what Paul said in order to make it seem as if he really isn't saying the objectionable things that he is in fact saying.

Two tendencies seem to prevail. First, there are those who welcome the un-Christian things that Paul teaches: i.e., that women are really second class citizens. Second, there is the more liberal element who tell us that if we really understand what Paul was saying we would know that it isn't as bad as it seems; in fact, they will point out instances of his magnanimity, for example, to prove that he wasn't "sexist."

In certain instances we know that Paul fully understood the spirit of Jesus' teachings as well as anyone. However, in other instances Paul was led far afield, making mistakes like the rest of us.

If Peter sometimes exasperated Jesus,
And Peter took him and began to rebuke him, saying, "God forbid, Lord! This shall never happen to you." But he turned and said to Peter, "Get behind me, Satan! You are a hindrance to me; for you are not on the side of God, but of men." (Matthew 16:22-23)

then there must have been times when Paul said things that made Jesus turn over in his grave!—(which by the way, though he wrote our first Christian literature long before the gospels, I believe Paul never mentions the empty tomb, giving credence to a spiritual resurrection). The scripture just quoted from the Revised Standard Version has instead these closing words in the Good News Bible translation: ". . .these thoughts of yours don't come from God, but from man." I think Jesus on occasions could have said the same thing about Paul (despite what Paul claims: Galatians 1:11-12).

Just as the Biblical scientific world view was distorted by the inadequate scientific knowledge of the day in which it was written, I am afraid that to a large extent the more primitive social perspective of the day in which Paul lived heavily influenced his teachings concerning Christian theology.

Paul reminds me of the rookie "born again" Christians of today who spring to life as fully grown theologians with all the answers. One minute they are down-and-out sinners with little connection to the church and even less contact with healthy Christian teaching, and the next minute they are theological authorities spouting such primitive beliefs as "God will bless you with success, wealth and good health if you only accept Jesus as your personal savior." They can espouse such doctrine with a total disregard of the Biblical witness that God's chosen are not promised comfort and popularity, but instead are often subjected to suffering and even martyred for their faith. Indeed, Jesus often almost discourages us from following him because of the pain and sacrifice involved,

"Behold, I send you out as sheep in the midst of wolves. . . they will deliver you up to councils, and flog you. . . you will be hated by all. . ." (Matthew 10:16-23)

to note just one warning among many.

But who was this Paul? The important things to know about him was that he was a great and courageous missionary for the infant church, and that he wrote a major portion of our New Testament. Paul began his career in a rabbinical school under the tutorage of one of the great Jewish teachers, Gamaliel, in

Jerusalem. He became a fanatical anti-Christian activist going about persecuting Christians because of their threat to Judaism. This meant that he was heavily steeped in Old Testament tradition.

While on a Christian-hunting safari, he had his famous conversion three or four years after the death of Jesus. Three accounts of that conversion have been preserved for us (Acts 9:1-19, 22:3-21, 26:9-18). He believed that God had called him to take this new faith, Christianity, to Asia Minor and Europe where he successfully established many churches. It is frightening to think what the church would have suffered in the way of stunted parochialism had not Paul risked his life and worked so assiduously to spread the gospel to other parts of the world. Add to this missionary work the fact that he wrote the first Christian literature preserved in the New Testament as letters to various churches and individuals, and we have, in Paul, the single most effective force in the early church.

Despite this commendation Paul was abundantly human, and while he echoed brilliantly much of what Jesus taught, he missed the mark on many other issues, most probably because of the influence on his thinking by the social mores of the day in which he lived as mentioned earlier. In other words, we must apply once more the measure of the nature and spirit of Jesus to what Paul had to say in order that we might sort out what he understood about God from what he misunderstood about God. (Parenthetically speaking, I always wonder why Paul used "God talk" all of the time? After all, Jesus just talked in plain American like us common folks. He told many stories and spoke in a clear and simple conversational manner for the most part while Paul, on the other hand, was so ornate, flowery, and pontificating with his "God talk" and theologians have been emulating Paul ever since).

The remainder of this chapter will be devoted to, first, some of the issues about which Paul was in error because he did not understand Jesus. Then we can examine the ideas of Jesus which Paul is able to fully appreciate.

We might as well begin with the issue of slavery. No matter how creatively you try to interpret Paul's ideas concerning slavery, you cannot characterize Paul as one who condemns slavery. You would stand about as much chance of interpreting the message of the National Rifle Association as intending that we should have serious gun control laws. If Paul were fully in tune with God's will for human relationships, we would never be able to read:

Slaves, be obedient to those who are your earthly masters, with

fear and trembling. . . (Ephesians 6:5)

which is the beginning of a five-verse passage that clearly indicates that Paul accepted this institution. He must have had this letter in front of him when he wrote Colossians or vice versa, for he repeats the message in Colossians 3:22 through 4:1.

In his letter to Philemon, who by the way is a slave owner, a letter which deals exclusively with this issue, Paul misses his chance to take any significant stand against slavery. One looks with disappointment for a simple statement saying, "Slavery is wrong; no human being can own another as property." and from a man who was especially known for his verbosity. We cannot exonerate Paul by pointing out that he said the master must treat the slave with kindness and love as Colossians and Ephesians have suggested. There needed to be a clear condemnation of slavery by Paul spoken to the people of his own day, as well as for the many people in the centuries since. Passages of Paul's have been used as Biblical support and justification for slave trade ever since.

In the same vein, Paul could not shake loose from the traditions of his day regarding the obvious inferior status of women and the fact that they were viewed as property of men who, themselves, were created superior by God. A quick glance might lull one into thinking that Paul was talking equality when he said,

Wives, be subject to your husbands, as is fitting in the Lord.

Husbands, love your wives, and do not be harsh with them.

(Colossians 3:18-19)

but there is a clear message of a chain of command, wherein wives must obey husbands and wherein husbands have control over the situation. Paul continues in another letter,

For the husband is the head of the wife. . . so let wives also be
subject in everything to their husbands. (Ephesians 5:23-24)

The ideas of Paul regarding the place of women in the ministry
and the life of the church are still being reverenced today. As
difficult as it is to imagine, there are still churches today which are
so antiquated as to refuse to let women preach and provide
leadership in the church. This is true because Paul was a prisoner
of the tradition of the day in which he lived and did not have the
vision of God on the matter:

. . .the women should keep silence in the churches. For they are
not permitted to speak, but should be subordinate, as even the
law says. If there is anything they desire to know, let them ask
their husbands at home. (I Corinthians 14:34-35)

In conjunction with this, Paul seemed to have some problem
with marriage (perhaps a bad marriage experience of his own?).
Here are a few of his ideas that bewilder and perplex us:

It is well for a man not to touch a woman. . . .I wish that all were
as I myself am (unmarried?). . . .To the unmarried and the
widows I say that it is well for them to remain single as I do. But
if they cannot exercise self-control, they should marry. (I
Corinthians 7:1, 7-9)

It sounds very much like Paul is saying we should only marry
if we cannot control ourselves. What ever happened to love? The
astute reader will note that Paul soon appears to add a reason for
his strange thoughts on marriage:

I mean, brethren, the appointed time has grown very short; from
now on, let those who have wives live as though they had none. . .
(I Corinthians 7:29)

Paul is misled by what he thought was to be a speedy return of
Jesus—another one of his mistakes. But why should that have
anything to do with marriage?

What are the possible explanations for Paul's mistaken notions
concerning slavery and women, as well as other issues?

a. We could say that Paul is right and that everything he said is God's will. Plenty of conservatives would like this one; however, this won't satisfy those who are a little further along in their evolutionary journey.

b. We could say that Paul definitely said these things but that he was dead wrong. This one won't cause me to lose sleep.

c. We could say Paul never said such things; they are later additions to his work by unknown persons. We said it occasionally happened to Jesus; let's be fair and give Paul the benefit of the doubt, also. There are good reasons why this is not quite as likely to have happened to Paul's works. Jesus wrote nothing himself, and many years elapsed before his oral teaching found its way into recorded form as we know it today. On the other hand, Paul did write, and his letters appear to be less tampered with than the process that led to the Gospel's final form.

d. Another possibility is to suggest that Paul said these things, but that they represent an earlier stage in his career. He could have gone through a process of maturing in which his later letters would more closely represent God's will. The fly in this ointment is that we do not see any pattern of change or any indication of growth and maturity concerning these subjects. Some of the above complaints actually come from his later writings. Following is a rough chronology of Paul's letters in order that the reader might do her or his own investigating:

I II Thessalonians	c. 50-51 A.D.
Galatians	c. 51-52
I II Corinthians	c. 53-56
(& III & IV if they exist)	
Romans	c. 56-57
Philippians	c. 59-61
Colossians	c. 59-62
Ephesians	c. 59-62
Philemon	c. 59-62

For example, one could refer to the marvelous passage that says:

There is neither Jew nor Greek, there is neither slave nor free, there is neither male nor female; for you are all one in Christ Jesus. (Galatians 3:28)

However, chronologically Galatians seems to come earlier in Paul's career. On the other hand, as wonderful as is this idea from Galatians, on careful inspection it does not liberate any slaves or women. It seems to say only that in the eyes of God we are equally precious despite the status we give one another here on earth.

   e. I suggest one final explanation (there may be others). We might simply be misinterpreting Paul. Perhaps those selected passages are not as harsh as they appear, and we just need to be more generous with Paul and his intended meaning. That may be your solution. As for me, I think the passages seem fairly dramatic and poignant, so I will opt for b of the above and be comfortable with it.

We might pause at this point and ask why Jesus would use sexist imagery for God, referring to God as "Father." First, Jesus wanted to communicate the idea of parent for God in order to use the parent-child love relationship as a model. In this situation Jesus was *using his cultural* setting to communicate an idea, whereas Paul was *being influenced by his culture* in the values he espoused. Jesus used the imagery to teach another idea. He was not concerned with sexism when he used the word "Father," just as he was not suggesting that heaven was a physical house with rooms when he said, "In my Father's house are many rooms. . ." (John 14:2a). Paul, on the other hand, was preaching sexism point blank.

Secondly, Jesus gave a place of equality and respect to women that was unheard of in his day—even to the point of shocking persons. The fact that Jesus would be so bold as to start up a conversation with a strange woman at a well is unparalleled (John 4:7-29):

Just then his disciples came. They marveled that he was talking with a woman, but none said, "What do you wish?" or, "Why are you talking with her?" (John 4:27)

We must not forget that Jesus was received into the home of Mary and Martha where Martha comments about how Mary is not preforming as the "woman of the house doing the woman's duties" and Jesus defends Mary's stepping out of the traditional role (Luke 10:38-42).

The record of Jesus' teaching and activities, we must remember, was subject to the modification and alteration of those who were a part of the process of preserving and formulating the story into its written form over a period of time. The teaching of Jesus is not exempt from the cultural bias of his biographers. For example we read,

> Soon afterward he went on through cities and villages, preaching and bringing the good news of the kingdom of God. And the twelve were with him, and also some women who had been healed of evil spirits and infirmities: Mary, called Magdalene, from whom seven demons had gone out, and Joanna, the wife of Chuza, Herod's steward, and Susanna, and many others, who provided for them out of their means. (Luke 8:1-3)

This is a fantastic passage. The authors who were preserving this information were describing it from their cultural perspective and yet the startling fact that Jesus had women followers was not edited out. This from the same persons who, in recording this information, allowed their cultural biasses to interpret the healing as that of exorcising demons. They had the intrepidity, no doubt against their better judgment, to include the revelation that women were supporting Jesus and his male disciples financially.

What makes for interesting speculation is that there is conceivably much that Jesus said and did that has been lost to us. I would like to think that Jesus made some significant statements concerning many things, like the slavery issue and women's status, that never got remembered:

> But there are also many other things which Jesus did; were every one of them to be written, I suppose that the world itself could not contain the books that would be written. (John 21:25)

But I digress. Returning to Paul, we find that he had a tendency to favor a predestination or at least a theology which understood God to be in greater control over the world's events and our personal lives than we care to imagine.

Reminiscent of the way in which God manipulated Pharaoh's mind so that at one moment he was ready to release the Hebrew people from bondage in Egypt and the next moment he wouldn't because God had hardened Pharaoh's heart (Exodus 7-12), we have Paul's various statements about God's control over our destiny:

> Therefore God sends upon them a strong delusion, to make them believe what is false, so that all may be condemned who did not believe the truth but had pleasure in unrighteousness. But we are bound to give thanks to God always for you, brethren beloved by the Lord, because God chose you from the beginning to be saved, through sanctification by the Spirit and belief in the truth. (II Thessalonians 2:11-13)

There is a strong thread running through Paul's theology that God made the decision who would and who would not be saved before we even came into being. This is a predestination that most Christians have outgrown today, notwithstanding the remnant of predestination in the belief that many Christians still hold that "when your time comes" to die you will indeed die at that appointed time. This provides a certain factor of safety for us in a dangerous world because we just know that God has appointed a very long time for us on this earth. This single element of predestination seems to be the only part that we cling to tenaciously.

However, Paul credits God with far more control over this world:

> For he has made known to us in all wisdom and insight the mystery of his will, according to his purpose which he set forth in Christ as a plan for the fullness of time, to unite all things in him, things in heaven and things on earth. In him, according to the purpose of him who accomplishes all things according to the counsel of his will, we who first hoped in Christ have been

destined and appointed to live for the praise of his glory. (Ephesians 1:9-12)

Tangled up in a very beautiful passage we find these confused words regarding predestination:

We know that in everything God works for good with those who love him, who are called according to his purpose. For those whom he foreknew he also predestined to be conformed to the image of his Son, in order that he might be the first-born among many brethren. And those whom he predestined he also called; and those whom he called he also justified; and those whom he justified he also glorified. (Romans 8:28-30)

The eighth chapter of Romans has so much beauty and power in it, that it is a shame that it seems to contain the theology that God is running the show and we become little automatons.

In the next chapter Paul delves into a little history concerning Rebecca and her children, Jacob and Esau, suggesting that God had predestined their history even before they were born (Romans 9:9-13)

It is very important for Paul's theology that God is credited for everything. It is his way of glorifying and praising God, I would imagine. In doing so, he takes away our own freedom. Also in doing so, he necessarily credits God with some wicked acts.

A part of Paul's theology is that humans are too evil and sinful to even make a response to God's love: God makes the overture, and then God causes us to respond or not respond as it pleases God:

What shall we say then? Is there injustice on God's part? By no means! For he says to Moses, "I will have mercy on whom I have mercy, and I will have compassion on whom I have compassion." So it depends not upon man's will or exertion, but upon God's mercy. (Romans 9:14-16)

Paul asks if there is any injustice on God's part because God controls everything that happens, such as who will and who will not be saved. Paul answers his own question with a resounding, "No!, God is just." I answer the same question with a resounding,

"Yes." Paul's theology takes away our freedom, which in turn takes away any responsibility we have for our actions, and in the end makes God unjust. I would urge Paul to go back and read the Garden of Eden story about the birth of right and wrong (Genesis 3). Paul's theology makes God out to be a monster, and we can blame God for the human devastation in wars as well as everything else bad that happens.

Paul anticipated I would come along and say all these things; consequently he fortuitously wrote:

> You will say to me then, "Why does he still find fault? For who can resist his will?" But who are you, a man, to answer back to God? Will what is molded say to its molder, "Why have you made me thus?" (Romans 9:19-20)

No, I am not questioning God. What I am questioning is Paul's ridiculous ideas concerning God.

Paul is telling us that God's ways only seem unjust because we do not know any better. If we knew God's reasons, it would appear all right to us. With this kind of theology our reason becomes useless because God's ways will not make sense to us. Paul discards reason but yet expects us to accept his reasoning.

Paul is wrong; we are not predestined. We are responsible for our own actions and our own decision to respond or not to respond to God. God does not do bad things, and God's ways do make sense and they are reasonable.

As we continue an examination of Paul's theology we must not overlook his comments concerning "speaking in tongues." Paul understands the ability to speak in tongues to be a gift from God and consequently an appropriate activity:

> . . . to another various kinds of tongues, to another the interpretation of tongues. (I Corinthians 12:10)

If by tongues Paul meant some kind of audible response coming from a deep emotional worship experience such as a groan or an equivalent of an "amen," I would say that was just fine as it constitutes an experience common to us all. Unfortunately, Paul meant much more than that. He believes that, while it is only babble to most persons, there are a select few who can "interpret" such noise. Evidence that Paul does not think speaking in tongues is only an emotional outburst and that it contains intelligible thoughts is found in his instructions (I Corinthians 14:27-33) that the phenomenon should be "ordered" and "limited." Only two or three at a time should speak and *only* if there is someone present who can interpret or explain.

I have been witness to such monosyllabic utterances, (Why is it always the conservatives? That should tell us something, but not the same something that the conservatives think it is telling us) and find it embarrassing. But that does not constitute grounds for its validity or lack thereof. Glossolalia is more like a fad; persons don't succumb until they observe someone else partaking.

Paul does put speaking in tongues low on his priority list of tasteful Christian activities:

He who prophesies is greater than he who speaks in tongues, unless someone interprets,, so that the church may be edified. Now, brethren, if I come to you speaking in tongues, how shall I benefit you unless I bring you some revelation or knowledge or prophecy or teaching?. . . I thank God that I speak in tongues more than you all; nevertheless, in church I would rather speak five words with my mind, in order to instruct others, than ten thousand words in a tongue. (I Corinthians 14:5-6, 18-19)

Then Paul utters that little comment that conservatives have jumped on with all four feet—the comment concerning this phenomenon being a "sign," and I have heard individuals say that you don't have the Holy Spirit unless you have the evidence: speaking in tongues:

Thus, tongues are a sign not for believers but for un- believers. . . (I Corinthians 14:22a)

Paul may downplay the activity to some degree, but the fact remains that he gives credence to it:

If any speak in a tongue, let there be only two or at least three, and each in turn; and let one interpret. But if there is no one to interpret, let each of them keep silence in church and speak to himself and to God. (I Corinthians 14:27-28)

If speaking in tongues is only to be employed when there is some qualified person who can explain or interpret for us, this should bring about the demise of this activity soon and for all time.

Now we get down to some very serious business: salvation by faith and the idea of the atonement.

We do not need to quote Paul at length concerning how we are saved, for it is a prominent theme in his theology. It probably is his top topic. One brief sentence will suffice:

> For by grace you have been saved through faith; and this is not your own doing, it is the gift of God—not because of works, lest any man should boast. (Ephesians 2:8-9)

Paul is concerned with the majesty and power of God and in desiring God to be in control of everything. In contrast, Paul is convinced of our worthlessness and sinfulness and of the fact that we cannot do anything for ourselves in the way of goodness. We are even incapable of making a response to God's love. It has to be God who gives us the gift of salvation. Our task is only to believe—to have faith. "Works" was anathema to Paul. The book of James would have caused Paul to turn over in his grave. Since Martin Luther was an avid fan of Paul, we read this interesting passage in one of his biographies:

> Luther read the New Testament in the light of the Pauline message that the just shall live by faith and not by works of the law. That this doctrine is not enunciated with equal emphasis throughout the New Testament and appears to be denied in the book of James did not escape Luther, and in his preface to the New Testament of 1522 James was stigmatized as "an epistle of straw." Once Luther remarked that he would give his doctor's beret to anyone who could reconcile James and Paul.[1]

I, on the other hand, would applaud the book of James as providing a beautiful balance between faith and works . The two are inseparable—a natural part of each other:

> So faith by itself, if it has no works, is dead. But some one will say, "You have faith, and I have works." Show me your faith apart from your works, and I by my works will show you my

faith. . . You see that a man is justified by works and not by faith
alone. (James 2:17-18,24)

This would be heresy to Paul, but I much prefer the all
important balance of James to Paul's warped perspective of God
and life.

For Paul, the "atonement" is a necessary extension of salvation.
Paul believed in "original sin," condemnation by proxy, and saw
Adam and Eve disobeying God and thereby ensnaring all of us into
corporate guilt. I cannot understand why so many Christians cling
so rabidly to the idea of "original sin." After all, Adam and Eve are
mythical figures, and while it is a profound myth full of religious
truth, original sin is not one of its enlightened revelations. There
was no "first fall" that forever condemned the human race. Sin, as
both state of relationship with God and as individual acts, is so
common because life is very rich in resources and temptations. For
us to follow God's way is more difficult, for it means selecting the
one best choice (the long-range benefit or satisfaction) over the
many other choices that promise excitement and alluring (short
term and fleeting) treasurers.

Enter by the narrow gate; for the gate is wide and the way is
easy, that leads to destruction, and. . . the gate is narrow and the
way is hard, that leads to life, and those who find it are few.
(Matthew 7:13-14)

Jesus had a better handle on the problem. In fact, I don't need
any excuse such as original sin or even a devil; I do very well at
sinning all by my free, responsible self. I can't remember Jesus
saying anything about original sin just as he didn't seem to be
cognizant of speaking in tongues.

Hand in glove with original sin is the "atonement" in which
Paul sees some kind of mystery:

For as by one man's disobedience many were made sinners, so
by one man's obedience many will be made righteous. (Romans
5:19)

Christ redeemed us from the curse of the law, having become a
curse for us. . . (Galatians 3:13)

. . .and through him to reconcile to himself all things, whether on earth or in heaven, making peace by the blood of his cross. And you, who once were estranged and hostile in mind, doing evil deeds, he has now reconciled in his body of flesh by his death, in order to present you holy and blameless and irreproachable before him . . . (Colossians 1:20-22)

. . .having canceled the bond which stood against us with its legal demands; this he set aside, nailing it to the cross. (Colossians 2:14)

And forever after, theologians have had great fun playing with complicated theories of how Jesus "paid the price," "ransomed us from the devil," or made God get over a tantrum and love us once again. I prefer the simple idea expressed by one early church theologian, Abelard (1079-1142):

. . .decidedly modern, in his conception of the atonement. Like Anselm, he rejected all ransom to the devil; but he repudiated Anselm's doctrine of satisfaction no less energetically. In Abelard's view the incarnation and death of Christ are the highest expression of God's love to men, the effect of which is to awaken love in us.[2]

This "moral influence" concept of what the cross means has appeal for me. What Jesus did by going to the cross was to reveal constraining love: just how much God loves us as acted out by Jesus with the purpose of calling forth a response from us to love God in return. Paul was busy wading around in unrealistic conjecture trying to make of the cross experience something magical and mystical, and most Christians remain lost in the quagmire today.

That classic historian, H. G. Wells, had some interesting comments concerning this subject in his venerable work, *The Outline of History*:

It is a fact in history that the teachings of Jesus of Nazareth had in it something profoundly new and creative . . . There was nothing in his teaching, so far as we can judge it at this distance of time, to clash or interfere with any discovery or expansion of the history of the world and mankind.

He is referring mainly to ideas like evolution at this point:

> But it is equally a fact in history that St. Paul and his successors added to or completed or imposed upon or substituted another doctrine for—as you may prefer to think—the plain and profoundly revolutionary teachings of Jesus, by expounding a subtle and complex theory of salvation, a salvation which could be attained very largely by belief and formalities, without any serious disturbance of the believer's ordinary habits and occupations. . .official Christianity throughout the world adopted St. Paul's view . . .that Jesus was not so much a teacher of wonderful new things, as a predestinate divine blood sacrifice of deep mystery. . . upon the theories of Paul, and not upon the injunctions of Jesus, doctrinal Christianity built itself.[3]

Before closing this chapter, we must exonerate Paul. By applying our test of measuring everything by the "spirit of Jesus" we find that Paul was able to understand some of the great ideas of Jesus and even expand on those teachings. Everyone appreciates the "love" chapter of I Corinthians 13: "Love is patient and kind. . ." The great ideas of Romans 12 culminate with a beautiful parallel of the sermon-on-the-mount kind of love found in Matthew 5:38-48! These two passages (Romans and Matthew) are in such marvelous accordance that Paul had to have understood perfectly the pacifism of Jesus!

One of my favorite passages in Paul is,

> Then let us . . .decide never to put a stumbling block or hindrance in the way of a brother. . . .it is right not to eat meat or drink wine or do anything that makes your brother stumble. (Romans 14:13,21 and everything in between and paralleled in I Corinthians 8:9-13)

And of course Galatians 3:28 quoted above about "neither Jew or Greek. . ." etc.

Paul has so much to offer, but we still need to recognize his human frailty and mistakes and constantly test him by asking, "Is this really what Jesus taught?"

NOTES:

[1] Roland H. Bainton, Here I Stand: A Life of Martin Luther (New York: Mentor Books, 1959), P. 259.

[2] Williston Walker, A History of the Christian Church (New York: Charles Scribner's Sons, 1959), p. 241.

[3] H. G. Wells, The Outline of History (New York: Garden City Books, 1956), p. 775.

18. Is There Any More Bible Around?

In the eighth chapter, we examined the way in which the Bible grew to finally include the 66 books of the present canon. In the process some books did not "make the cut" while some of those that did were accepted with reluctance. Grumbling over what did make it but shouldn't have as well as what didn't make it but should have was the subject of much arguing for centuries. Chapter eight listed the fifteen books of the apocrypha that came close, but did not quite make the canon. These books appear in Roman Catholic Bibles and are beginning to make their appearance in some editions of "Protestant" Bibles. They were written between the Old and New Testament periods, roughly 200 BC to about 90 AD, and include the following:

> I and II Esdras
> Tobit
> Judith
> additional chapters to Esther
> Wisdom of Solomon
> Wisdom of Jesus the Son of Sirach or Ecclesiasticus
> Baruch
> Epistle of Jeremy
> Song of the Three Holy Children
> Susanna
> Bel and the Dragon
> Prayer of Manasses
> I and II Maccabees

There are other books purporting to be Old Testament literature called Pseudepigrapha that date from almost the same period of time as the apocrypha (c.200 BC to c.100 AD), but they were not considered inspired enough to make the Bible nor even the level of the "near miss" category, apocrypha. Some of these books have names such as,

> Testaments of the Twelve Patriarchs
> Psalms of Solomon
> Lives of the Prophets
> Jubilees
> Testament of Job
> Enoch
> I and II Adam and Eve
> Assumption of Moses
> Apocalypse of Abraham
> III and IV Maccabees
> Testament of Reuben
> Testament of Judah
> Testament of Joseph
> Testament of Issachar

This does not exhaust the list.

There are yet other books with New Testament subject matter that vied for the honor of scripture, but did not receive enough support from the committees who were making the decisions at the time. The following seem to have been written between the years c. 90 AD and c. 150 AD:

> I Clement (c. 95)
> The Didache (c. 110)
> Gospel of the Ebionites (c. 150)
> Gospel according to the Hebrews (c. 125)
> Gospel according to the Egyptians (c. 135)
> Gospel of Peter (c. 130)
> Shepherd of Hermas
> Epistle of Barnabus
> Epistle to the Laodiceans

There are many other Gospels and Acts that date from the second half of the second century. Included are the following:

Acts of Peter
Acts of Paul
Acts of Thomas

The list goes on. There are "gospels" and "acts" written in the name of nearly everyone of prominence in that day.

While some of this literature contains good material, common sense, and advice which are consistent with the Christian faith, others of it drift a little towards the extreme. Some of it makes interesting reading, so I will share some examples.

As a little boy of five years, Jesus is out playing in the mud after a rain shower. His disciple, Thomas, is relating this story. He makes some little mud birds while his playmates were presumably making mud pies. Joseph is called to come and discipline Jesus for profaning the sabbath by making mud birds. Jesus never seemed to get anything right on the sabbath! What was Jesus' response to this?

> Then Jesus clapped together the palms of his hands, and said to them: Go, fly away; and while ye live remember me. So the sparrows fled away, making a noise. (II Infancy 1:8-9)

According to these extrabiblical books Jesus was not always as nice as we know him to be as an adult.

> Another time Jesus went forth into the street, and a boy running by, rushed upon his shoulder; At which Jesus being angry, said to him, thou shalt go no farther. And he instantly fell down dead. . . (II Infancy 2:7-9)

> They brought him then to a more learned master, who, when he saw him, said say Aleph. And when he had said Aleph, the master bade him pronounce Beth; to which the Lord Jesus replied, Tell me first the meaning of the letter Aleph, and then I will pronounce Beth. But this master, when he lift up his hand to whip him, had his hand presently withered, and he died. Then said Joseph to St. Mary, henceforth we will not allow him to go out of the house; for every one who displeases him is killed. (II Infancy 20:13-16)

And this is the same guy who told us what it means to be a good neighbor?

We begin to see some good reasons why some books were left out of the Bible. They contained exaggerated stories and legends that had no basis in fact. But then some of the books that were included in the Bible also contain similar fiction.

Most apocryphal books tend to copy Old or New Testament books respectively, usually trying to expand on the canon material by adding greater detail, obviously of a highly imaginative nature.

Through a very difficult process with much disagreement, the church finally reached a consensus concerning which books they could consider inspired so as to make clear boundaries for what could be called "scripture."

However, just as we would be wrong in believing that everything that is found in the Bible is the inspired word of God or actual history, we would be even more foolish to think that everything that is not in the Bible is uninspired.

This brings us to a delicate question, "What do we as Christians think about the sacred writings of other religions?" Most religions have early manuscripts that concern origins of their faith, its history, its rules or laws for personal conduct and worship. Obviously the adherents of each particular faith revere those writings as sacred truth just as Christians do their own. In some instances other religions include Christian scriptures or writings of religions other than their own as sacred also, but in most cases the followers of each respective religion believe their own sacred literature to be *the only*, or at least a far superior, "holy" edict.

An interesting question to ask is which religion has the "best Bible:" for example, the highest ethical standards, a greater understanding or explanation of life and the universe, and so forth? Does any religion own a corner on the market of truth? Or are all of them "good" and of equal worth? Or is one at least closer to the divine truth than the others?

It is very important that we separate a religion, its doctrine and teachings, from its followers. We who profess a faith seldom do well practicing that faith out in the field. Because sometimes our conduct is an embarrassment to our professed faith, our religion should not be judged by our behavior! How a people live is not indicative of the strength or value of their religion. There are always too many "followers" who are only nominal in the faith, and many do not even know much about their sponsoring faith. It follows that none of us is perfect nor capable of being a faithful living example of what our religion may teach.

Christians through the centuries have had periods of a very poor track record. Despite Christianity being a religion of love, peace, and justice, Christians have owned slaves, perpetrated atrocities, and practiced unbelievable behavior. This is in no way an indictment upon Christianity, the religion.

Consequently, in the remainder of this chapter, we will look simply at a sampling of the written documents that some of the major, more successful religions consider as sacred, documents upon which they found their faith. We will chose to ignore the religion as it is practiced by its adherents.

When one examines the sacred writings of many different religions it is easy to understand why the religions seem confusing and unwieldy. Like Christianity, they are represented by many different points of view and interpretations. As one reads the sacred writing, the reason for these different schools of thought in each religion becomes evident. The literature comes from a more remote period of time when less was known about our world and human nature. For many persons part of its charm, I suppose, is its antiquity and confusing orientation. Much of it, if it were offered for publication today as a creative and original work, would not be found marketable! In a word, "ridiculous" would be the description for it.

As I read through this literature, I kept asking myself the question, "Why do people think so highly of this stuff?" I might offer these possibilities:

a. As mentioned, it is old and anything old is venerable.

b. It is often confusing, which is another fatal attraction. It is like the preacher who, when his ideas or arguments at a particular point in the sermon are weak, shouts and pounds the pulpit. If the preacher shouts, it must be important! For many of us, if it is hard to understand and full of confusing imagery, it has to be deep—like Revelations.

c. People are conditioned from early childhood to respect and "worship" this sacred literature.

d. It then follows that it is blasphemes to question or doubt such holy writings.

e. Many of the adherents are moderately uneducated masses.

f. More likely than not, the vast majority of a religion's followers, being no different than Christians, do not even read their own respective scriptures.

g. Folks looking around at other religions do not see "anything better" due to their ignorance of the writings of other faiths. Similarly 99% of all Christians do not even know the titles of scriptures of other religions, let alone any of their contents (they probably could not even name the books of the Bible). Because of their unfamiliarity with the literature, the only other likelihood of becoming acquainted with another religion is to watch the actions of its followers, which could be more detrimental than enlightening.

h. You may insert at this point other good reasons you think are just as appropriate.

How do other religious writings compare with the New Testament? This is a question that all serious Christians should ask. There are two ways in which people generally arrive at the conviction that their faith is the "right" religion and their religious literature is "the truth." First, a person raised in a faith is conditioned from early childhood by the doctrines and teachings of that religion. In such case the individual simply "knows" that she or he has the right and true religion.

Secondly, a person could choose to carefully examine each major religion and make honest comparisons in a search for "the" true religion. Few do. This is very difficult to do since none of us grow up living in a vacuum. We cannot escape having some religious values fostered upon us by our social environment. Consequently, we will be conditioned enough that we will never be totally free of prejudice in our examination of different religious traditions. The least we can hope for is an honest effort to be as open as possible to new and different ideas or philosophies.

I believe that any individual who is serious concerning her or his religious convictions—a person who cares about our world, people, and finding truth—should try to familiarize herself or himself with other sacred writings, enough so as to have a fair idea of what is out there in the way of other "sacred" writings. No one should spend his or her study time exclusively in this kind of discipline because there are just far too many things to read and learn in our marvelous world of literature—poetry, history, science, fiction, etc. However, we should try to become acquainted with the main documents, or at least a good representation, of other major religions.

I have thoroughly enjoyed trying to make comparisons between the various writings. I am not free of bias; however, if I can be openly critical of my own faith's sacred literature and accept its weaknesses and errors, then I believe I will come a little closer to being fair with other religious literature.

Granted, we are trapped in a circular process. We need some standard by which to judge the value of something, a judgment that one idea is superior to another? If we use Q to measure X, Y, and Z, then Q becomes the ultimate standard and nothing else will be able to equal Q. I am conditioned by the teachings of Jesus and will use the Christian faith by which to judge everything else. Therefore I believe the Christian teachings are far superior to all others—a circular argument that is impossible to avoid. Necessarily, then, we will all start from a prejudiced position.

What values do I look for in a religion's writings? There are two elements that I consider important. I want to find ethical teachings that teach us how to live together in relationships of all levels in order that each individual may find a maximum of fulfillment, meaning, and enjoyment from life. (Let's not become bogged down in a discussion concerning hedonism.) I am simply talking about searching for an understanding of the best conduct for human living.

Next, I look for a religion able to tell me about the universe. I want it to satisfactorily explain God or gods or any divine or supernatural power that might exist and the meaning and purpose of life (and possible afterlife), and seek to answer questions that are central to life such as why there is pain and evil in the world. I repeat: I search for 1. ethics, and 2. explanations of the universe—a humble order!

What do the other major religions writings have to offer? Let me boldly offer my impressions of their literature and make some comparisons of their literature to the teachings of Jesus.

The limited and brief nature of this exploration necessitates a superficial treatment of the literature in an attempt at an accurate "general impression." In every case I was hoping to find some significant thoughts, and while there were many good ideas, overall I was disappointed. One general impression is that much of the literature is repetitive ad nauseam! There is so much repetition that often one could condense a hundred pages of the material down to just four or five and lose nothing! *The Koran* and *The Egyptian Book of the Dead* are two such examples.

I have already given a critique of the Old Testament in this book. Obviously, and happily so, it is not the extent of the Jewish religion's sacred literature. The Old Testament is only the foundation for a later extensive library. As mentioned earlier, there is much additional religious teaching that originally circulated orally and developed over centuries, finally being compiled in the Mishna, which consists of commentary on the Old Testament or at least the law generally. This is followed by an even more extensive commentary upon the Mishna known as the Gemarah. Both could be referred to under the heading of Talmud—although it all depends upon which author one reads as to what these terms designate.

One could debate the parameters of "scripture." Does Jewish sacred literature end with the Old Testament or continue indefinitely? If one wants to evaluate the Talmud as a parallel to other "scriptures" such as the Koran, one finds that it is not easily accessible. I get the impression that it is not generally used by the lay person, but we are encouraged to study it only with a rabbi or simply rely on the religious leader for instruction. One does not simply *read* the Talmud. One becomes "involved" with it through meditation, reason and discussion. This is how most religions feel about their sacred literature.

The Talmud is comprised of stories, religious laws, wise sayings, and discussions. It is the struggle to find the proper response or God's will for all of life's situations no matter how trivial—it tends to be thorough. It is an attempt to use reason and logic in finding answers that should be tested against all possible objections. Consequently, it literally invites questioning and challenges as a part of the process at arriving.

It does not claim to be a book about ethics, history, religion, philosophy—but a vast literature or anthology. In a few words, the Talmud is complex, diverse, unique, sprawling, and ponderous. As a handbook of rules to live by, it certainly does not exceed other teachings such as Confucius or the *Tao Teh Ching*. As a matter of fact, it reminds me of the teachings of Confucius. Let me give some examples of the Talmud's common sense proverbs:

Who is truly rich? He who is happy in his portion. (Abot, 4, 1.)

The Divine test of a man's worth is not his theology but his life. (Baba Kama, 38a.)

A man should accustom himself to be pleasant to people. (Taanit, 4.)

He that feeds the hungry feeds God also. (Agadat Shir ha-Shirim.)

These are all very good ideas; we can find no fault in them. But then when we encounter those embarrassing passages that are obviously ridiculous or simply very bad theology, there is usually a tendency to "cover up" the problem instead of admitting that the ideas are wrong or foolish. This is true for all religions. One of the most common tactics is to say that there is a deeper meaning to the passage in question and that we must ignore the literal meaning as being superfluous. I know where of I speak, for I have been guilty of doing that very thing in this book in my defense of Christianity and the teachings of Jesus. Let me cite an example from the Talmud of a passage that I believe to be "sick" or disgusting.

> God had the same reason for giving Palestine to Canaan before it came into the rightful hands of Israel that He had for giving Bathsheba in marriage to Uriah, the Hittite, before she became the wife of David, her rightful mate. (Zohar, i, 73b.)

A Rabbi might try to tell you that there is a deeper meaning beneath those words which you simply don't understand. I say, "I think not." Let's just tell the truth—it was a sad mistake that those words were ever uttered. I'm sure that followers of every religion are guilty of trying to justify some embarrassing material in their sacred literature by just such a gimmick.

Are there any other "Bibles" out there that can be considered comparable to the teachings of Jesus?

We could begin with *The Koran*, which is the infallible word of God (Allah) for Muslims. Because it is a highly praised book, I was expecting something out of the ordinary, and perhaps those high expectations explain my disappointment. The significant ideas could be singled out and would barely fill a 10-page pamphlet—so cumbersome is the repetition. This adds to the impression that it may have been the work of one person as it certainly seems to hang together very well with a minimum of contradictions.

For starters, we are always told *The Koran* loses in translation. Translating it out of its native language costs the book much of its richness. That depends upon what it is all about. If it is poetry or unique imagery, yes, it would be difficult to capture the essence when moving from one language to another. In the case of *The Koran*, I don't see that as a problem. Perhaps a flowery and colorful language is lost, but the ideas are plain and simple.

The Bible doesn't lose anything in translation! It has been translated into countless languages and dialects and never has been accused of losing its power and meaning! Rather one might say that that is evidence of its value—that it can be translated with power into any language!

An inherent weakness in *The Koran* is that it often tries to "prove" itself. Apparently anticipating future criticisms as it was being written, it continually and defensively professes its truth and constantly condemns those who disagree:

> The unbelievers say: 'Give no heed to this Koran. . . . They shall abide in Hell forever, because they have denied Our revelations.' (between 41:22 & 41:29)

> This book is not to be doubted. (2:1)

> If they say: 'He has invented it himself,' say to them: 'Invent ten chapters like it.' (between 11:19 & 11:15)

I get an uneasy feeling when someone becomes so defensive.

Like the Bible, it does have contradictions, however, I think, on the whole, there are fewer of them in The Koran. As I suggested, it seems to be more of a theological whole in contrast with the wide variety of material and ideas found in the Bible.

An example of one of its contradictions is that it clearly seems to teach the Old Testament ethic of "an eye for an eye" at one point, but then turns around to suggest the New Testament "turn the cheek" of Jesus' teachings:

> Let evil be rewarded with like evil. . . .Those who avenge themselves when wronged incur no guilt. (between 42:35 & 42:44)

> Requite evil with good, and he who is your enemy will become your dearest friend. (between 41:30 & 41:38)

If I seem to be guilty of lifting isolated verses out of context, do not be alarmed; it is the nature of *The Koran* that so much of it is composed of little proverbs that stand alone with no relation to what comes before or after, much the same as is true of some of the Sermon on the Mount material or the book of Proverbs.

Criticisms of Islam that it is a violent religion come not only from some historic incidents, but are probably interpreted from such passages as:

> Fight for the sake of Allah those that fight against you, but do
> not attack them first. . . .Kill them wherever you find them.
> Drive them out of the places from which they drove you. Idolatry
> is worse than carnage. (between 2:190 & 2:194)

> Fighting is obligatory for you, much as you dislike it. (2:216)

Such ideas are glaringly alien to the teachings of Jesus.

Similar to Paul's treatment of the status of women, *The Koran*
places women in an inferior position. But then, like Paul's letters, it
was a victim of the social mores of the day in which it was written:

> A male shall inherit twice as much as a female. (between 4:10 &
> 4:12)

> Men have authority over women because Allah had made the
> one superior to the other, and because they spend their wealth to
> maintain them. (4:34)

> Blessed are the believers. . .who restrain their carnal desires
> (except with their wives and slave-girls, for these are lawful to
> them) (23:1)

The parenthesis in the above quote is part of the text and not
my editorializing. These words are very harsh; however, it is
difficult to see that the meaning has suffered any in the process of
translation to make much difference.

Some of the strengths in *The Koran* are repeated more than
generously throughout the text: Allah forgives, we should give
alms, and we must believe in Allah! This last admonition is
tempered with the threat that if you do not believe in Allah you
will go to hell.

Other strengths of *The Koran* include the importance of prayer
and,

> They ask you about drinking and gambling. Say: 'There is great
> harm in both. . . (2:219)

Another religious text that has received much praise and regard
is the *Bhagavad-Gita* of Hinduism. This religious work is more
"poetic" than *The Koran*, and no doubt may have lost some of its
frills in translation. However, the ugly parts come through loud and
clear; there is no denying the meaning of the message!

The best parts of this book concern self-control and some personal relationships. We should give alms, be friendly and compassionate, be forgiving, and control our passions.[1] We must be humble, upright, and clean in mind and body.[2] We should have an even temper, tranquil mind, and gentle nature, while not being hypocritical, arrogant, cruel or hateful.[3]

Three negatives that I find in the *Bhagavad-Gita* that definitely run contrary to the teachings of Jesus make it hard to understand why Gandhi could consider it so wonderful. First, like most Eastern religions there is a denial of the goodness of this physical world. Our aim should be to control our passions to the point that we do not really have an appreciation of this beautiful world. We are to be ascetic-minded and not aesthetic-minded. It is important to not enjoy the things of this life, but instead one should practice self-denial:

> For when a man's heart has reached fulfillment through
> knowledge and personal experience of the truth of Brahman, he
> is never again moved by the things of the senses.[4]

This gives us the impression that this world that God has created is somehow not a very nice place. It means denigrating all the beautiful, physical gifts God has given us. The impression given by the asceticism of the *Bhagavad-Gita* is that God's world is a bad place and the sooner we can get out of it, the better.

Another problem with this Hindu gospel is that it encourages the caste system. Krishna, the mouth-piece for God, says, "I established the four castes. . ."[5] Krishna also says that "caste-mixture" is wrong. One of the bad things that could happen is that

> They would all be lost. The result would be caste-mixture and
> universal destruction.[6]

Even though most if not all social systems have an informal or unwritten caste system, when it is given the blessing of a religious endorsement, it becomes God's way, and its destruction of human life is most difficult to eradicate.

Perhaps the most dramatically disappointing theology of the *Bhagavad-Gita* is the dialogue that opens the book. The format of the work is a dialog between four speakers very similar to Plato's method of writing. The actor who is purported to be the spokesperson for truth is Sri Krishna with the other three apparently acting as foils for him in the process of exposing the truth. At the beginning of the work, the reader must be informed who is the spokesperson for truth, or else the reader will be completely misled, the reason being that Arjuna seems to be speaking for the "right" or moral position and Krishna speaking for the "wrong" or immoral position! Arjuna sounds exactly like Jesus speaking, representing the compassionate and humane philosophy. In contrast Krishna contradicts these ideas and sounds callous and cold-hearted. But in fact, Arjuna's ideas are to be understood as foolish and wrong—that "turn-the-other-cheek" and "go-the-second-mile" stuff that Jesus talked about—whereas Krishna is revealing the proper ethic, the right.

We will illustrate with a few lines from the *Bhagavad-Gita*:

Arjuna: ". . .What can we hope from This killing of kinsman? What do I want with Victory. . . Knower of all things, Though they should slay me How could I harm them? I cannot wish it. . . Krishna, hearing The prayers of all men, Tell me how can We hope to be happy Slaying the sons Of Dhritarashtra? Evil they may be, Worst of the wicked, Yet if we kill them Our sin is greater. How could we dare spill The blood that unites us? Where is joy in The killing of kinsmen?. . .I shall not struggle, I shall not strike them. Now let them kill me, That will be better."[7]

This sounds like a person who is loving and kind; like Jesus. Wrong! Arjuna is a fool!

Krishna: "Arjuna, is this the hour of battle the time for scruples and fancies? . . .What is this weakness? It is beneath you. . . .The truly wise mourn neither for the living nor for the dead. . . ."

And Jesus was silly enough to suggest, "Blessed are those who mourn. . ." (Matthew 5:4)

". . .Therefore, you should never mourn for any one. Even if you consider this from the standpoint of your own caste-duty, you ought not to hesitate; for, to a warrior, there is nothing nobler than a righteous war. Happy are the warriors to whom a battle as this comes. . ."[8]

Prior to the *Bhagavad-Gita*, which is the most popular sacred writing of Hinduism, the Hindus had The *Upanisads*, which might more aptly be called scriptures for them. *The Upanisads* are somewhat less concerned with ethics; however, they have their share of little proverbs and wise sayings. There is a somewhat greater emphasis on ways of meditation, mystic thoughts, cosmogony (theory of origins of the universe), cosmology (nature of the universe), and unclear passages with meanings that I'm sure have been lost long ago.

I will share some samples of interesting passages from some of the Upanisads. If it seems they might be ideas with the meaning distorted by being lifted from the context, I tried to be careful to make sure they were passages whose meaning remained unsullied by isolation.

Central to the faith is meditation:

Let a man meditate on the syllable Om. . .(Khandogya Upanishad: First Prapathaka, First Khanda, 1)

'What is the origin of this world?' 'Ether,' he replied. For all these beings take their rise from the ether, and return into the ether. (Khandogya Upanishad: First Prapathaka, Ninth Khanda, 1)

In the beginning this was non-existent. It became existent, it grew. It turned into an egg. The egg lay for the time of a year. The egg broke open. The two halves were one of silver, the other of gold. The silver one became this earth, the golden one the sky. . . (Khandogya Upanishad: Third Prapathaka, Nineteenth Khanda, 1-2)

If a man wishes to reach greatness, let him perform the Diksha on the day of the new moon, and then, on the night of the full moon, let him stir a mash of all kinds of herbs with curds and honey, and let him pour ghee on the fire . . .If in his dream he sees a woman, let him know this to be a sign that his sacrifice has succeeded. (Khandogya Upanishad: Fifth Prapathaka, Second Khanda, 4,8)

But those whose conduct has been evil, will quickly attain an evil birth, the birth of a dog, or a hog. . . (Khandogya Upanishad: Fifth Prapathaka, Tenth Khanda, 7)

In this same Upanishad we read a clever way of ascertaining a person's guilt of theft. If the person denies the crime, heat a hatchet until it is very hot and then ask the suspect to grasp the hatchet. If the person is burnt, she or he is guilty and will be killed. If the person is not burnt, that person is innocent (Sixth Prapathaka, Sixteenth Khanda, 1-2).

Some insensitivity is found in the Brihadaranyaka Upanishad where we read:

. . .speech is Brahman; for what is the use of a dumb person?

. . .sight is Brahman; for what is the use of a person who cannot see?

. . .hearing is Brahman; for what is the use of a person who cannot hear? (Fourth Adhyaya, First Brahmana, 2, 4, 5)

A Hindu apologist might say that you need to have the deeper meaning of these passages to fully appreciate what is being indicated, and I say that is debatable.

One more revealing quotation:

Therefore let him approach a woman whose garments are pure, and whose fame is pure, and address her. If she do not (sic) give in, let him, as he likes, bribe her. And if she then do not give in, let him, as he likes, beat her with a stick or with his hand, and overcome her, saying: 'With manly strength and glory I take away thy glory,'—and thus she becomes unglorious. If she give in, he says: 'With manly strength and glory I give thee glory. . .' (Brihadaranyaka Upanishad: Sixth Adhyaya, Fourth Brahmana, 6-8)

Going back to an earlier period, Hinduism had still more primitive texts, hymns and prayers for worship entitled Rig-Veda of which I am unfamiliar.

I mention next *The Egyptian Book of the Dead* which some have claimed to be one of the most influential books in history. It may have had extensive influence, but I question the extent of its value.

The chief merits of this work would revolve around the similarities with Christian ideas concerning a life after death. Given the fact that these texts were composed some 3000 years or more before the time of Jesus makes it more interesting. The central theme involves the reciting of prayers and chants in order to insure that the soul of the departed will be reunited with its spiritual body in "heaven" or the realm of the gods which is in the sky.

There seems little doubt that Egyptian theology had, as had also Babylonian theology, some influence on Hebrew theology. Therefore, it is strange that Hebrew theology in the Old Testament makes so little of life after death. It is as if the Egyptian theology bypassed Jewish thought, going on to influence Christian thinking.

Just as their thinking about a resurrection in an afterlife is a little confused, so also is their belief about a god or gods and goddesses.[9] Some would insist that the Egyptians held to a monotheism long before that teaching appeared in the Old Testament. However, the proliferation of their goddesses and gods give no doubt to the popularity of polytheism for them.

There really isn't much else contained in their religious texts; any illusions to rules of behavior for the living are vague at best, with simple references to the deceased not having lied or done evil things on earth.

Constant preoccupation with a spiritual resurrection in an afterlife is the one unique offering of the ancient religion of Egypt, and I had the distinct impression while reading through these writings that that gift applied only to the important persons in society and not to the common folk; or was I letting the pyramids influence my thinking?

We can sample the sacred literature of the Buddhist tradition by looking at some of the Mahayana texts. The Buddha-Karita of Asvaghosha is a legend of the history of Buddha.

The Buddha's father tries to shield his son from all of the unsavory experiences of life—old age, disease, and death. These things take away the pleasure of life. Nevertheless, the Buddha encounters the bad things of life and is distressed. The highlight of the literature occurs when the Buddha experiences the suffering of the creatures of this world. He is out enjoying the countryside when he comes upon some persons plowing a field. Buddha notices the little insects in the ground being killed because of the plowing, the toil of those plowing, and the suffering of the cattle pulling the plow. He is full of compassion because of the pain and destruction to these forms of life:

> . . .he went over the ground slowly, overcome with sorrow—pondering the birth and destruction of the world, he, grieved, exclaimed, 'this is indeed pitiable.' (Book 5:7)

Unfortunately, that is as good as it gets. From this point the literature starts down hill, He arrives at the secret to the ideal life: we must be free from any significant relationships with this world, we must free ourselves from the desire of worldly objects, and then we will be free from pain and sorrow. Thus the answer is to try to escape from this world through meditation and focusing our minds on the attainment of Nirvana.

The Eastern religions seem to take pride in running away from life and reality, probably because life for them has often been hard. Consequently for them, life is not reality. What we call the physical world is nothing but illusion. Things are but names, an extreme Pyrrhonism (skepticism).

Buddha's move towards a monastic life leads him to abandon his family. His wife—foolish as she is, having only common sense, a love for family, a sense of understanding of responsibility concerning human relationships—has the audacity to comment:

> 'If he wishes to practice a religious life after abandoning me his lawful wife widowed—where is his religion, who wishes to

follow penance without his lawful wife to share it with him? (Book 8:61)

'Alas! the mind of that wise hero is terribly stern—gentle as his beauty seems, it is pitilessly cruel,—who can desert of his own accord such an infant son. . . (Book 8:68)

Even his father seems more intelligent than Buddha:
"". . .do not show disregard for thy unhappy kindred —compassion for all creatures is the true religion. Religion is not wrought out only in the forests, the salvation of ascetics can be accomplished even in a city; thought and effort are the true means; the forest and the badge are only a coward's signs."' (Book 9:17-18)

But Buddha is adamant:
'. . .I maintain that the absolute attainment of our end can only be found in the abandonment of everything.' (Book 12:80)

There is some direction for living a good life, however. Found in the Larger Sukhavati-Vyuha are ideals that we should incorporate into our personality and behavior: be gently, charming, compassionate, agreeable, satisfied, not foolish, not suspicious, not crooked, not wicked, etc. (section? 10)

One final sage piece of advice from the Amitayur-Dhyana-Sutra: it is suggested by the Buddha that for meditation we should—"if not blind from birth"—set down and gaze at the setting sun! (Part II:9) It is interesting that he should mention that part about those not blind from birth.

I suppose the mystic flavor to Buddhism and other Eastern religions appeals to the strange in many of us. While retaining some of the Oriental mysticism, there is a religion that does emphasize a more practical life style. That would be Confucianism though some might not call it a religion. It does have some significant "religious" texts that are worthy of examining.

While the Analects, The Great Learning, and the Doctrine of the Mean may not all be the words of Confucius as it is believed some of the material may originate with his disciples, it certainly is in the Confusius tradition and style.

In the teachings of Confusius, we have the practical wisdom of common sense—proverbs of propriety or correct attitudes. We find little or no metaphysics. Most persons are familiar with the "Confusius says" style. From book IV of the Analects:

The Master said, 'The cautious seldom err.' (Chapter XXIII)

The Master said, 'The superior man wishes to be slow in his speech and earnest in his conduct.' (Chapter XXIV)

The Master said, 'Virtue is not left to stand alone. He who practices it will have neighbors.' (Chapter XXV)

The negatively stated "golden rule" is found more than once in these writings and comes from a time before Jesus:

'What I do not wish men to do to me, I also wish not to do to men.' (Book V, Chapter XI)

'. . .not to do to others as you would not wish done to yourself. . .' (Book XII, Chapter II)

The sage advice continues:

'Now the man of perfect virtue, wishing to be established himself, seeks also to establish others; wishing to be enlarged himself, he seeks also to enlarge others. (Book VI, Chapter XXVIII, 2.)

The advice is predicated on the assumption that the selfish motive is not too dominant.

What are other virtues? Four characteristics of a superior person are humility, respect, kindness and justice (Book V, Chapter XV). When asked about benevolence, the Master said, 'It is to love all men' (Book XII, Chapter XXII, 1). That seems to reach close to the level of the Christian ethic. However, when it comes to pacifism, Confucius cannot go that far (Book XIV, Chapter XXXVI, 1-3). If we are looking for a religion other than Christianity that teaches pacifism, we will find only one among the major religions. Outside of Christianity the religious literature with the greatest ethical standard would have to be Taoism.

The *Tao Teh Ching* is short as sacred texts go and consequently avoids the clumsy and nonsensical repetition of most other religious literature. It is still in the Oriental family of religions. It is composed of many proverbs with pithy sayings:

A journey one thousand miles long Begins with the first step (Chapter 64)

I have three treasures. Keep them and treasure them. The first is compassion; The second is frugality; The third is: Dare not be first in the world. (Chapter 67)

Those who know do not speak; Those who speak do not know. (Chapter 56)

Central to this religious writing is an attitude of quietude or "laid-back" life style. The theme is stated in the phrase *we wei*, which should be interpreted as "going with the flow." The idea is not to rock the boat, let nature take its course, relax and avoid tensions, be in harmony with all around you, and practice no self assertiveness. This means to be in tune with nature and at peace with one's neighbors:

. . .the Sage handles affairs non-assertively. . . (Chapter 2)

Practice non-interference. . . (Chapter 3)

The softest things in the world Can match and overcome the hardest. (Chapter 43)

While some persons think they can see a similarity between *Tao Teh Ching* and the sermon on the mount, the former religious document is too "laid back." Jesus preached meekness and gentleness, but never excluded direct, dramatic and decisive action! His life was not one of *we wei*, but rather one of aggressive love. Jesus would not have challenged the religious leaders of his day calling them bad names (Matthew 23:13-28) were he a Taoist. Jesus would not have stormed into the Temple turning over the tables and driving people out (John 2:13-16) were he a Taoist. As in all areas of life, Jesus had a fine sense of balance between action and inaction.

Tao Teh Ching is said to teach pacifism. There is no doubt that there are pacifist teachings in the book, but the question will always remain, "How far does it go?"

He who uses Tao to assist the ruler of a people Will not employ armed force to dominate the world. (Chapter 30)

Fine weapons are inauspicious instruments They are probably detested by the people. Therefore, he who is possessed of Tao rejects them. . . .

He uses them only under dire necessity, And in this case priority is given to moderation. . . . Mass slaughter is to be bewailed with grief and sorrow. Victory is to be mourned with funeral rites. (Chapter 31)

I have never seen any remorse from the general population of the United States after a war as the above lines so eloquently suggest is proper. Instead, we cheer a victory as we do a football game victory!

Even though love does not quite reach the heights in the *Ta o Teh Ching* as it does in Christianity (note the lines just quoted—an equivocation on pacifism not found in Jesus), this religious literature stands above all other and second only to the teachings of Jesus.

Native American religion should be represented even though the literature is for the most part oral, just as was the first Christian teaching. A second problem is that there are so many traditions that it is impossible to focus on much consensus. The various traditions do not agree on a "Great Spirit" or a "happy hunting ground" but have confused teachings about what happens after death and how many and who are the gods.

Reverence for nature is an important facet in the Native American teaching and religion generally. Even though the beliefs took on a form of placating the elements of nature—animals and storms, for example, out of fear and necessity, yet that vital respect for creation and our environment is a lesson that remains lost on the rest of us at this time.

The various geographical groups had different unwritten ethical standards directing their relationships although there is little or no mention of them.[10]

Ordinarily I would not mention something like the *Book of Mormon* because it is, I suppose, related to Christian literature. I made some significant comments in chapter ten which I will not repeat here. The reason why I mention this religious work is that it is so familiar to many persons in our country even if in name only, and if one travels enough, she or he will find a copy in a motel room along with the Bible. Add to this the fact that I have spent an inordinate amount of time with the *Book of Mormon* and the study of Mormonism. I could not pass up an opportunity to comment briefly, at least, about a marvelous phenomenon.

The Book of Mormon has carefully and cleverly recreated the style of the Old and New Testaments even down to the "King James" language. I will share just a few observations that raise too many questions for me.

It has some interesting anachronisms—for example, "synagogues" in Alma 21:4 and the word "church" long before the time of Jesus.

Examples of other problems include: God making a black skin a curse (II Nephi 5:21). We find New Testament ideas written in about 500 BC. It parallels the Bible all too neatly and boringly. Even the Bible gives much, much more prominence to women.

The *Book of Mormon* has mainly copied the Old and New Testaments and it contains and contributes absolutely nothing new of any significance.

There are many more problems with this fascinating literature. An astute reader might pick up some idea of what it is all about by reading between the lines of *History of Joseph Smith* written by his mother, Lucy Mack Smith.

Still another piece of literature that serves as a foundation for one of the world's religions is what appears to be the Zoroastrian Bible known as the *Avesta*. F. Max Muller, an authority on sacred books, says:

> The sacred code of Zoroaster or of any other of the founders of religions may appear to us to be full of absurdities, or may in fact really be so. . .if Zoroaster was what we believe him to have been, a wise man, in our sense of the word, he could not have written the rubbish which we find in the Avesta.[11]

Would I be repeating myself if I mentioned that this work is also very repetitive? This seems to be a malady that few "sacred" writings can avoid.

The best that the *Avesta* seems to offer, and that is not much to write home about, is a few remarks about minimal ethics and some vague references to a possible afterlife. There are admonitions against striking or hurting other persons with attendant punishments. Penalties run accordingly: hurting someone warrants 30 stripes; drawing blood, 50 stripes; breaking bones, 70 stripes; and (I'm not sure what we are to make of the following law, be it a lack of respect for taking human life, or a sign of refined and enlightened ethical standards because there is no capital punishment) for taking another's life, only 90 stripes.[12]

We are to be pure, a cleanliness which includes clean thoughts, words, and deeds.[13] This is left as a general rule without details as to specific situations.

There is ample evidence of a belief in life after death:

> What shall be his reward, after his soul has parted from his body, who has cleansed from the Nasu the man defiled by the dead? Ahura Mazda answered:—"The welfare of Paradise thou canst promise to that man, for his reward in the other world."[14]

> . . . and grant that reward which Thou hast appointed to our souls. . .for this world and the spiritual. . .[15]

Examples wherein this sacred work gets goofy is the strange obsession the material has with how dead bodies seem to defile us (there is an inordinate preoccupation with this thought), and the sometimes bizarre ideas,

> Which is the urine wherewith the corpse-bearers shall wash their hair and their bodies? Is it of sheep or oxen? Is it of man or of woman?[16]

> The answer, if you are seriously concerned, is sheep and oxen. They shall therefore cause a yellow dog with four eyes, or a white dog with yellow ears, to go three times through that way. . . then the Drug Nasu flies away to the regions of the north, in the shape of a raging fly. . .[17]

I can quickly see where the use of drugs could be an asset in certain religions in order to realize some of the benefits.

It might be worth examining the religious texts of one last faith, the Bahai. Bahaullah, the founder and author of the Bahai's words from God, lived during the 1800's AD. In order for a religion to be real, doesn't it have to be at least 1500 years old? Despite the "modern" nature of this faith, it has some unique claims for world recognition as a religion. Foremost among its claims is the assertion of the Bahais that they are the final revelation, the ultimate religion, the faith that has summed up all of the rest of the world's religions and taken the best of them all. If you are not impressed yet, let me share the significant strengths of the faith.

Their scriptures make it clear that Bahai is a religion of love and kindness. It preaches peace and concern for all persons. Two of its unique, though related, tennants is that we should strive for a one world government and one common language for all peoples:

> Let your vision be world-embracing, rather than confined to your own self. . .'It is not his to boast who loveth his country, but it is his who loveth the world.'. . . Languages must be reduced to one common language to be taught in all the schools of the world.[18]

Along with the emphasis on love and goodness, this superb and progressive idea of the world as one country with one common language is the best this religion has to offer, even though it will scare the Hades out of the political right wing. However, just when you think the Bahai scriptures may be on to something, Bahaullah pulls the rug out from under a great idea with the suggestion that the best form of government, aye, even "one of the signs of God," is a monarchy.[19] Though this is tempered with the suggestion that uniting a king with a republican form of government would be rewarding.

Its claim to be the ultimate revelation and the last word in religions, however logical an extension of the one-country-one-language philosophy it seems to be, is not as sound as I'm sure the Bahais would like. All the religions have been revelations from

God and worthy, we are told. Jesus, Muhammad, Bahaullah, and the others are all prophets of equal worth preaching the same message:

> . . .neither the person of Jesus nor His writings hath differed from that of Muhammad and of His holy Book. . .[20]

> . . .all their utterances are, in reality, but the expressions of one Truth.[21]

> . . .thou hast inquired which of the Prophets of God should be regarded as superior to others. Know thou assuredly that the essence of all the Prophets of God is one and the same. Their unity is absolute.[22]

As nice as the religious tolerance of the Bahais seems to be, there are two serious problems with it, in addition to the fact that it may not be as magnanimous as it *makes itself* out to be. A closer scrutiny of their claim to be an amalgamation of all religions and the final authority or revelation reveals:

> The Prophetic Cycle hath, verily, ended. The Eternal Truth is now come.[23]

> In this most mighty Revelation all the Dispensations of the past have attained their highest and final consummation. Whoso layeth claim to a Revelation after Him, such a man is assuredly a lying impostor.[24]

The Bahais are saying in the scriptural passages above that in essence theirs is the true religion. While making such a claim, yet Bahaullah has the audacity, if I am interpreting their scripture correctly, to call the Jews, "these small-minded, contemptible people" because the Jews contend that all revelation has come to an end—a claim that can't be made until Bahaullah, himself makes it.[25] This certainly borders on anti-Semitism.

The two problems presented by the pronouncement of the value and worth of all religions is (1) how do we know who are the false prophets that Jesus, for example, spoke about? Are we to accept Satan worship and all other weird cults? We are given no help in determining whom to believe. Certainly we cannot believe all claims—a total absurdity. (2) An extension of that thought is the fact that Bahaullah appears to be totally blind to the stark contradictions between the various religions and even within a single religion. Yes, I know, he has a mystical solution for that problem that most of us are unable to understand. I suppose that leaves most of us floundering out there with little help at the mercy of all kinds of strange religious ideas and cults.

I will briefly mention a few other weaknesses, though not all. Does the scriptures of Bahai support the caste system or not?

> To transgress the limits of one's own rank and station is, in no wise, permissible. The integrity of every rank and station must needs be preserved.[26]

Another weakness is the implication that apparently God can change her or his mind:

> He hath now made interest on money lawful, even as He had made it unlawful in the past.[27]

This is a definite reference to *The Koran* and the Old Testament, both of which at some point tell us, "No interest allowed." Having God change her or his mind is one way in which Bahaullah resolves contradictions.

Another weakness is seen insofar as Bahai is not a pacifist religion.[28]

Yet another weakness is the fact that Bahai, for all of its universal pretensions, is heavily influenced by its Eastern origins and by *The Koran*, the book that conditioned Bahaullah. One example is the conviction that this physical world and physical things are bad.[29]

The Koran has unfortunately had too great of an impact on the writings of Bahai. Like *The Koran*, Bahaullah's writings, also, are tiresomely repetitive and extremely defensive in nature. They spend an inordinate amount of effort trying to convince readers that they are the truth as well as trying to justify their existence, as does *The Koran*. Also mimicking *The Koran*, Bahaullah's writings are constantly praising God, sometimes interrupting in mid-sentence in order to do so.

There is one final criticism, though I have not exhausted all of the possibilities, regarding the defensive posture: We are told we cannot question God, which translates into never questioning the writings of Bahaullah since he is God's spokesperson.[30]

To be frank, all "sacred" writings are the products of human beings and subject to all of our weaknesses, prejudices, and mistakes. They all exhibit human frailties; yet, I believe that the "word of God" occasionally sneaks through. God was able to somehow communicate her or his spirit to many prophets. Nevertheless, in contrast to the teachings of Jesus I have found all other "sacred" writing wanting.

Let me quote from Geddes MacGregor concerning the worth of our Bible:

> What is this book which, having been accounted so precious by Christians in the days of the Emperor Diocletian that they suffered the most cruel tortures rather than give up copies of it to the Roman authorities, now has a demand exceeding the most popular novel of the year?[31]

And we read at the end of the sermon on the mount (Matthew 7:28) the words, ". . .when Jesus finished these sayings, the crowds were astonished at his teachings. . ." The reason for the astonishment is obvious. Nowhere else can one find such a concentration of great ideas! The sermon on the mount (Matthew 5, 6 & 7) alone is enough; what more could anyone desire in the way of great truth?

Besides the unbelievable beauty and power of the sermon on the mount, consider a few of the other great words from the gospels alone which makes the sacred literature of all other religions pale into insignificance.

— the good Samaritan parable, Luke 10:25-37.
— the prodigal son parable, Luke 15:11-32.
— the incident where Jesus tells the wealthy person to sell all he has and give it to the poor, Luke 18:18-25.
— the eleventh hour workers parable, Matthew 20:1-16.
— the parable of the final judgment, Matthew 25:31-45.

— the parable of the rich man and Lazarus, Luke 16:19-31.
— the lost sheep parable, Matthew 18:10-14.
— other parables of the kingdom, Matthew 13.
— the great commandment, Matthew 22:34-40.
— the incident of the woman caught in adultery, John 8:1-11.
— Jesus washing the feet of the disciples, John 13:4-9.
— the cross itself!
— the comment from the cross forgiving those who killed him! Luke 23:34.

Everything you ever needed to know to get to heaven you learned from Jesus even if your minister was afraid to tell you.

If a definition of scripture or the Bible could be "words through which God speaks to us," then there is much more of the Bible around. For instance, the following thoughts from *The Velveteen Rabbit* come close:

"What is real?" asked the Rabbit one day, when they were lying side by side near the nursery fender, before Nana came to tidy the room. "Does it mean having things that buzz inside you and a stick-out handle?" "Real isn't how you are made," said the Skin Horse, "It's a thing that happens to you. When a child loves you for a long, long time, not just to play with, but really loves you, then you become real." "Does it hurt?" asked the Rabbit. "Sometimes," said the Skin Horse, for he was always truthful. "When you are real you don't mind being hurt." "Does it happen all at once, like being wound up," he asked, "or bit by bit?" "It doesn't happen all at once," said the Skin Horse. "You become. It takes a long time. That's why it doesn't often happen to people who break easily, or have sharp edges, or who have to be carefully kept. Generally, by the time you are real, most of your hair has been loved off, and your eyes drop out and you get loose in the joints and very shabby. But these things don't matter at all, because once you are real, you can't be ugly, except to people who don't understand."[32]

NOTES:

[1] Swami Prabhavananda & Christopher Isherwood, translators, <u>The Song of God: Bhagavad-Gita</u> (New York: Mentor Books, 1961), p. 99.

[2] Ibid., p. 101.

[3] Ibid., p. 114.

[4] Ibid., p. 64.

[5] Ibid., p. 51.

[6] Ibid., p. 47.

[7] Ibid., pp. 32-34.

[8] Ibid., pp. 35-38.

[9] E. A. Wallis Budge, editor, <u>The Egyptian Book of the Dead</u> (New York: Dover Publications, Inc., 1967), pp. lxx, xcii-xciii.

[10] Ruth M. Underhill, <u>Red Man's Religion</u> (Chicago: The University of Chicago Press, 1965), p. 9.

[11] F. Max Muller, translator, <u>The Upanisads, Part I</u> (New York: Dover Publications, Inc., 1962), p. xix.

[12] James Darmesteter, translator, <u>The Zend Avesta of Zarathustra</u> (Edmonds, Washington: The Near Eastern Press, 1984), pp. 18-19.

[13] Ibid., p. 23.

[14] Ibid., p. 38.

[15] Ibid., p. 43.

[16] Ibid., p. 30.

[17] Ibid., p. 30.

[18] <u>Tablets of Bahaullah</u> (Wilmette, Illinois: Bahai Publishing Trust, 1988), pp. 87-89.

[19] Ibid., p. 28.

[20] <u>Gleanings from the Writings of Bahaullah</u> (Wilmette, Illinois: Bahai Publishing Trust, 1983), p. 21.

[21] Ibid., p. 53.

[22] Ibid., p. 78.

[23] Ibid., p. 60.

[24] Ibid., p. 244.

[25] Ibid., p. 24.

[26] Ibid., p. 188.

[27] <u>Tablets,</u> p. 133.

[28] <u>Tablets,</u> p. 165 & <u>Gleanings,</u> pp. 250-251.

[29] <u>Gleanings,</u> pp. 100 & 328.

[30] Ibid., p. 333.

[31] Geddes MacGregor, <u>The Bible in the Making</u> (New York: J. B. Lippincott Company, 1959), p. 14.

[32] Margery Williams, <u>The Velveteen Rabbit.</u> (New York: Doubleday & Co.)

19. King James:
The Version Jesus Used

I still remember the furor over the Revised Standard Version of the Bible when it was first published. I was about 14 or 15 years old and remember how the people of the church in which I grew up became upset over this new translation. The Revised Standard Version New Testament had been published about six or seven years earlier by that time, and members of my church were quite disturbed over the way in which this new translation had distorted the Bible. For them the King James Version was the only true translation; anything else was a travesty of God's word.

The history of the various translations of the Bible is a history of firm, and sometimes, violent resistance. We grow accustomed to familiar and beloved words. We trust them. New translations bring "modern" words that sound crude, and they grate on our ears. These new editions seem to "violate" the beautiful and true.

Resistance to new translations is exemplary of the problems with which this book has been trying to come to grips. Too many Christians live in fear that any change, challenge, or "liberal" interpretation of scriptures will undermine the truth of God's word. The King James Version had been around long enough to become a trusted friend; and after all King James English was the language that Jesus spoke. I still hear Christians today refer to the "Saint James" Version.

It is true that we have become more accustomed to new translations today as they have been appearing with greater frequency, and perhaps we even think they have already "done their damage," so we seem to have grown a little more tolerant of the new versions.

Co-evolving with the proliferation of new translations has been the demise of memory work. We often hear it bemoaned that no one memorizes Bible passages any more. The problem may well be "Which translation should I memorize?" Heretofore, the answer had been, "We memorize the King James version, of course." Now there are too many versions of our favorite verses, a situation which may not be all bad. Perhaps now we are forced to remember "ideas" and "concepts" instead of just words, although that is not to say that when we memorized words we didn't clearly understand the ideas behind the words. It is just that the possibility does come to mind.

As a preacher, I find a decided advantage in the existence of multiple translations. When I "quote" a few verses in a sermon now, I don't have to be exact. Who knows *what translation* I may be using.

However, another and perhaps more precise reason for the decline in memorization could be that succeeding generations may not even be reading the Bible. This you cannot blame on the variety of translations since these new translations are offered in the hope of making the scriptures more readable and under-standable.

This chapter intends only to highlight the translation "problem" and to offer a rough evaluation of the differences among the main translations.

We should not begin without recalling the problem the early English translators encountered. John Wycliffe was the first to translate the Bible into English. When he died of natural causes in 1384, he thought he had escaped the church's wrath for the terrible sin of translating scripture out of the languages God spoke (Latin, Greek, Hebrew) into the vernacular. However, Christian church leaders later became so incensed over his crime that they dug up his bones in 1428 and burned them, throwing the ashes into the river.[1]

This first Bible in English managed to survive until William Tyndale decided to make another translation into English in the 1500's. Not being as lucky as Wycliffe, Tyndale, before he died, was strangled and burned at the stake in 1536.[2] Think of the many good church leaders from the middle ages who are turning over in their graves because they cannot get their hands on the many 20th century translators—talk about a noisy cemetery.

Skipping over other English translations—Coverdale, 1535; Matthew's, 1537; The Great Bible, 1539; Geneva Bible, 1560—the first English Bible that has direct relevancy for us would be the King James Version.

Strangely enough, although the King James Version from fifty years after the date of its publication in 1611 up until the middle of this century has been regarded as "the only true" Bible, it was not so at the time of its advent:

> When it first appeared, a London cleric claimed that it "sounds like yesterday's newspaper, and denies the divinity and messiahship of Christ." One chaplain accused the translators of pandering to King James' interest in witch-craft; and when they sailed for the new world in 1620, the Pilgrims refused to carry the KJV with them. It took 50 years for it to win the acclaim that it has kept ever since.[3]

The King James Version began when, in 1604 at the Hampton Court Conference, one John Reynolds, president of one of the colleges at Oxford, suggested that there be an authorized English Bible that all persons could accept.[4] James I, new to the throne, liked the idea and immediately made arrangements whereby about fifty scholars would make a new translation. These individuals relied on many different Bibles of an earlier genre including English, Latin, and other languages. They also tried to make use of the Hebrew and Greek manuscripts, but relied most heavily on the Tyndale, Coverdale and Geneva texts. It was more a project of revising the English versions than any attempt at a start-from-scratch new translation of the earliest manuscripts.[5]

After publication in 1611, there appeared many, many editions of this King James Version with a great many errors in each edition or revision. Of course we do not read the "original" King James Version today. After many subsequent revisions, the one that finally became somewhat standard was that of Benjamin Blayney of Oxford that appeared in 1769. Following this edition there were very few changes made in later editions.[7]

The charm of the King James Version, with its somewhat archaic language, is its. . .

reproduction of much of the flavor of the vivid and concrete word-picture character of Semitic expression, with its striking imagery, metaphors, personifications. . .[7]

Though criticism of the King James Version was severe, it remained "the" Bible until the Revised Version appeared in 1885 (the New Testament in 1881) in England.[8] A committee in the United States decided to publish its own version of the Revised Version in this country which appeared in 1901 and was known as the American Standard Version.[9] Although this latter version become popular in this country, it never was able to surpass the King James. But this new version (1885 and 1901) took advantage of very early manuscripts that were unavailable to the King James revisors.[10]

The Revised Version (American Standard) was not without its defects. It is not the easiest version to read and understand. The realization that this is true, in addition to the discovery of new manuscripts, progress in textual study, and archeological discoveries, made it possible to more closely approach a true and exact meaning of different words and idioms. With the progress made in these areas, there was constant interest in bringing out "better" versions.

Probably the two foci of any work are accuracy and clarity. We always want to come closer to the original meaning of the scriptures and be able to say it in language that is readable and understandable. To those ends many versions have and will come out periodically. Among the popular names in translations have been Goodspeed, Moffatt, and Phillips. The Rhemes-Douay (Rheims-Douai) is an earlier (1635) Roman Catholic version with the Confraternity being a more recent (1940's) Roman Catholic venture.

However the next giant step in publishing versions of the Bible came when a group of about 32 scholars began the Revised Standard Version in 1930. It followed closely the Revised Version but with modernization and with the advantage of more recent knowledge. The New Testament came out in 1946 and the Old Testament in 1952.[11]

Back in England the New English Bible appeared in 1970 under the supervision of many denominations. It ranks with the best in quality of translation as well as clarity.

Another step in developing a version that would be readable without losing any accuracy came in 1976 when the Good News Bible, Today's English Version, was published. It was a successful effort in using "plain, everyday, natural" language, and it has had an enormous appeal.

Approaching the ultimate in modern language—at least for now—is the highly successful and popular The Living Bible published in 1971. It is indeed only a paraphrase and not a translation. An example of the contrast between the King James and The Living Bible can be seen in an examination of respective scripture readings from Genesis 6:1:

And it came to pass, when men began to multiply on the face of the earth. . .

Now a population explosion took place upon the earth. . .

Perhaps the reader can determine which of the above is King James and which is The Living Bible. No publisher would print The Living Bible until Billy Graham endorsed it, and then it became immensely popular, chiefly among the conservatives. That in itself is a strange phenomenon because the conservative Christians are usually the most adamant against "change" and modernization especially when it comes to the Bible. Yet ironically they have accepted the most "far out" liberal version yet—one at which even "liberals" look askance. I am told that the secret that makes it acceptable is that The Living Bible is acknowledged as only a "paraphrase." However, you might think about that one for a while.

The latest translation—until this book becomes dated—is the New Revised Standard Version of 1990.

NOTES:

[1] Roy L. Smith, <u>Know Your Bible Series, vol. 1</u> (New York: Abingdon Press, 1955), p. 11.

[2] Ibid.

[3] <u>Circuit Rider</u> (A United Methodist Magazine) June 1989, pp. 8-9.

[4] Geddes MacGregor, <u>The Bible in the Making</u> (Philadelphia: J. B. Lippincott Company, 1959), p. 147.

[5] Nolan B. Harmon, editor, <u>The Interpreter's Bible, vol. 1</u> (New York: Abingdon Press, 1952), pp. 93-94.

[6] Ibid., p. 95.

[7] Ibid.

[8] Ibid., p. 97.

[9] MacGregor, p.214.

[10] Ibid., p. 195.

[10] F. F. Bruce, <u>History of the Bible in English</u> (New York: Oxford University Press, 1978), p. 186.

Biblical Reference Index in Chronological Order

Partial Subject Index

Some subject listings (i.e., Mary, Joseph, ark, etc.) in some instances will refer to more than one person or object. Some subjects (God, Jesus, Israel, Egypt, Paul, etc.) appear often enough that they are not included in this index. I want to thank my friend, Ruthie Peterson, for typing the final version of these two indexes.